The Lagos Consulate
1851−1861

The Lagos Consulate
1851–1861

Robert S. Smith

UNIVERSITY OF CALIFORNIA PRESS
Berkeley and Los Angeles

University of California Press
Berkeley and Los Angeles, California

© Robert S. Smith 1979

ISBN 0 520 03746 4

Library of Congress Catalog Number: 78-59455

Contents

List of Illustrations	vi
List of Maps	vi
Abbreviations used in the Notes and Bibliography	vii
Preface	ix

1	The Troubled Kingdom	1
2	The Reduction of Lagos	18
3	Before Campbell	34
4	To the Palaver Islands	49
5	Mr Consul Campbell	66
6	The Iron Coffin	91
7	The Last Consuls	111
8	A Deadly Gift?	128

APPENDIX	A	Treaty between Great Britain and Lagos, 1 January 1852	135
	B	The Treaty of Epe, 28 September 1854	138
	C	The Treaty of Cession, 6 August 1861	140

Notes and References	143
Bibliography and Sources	177
Index	183

Illustrations

1 Cruiser's boats about to board a slaver
2 Shipping slaves through the surf
3 On the 'road' from Lagos to Abeokuta
4 The Lagos steamer fetching the mail

Maps

1 The Yoruba and their neighbours, c. 1850.　　　　　*facing p.* 1
2 Lagos and Lagos River, based on the surveys of 1851 and 1859　　29
3 Lagos and Epe; Kosoko's kingdom in exile　　41

Abbreviations used in the Notes and Bibliography

References to secondary works in the notes, other than to works cited only incidentally, consist of the author's name and, where necessary for identification, the date of the relevant work. A description of each work is given in the Bibliography.

BFSP	*British and Foreign State Papers*
CMG	*Church Missionary Gleaner*
CMI	*Church Missionary Intelligencer*
CMP	*Church Missionary Proceedings*
CMR	*Church Missionary Record*
C.M.S.	Church Missionary Society
CO	Colonial Office
FO	Foreign Office
JAH	*Journal of African History*
JHSN	*Journal of the Historical Society of Nigeria*
LNR	*Lagos Notes and Records*
MP	Wesleyan (Methodist) missionary papers
PP	Parliamentary Papers
PRO	Public Record Office, London

Preface

The decade which opened with the intervention of the British at Lagos in December 1851, followed by the establishment of the consulate there eleven months later, and which ended in their annexation of the kingdom as a colony in 1861, was a time of transition for this southern Yoruba people from independence to colonial rule. But it has wider importance as a first step in the making of Nigeria, the most populous and among the richest of African states. It was also a prelude to that *Prelude to the Partition of West Africa* between the European powers about which Professor J. D. Hargreaves has written, for it exhibits in microcosm many of the features of these later years, as well as many individual divergencies. Lagos in its consular period was the focus and meeting place of the activities of Europeans of varied callings and characters – administrators and officials, naval officers and ratings, traders, and Christian missionaries – and of the Sierra Leonean and Brazilian 'emigrants' or 'liberated Africans', all impinging in their different ways on the society and politics of the indigenous inhabitants of the island kingdom.

A study of this period should have another, and perhaps deeper, significance in the light which can be thrown on the pre-colonial history of Lagos itself (destined to be the capital of Federal Nigeria and one of the country's nineteen component states) and of its neighbours among the southern Yoruba and, on the west, the Fon of Dahomey and the other Aja-speaking peoples. With the intrusion of the Europeans and, to a lesser extent, the arrival (or return) of the 'emigrants' there began the continuous written record of events and conditions in this part of Africa. The disturbed state of the hinterland became the subject of much anxiety and of many reports in Lagos. The kingdom had taken its own part in the wars which beset the Yoruba from the early nineteenth century, and for the rest of the century, under a series of British governors, Lagos was to emerge as a pacifier, though one with a rather heavy hand and with its own favourites among the protagonists. Here again the consular decade was a time of transition. The aim of this book is, therefore, to direct attention to a small corner of the West African coastline and a period of a mere ten years, in the hope that some insight may be gained thereby into a wider situation.

The book was written in Lagos but is based mainly on archival sources in London which were read during a part of two Long Vacations. The Foreign Office and Colonial Office material has been taken from the files in the Public Record Office, supplemented by extracts in British State Papers; the missionary material is from the printed journals, supplemented by the records of individual missionaries and files concerned with the Yoruba Mission.

The writer published a summary of the consular decade in the *Journal of African History*, volume XV, number 3 (1974), while Chapter 4 of this book is based on his article under the same title in the *Journal of the Historical Society of Nigeria*, volume V, number 1 (1969). The editors of these two journals are sincerely thanked for according permission to use this material. The writer is also grateful to the authorities of the Public Record Office, the Church Missionary Society, and the Methodist Missionary Society, and to the librarians of the Universities of Lagos, Ibadan and London and of the Foreign and Commonwealth Office in London for their helpfulness and the speed and efficiency of their services. He must also thank many others who gave their help in different ways, in particular: H.H. Adeyinka Oyekan II, the Oba of Lagos, for his co-operation and hospitality during two informative visits to his palace; the chiefs and other residents in Lagos and its neighbourhood who generously shared their knowledge of the traditional past, especially those listed on page 178 in 'Bibliography and Sources'; his former colleagues in the Universities of Ibadan and Lagos, Professor Babatunde Williams, Professor G. O. Olusanya, Dr E. R. Turton and Dr Robin Law, the last of whom generously allowed him to make use of his recently completed and unpublished article on Oba Adele of Lagos; Mr Christopher Fyfe, who provided information about Consul Campbell's earlier career and descendants; Mr and Mrs James Packman; Mr W. E. F. Ward; Professor R. J. Gavin; Rev. Canon J. J. H. Payne, M.B.E.; Miss Joan Wales and Mrs E. R. Brinton, O.B.E., who checked references for him in London; Dr K. V. Tomlins and the late Mr K. C. Murray, who read the manuscript and made valuable suggestions; Captain R. N. Mackie, from whose light aircraft he was able to observe the intricate topography of the central consular area from Badagry to Epe; Mr J. F. Brown and Mr D. Joannides, in whose boats he visited parts of the lagoon; Mr S. A. Ojobo, who acted on several occasions as his interpreter in Yoruba and helped with the maps, and Mr T. Makewu, who typed the last draft of the book. He continues to be indebted to Professor Michael Crowder for constant encouragement in his work as well as for valuable criticism. Finally, he acknowledges with gratitude the support of the authorities of the University of Lagos who provided him with research grants in the 1970–1 and 1971–2 academic years and have generously assisted in the publication of this book.

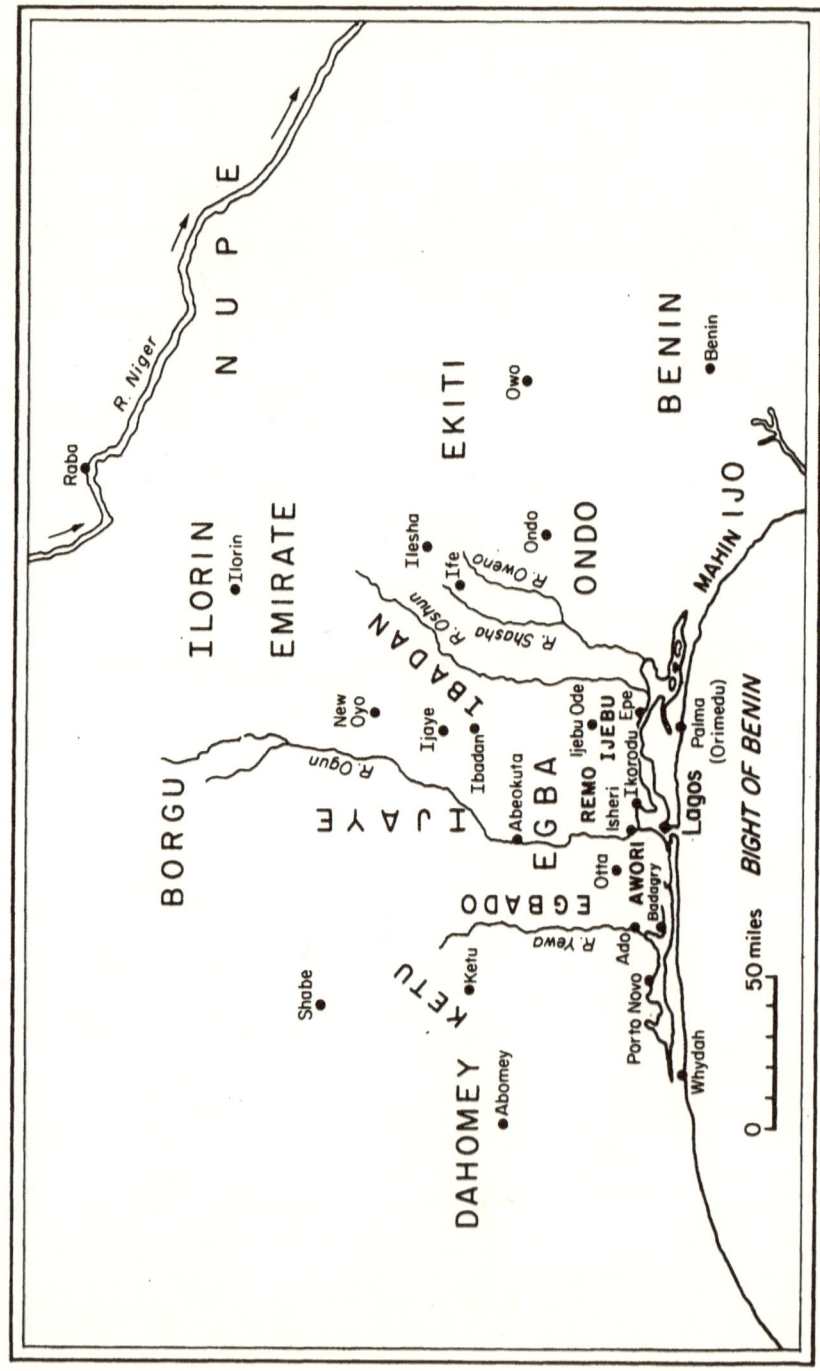

The Yoruba and their neighbours, c. 1850.

I

The Troubled Kingdom

For the Yoruba people the nineteenth century was a century of war.[1] It began in the north of their country with the disintegration of Oyo, the largest and once the strongest of their kingdoms, and its infiltration and invasion by followers of the Islamic revivalist Usman dan Fodio, and in the south with the almost simultaneous outbreak of war between the allied Ife and Ijebu and the Owu. The collapse of Oyo led to a regrouping of the remnants of the armies in the forests to the south. The warriors of the Hausa–Fulani Holy War were kept at bay, but the new political order intensified rivalries between the Yoruba themselves, especially among the states succeeding to the power of Oyo, and warfare became endemic. Moreover, from the 1840s onwards western Yorubaland – the country of the Egba and Egbado and the western fringes of Oyo – was under attack from the powerful Dahomeans. Thus from about 1817[2] to the imposition of a *Pax Britannica* in 1892–3 nearly the whole Yoruba country was in a state of chronic instability and almost constant war. It is this which forms the background to the troubled history of Lagos in the half-century preceding the British 'reduction' of the island in 1851, and to the consular and early colonial periods there.

War brings changes in its wake. But other forces making for change were also at work in Yorubaland during this time. The prohibition of the slave trade by the British in 1807 was followed by the establishment of a Royal Navy patrol on the west coast of Africa, the Anti-Slavery or Preventive Squadron, and by the fostering of trade in 'legitimate' products, especially those of the palm trees which grew with providential profusion in the very areas from which many of the slaves were taken. The humanitarian work was supplemented by that of the Christian missionaries, the first of whom reached Abeokuta from Badagry in December 1842. Officials and administrators followed hard on the heels of the traders and missionaries. The British, as R. Robinson and J. Gallagher put it, 'had not abolished their own slave trade to make life easier for the slavers of other nations',[3] and their cruisers, of which there were by 1850 some two dozen on the coast, continued to hunt Portuguese, American, French and Cuban slavers and to impose anti-slavery treaties on the coastal chiefs with such vigour that they created 'an undeclared British paramountcy along the shores of Sierra Leone, Liberia, the Ivory and Gold Coasts, Dahomey, the Niger Delta and as far south as the mouths of the Congo'.[4] In June 1849 the British Government supplemented these naval activities by setting up a consulate for the Bights of Benin and Biafra, which was to provide a base for the drive against the slave trade in this notorious area and to protect and encourage the growing legitimate trade in palm oil. The former trader John Beecroft was appointed as first consul, with his headquarters on the island of Fernando Po, and proved a doughty agent for his government's policies.

The centre of the slave trade at this time in the western half of the consulate was the kingdom of Lagos under its ruler Kosoko, until at the end of 1851 naval and consular intervention succeeded against determined local resistance in imposing a more pliant regime there. Some months later a vice-consul was posted to Lagos and the following year the consular area was divided, a substantive consul for the Bight of Benin being appointed to reside in Lagos. This 'quasi-protectorate', as it was soon seen to be, lasted until 1861, when the British Government annexed Lagos and the neighbouring territories as a colony. The expansion of this colony, at first gradual and even hesitant, was to bring together the greater part of Yorubaland under one government and to be the foundation of the former Western State of Federal Nigeria (now comprising the states of Lagos, Oyo, Ondo and Ogun). Meanwhile, in the Niger Delta the 'Old Coast' or 'informal' system[5] continued until 1885, when the consulate for the Bight of Biafra was transformed into a Protectorate of the Niger Districts, or Oil Rivers. This contrast between the histories of the two parts of the original consular area raises questions which are fundamental to the present study: why or, more properly, *how* did the consulate for the Bight of Benin, otherwise called the Lagos consulate, develop from its first years the character of a protectorate, and how was it that the British found it both feasible and desirable to abandon the old 'informal' system there after only ten years and to assume the obligations entailed by the proclamation of the new colony?

Lagos and its lagoon; kingship and kingdom

The original Lagosians belonged to the Awori who, with the Ijebu, are the most southerly of the Yoruba-speaking people, occupying an area west of Lagos and extending about forty miles inland.[6] Their town and island are known to them as 'Eko', though the name 'Lagos', deriving from the Portuguese word for 'lagoon' and probably contracted from the 'Lago de Curamo' applied to the eastern lagoon, is now far more widely used.[7] Their kingdom, never amounting to much more in size than a city-state, was among the smallest and, in early times, probably least important of the Yoruba states. These varied in size from the miniature kingdoms of Ekiti to Oyo whose empire at its height straddled the savannah in the north and the southern forests down to the coast; the predominance of Oyo is reflected in the fact that the word 'Yoruba', the name given by the Hausa to the inhabitants of that kingdom, came in the nineteenth century to be used for all speakers of this language. Nor does Lagos seem to have been of any importance until the rise of the slave trade there in the eighteenth century. The earliest reference to the area is in Duarte Pacheco Pereira's *Esmeraldo de Situ Orbis*, which, describing the coast at the end of the fifteenth and early in the sixteenth centuries, gives a discouraging account of the 'region of the river Lagua' where, apart from slaves, 'There is no trade . . . nor anything from which one can make a profit'.[8] Pacheco makes no mention of any settlement on the river nor does the map of West Africa of 1594 by Plancius give any name here, though the lagoon and the island are marked. The first reference to a settlement seems to be the name 'Ichoo' (for Eko) on the map by the Dutch cartographer Blaeu in 1659, while Dapper's map of 1686 also shows 'Ichoo'.[9] Lagos is altogether omitted from the map accompanying Snelgrave's account of Guinea published in 1734, and though some attempt is made to represent the lagoon, it is confused with the Benin River. Probably the fellow Awori kingdom of Otta, lying a few miles inland from Lagos, was an earlier and more important state. But Lagos possessed a physical feature of great importance for the future, for it was here that the first permanent break occurred in the miles of beach and dune of the outer coastline to the east of the Volta estuary, giving access, though across a bar of great difficulty and danger, to a deep-water anchorage and thence to the sheltered lagoon and to a vast system of inland waterways of which Lagos lay approximately at the centre.[10] Pacheco writes of this 'river Lagua' that 'The channel has two fathoms at high tide, but its entrance is very dangerous, with shallows of sand on which the sea breaks during the greater part of the year, so that the channel is scarcely seen; only small vessels of thirty to thirty-five tons can enter it'. This suggests that the harbour at least was known to Europeans, and perhaps in use, by the early sixteenth century.

As with all the Yoruba kingdoms, it is impossible to ascribe a date to the foundation of Lagos, or even to say with confidence in what century this took place. It seems likely, however, that the emergence of this settlement near the ocean's edge was later, perhaps by a century or more, than that of most of the other kingdoms. The Yoruba almost certainly originated as an inland people, for the sea plays no part in their traditions and Lagos is still the only Yoruba town on the coast. The traditions of early Lagos tell plausibly enough of the movement of a small group of Awori from the village of Isheri, some twelve miles to the north of Lagos island up the river Ogun,[11] seeking security from the troubles of the mainland – probably from the depredations of their more numerous Ijebu, Egba and Egbado neighbours – and in particular from a war remembered as the Ogun Ajakaiye, or 'war of the world'. They settled first at Ebute Metta ('three harbours') on the lagoon, in territory which was claimed later as belonging to the Ijebu, and then for greater safety moved across to the small island of Iddo. Here, two settlements developed, one at Oto ('separated') on the north shore opposite the near-by mainland, and one at Iddo ('a camp') from which this island, only about a square mile in extent, took its name. A third settlement on the west, called Ijora ('a gathering of kinsmen'), seems to be of later date. From here these first Lagosians expanded to the adjacent larger island, some 3¼ by 1¼ miles in extent,[12] lying in the lagoon immediately behind the narrow strip of sandy coastline and beside the channel, or 'Lagos river', connecting the lagoon with the Atlantic ocean. The western end of this island became Eko, a name derived probably from the farm (*oko*) of these earliest settlers, and this area, known as Isale Eko ('downtown Lagos'), is still the most closely inhabited part and regarded as the core of the town. Elsewhere on the island there were probably small Ijebu fishing villages, similar to those dotted around the shores of the lagoon, and doubtless some of these became absorbed into the main group of Awori. The first ruler, entitled the Olofin, continued to live on Iddo Island, while the ten eldest sons of the first Olofin are said to have ruled as sub-chiefs over different parts of Iddo and of the main island. From these latter are held to descend the group of ten chiefs called the Idejo.

Tradition has little else to tell about these early years. Then at some time during the reign at Benin of Oba Orhogbua, and therefore probably about the middle of the sixteenth century, Lagos was conquered by Bini armies advancing westwards along the coast,[13] travelling presumably by canoe through the creeks and lagoons (a journey said to take some eight days). The Olofin, though not the Idejo sub-chiefs, was replaced on his throne by a Bini nominee, and the title disappears from Lagos history (though it survives at Isheri). Ashipa, the first king of this second dynasty, has been described in Bini tradition as a son or grandson of the Oba of Benin.[14] Lagos tradition, understandably, does not mention this, one source indeed maintaining that the new ruler imposed by the Bini was an Awori prince from Isheri, the original home of the Olofin.[15] But in any event the connection between the new dynasty and Benin was close enough to imply a client relationship, though probably of a mild kind, of Lagos to Benin. All subsequent rulers of Lagos claim descent from Ashipa, using the titles Ologun, Eleko, and (in more recent times exclusively) that of Oba, the last being the general term in Yoruba for 'king' and also the title of the ruler of Benin. Meanwhile, either under Ashipa or his second successor, Gabaro, the royal seat was transferred from Iddo to Lagos Island or Eko, where a palace was built, the Iga Idunganran or 'pepper palace', named from the pepper bushes growing there.

The site of Lagos, so like that of Venice, suggests similarities with the history of that other city of the lagoons. As with the Venetians, the first settlers were refugees from the dangers of life on the mainland. The islands of Eko and Iddo, little better than mud-flats, were yet readily defensible against an enemy. But the lack of space and the poverty of the sandy soil made agriculture difficult, and from early times the Lagosians must have been dependent for an increasing part of their food on mainland neighbours: their fellow Awori to the north and west, the Egba still further north up the Ogun river (which enters the lagoon some twelve miles to the north of Lagos), and the Ijebu living to the east and around the lagoon. One important local source of food, however, and of exports to be exchanged against the imports from mainland markets, was fish from the inland waters, and the Lagosians were doubtless great fishermen before ever they became great traders. Their small fishing canoes were made by hollowing out the softwood trees which grew in the surrounding swamps, but for their larger canoes, especially those used in war, carved and burnt out from the great trees which grew only sparsely on the islands and around the lagoon, they were again dependent on their neighbours in the forests. Yet, unlike Venice, Lagos did not seek for either commercial or strategic reasons to extend her boundaries as she grew richer, apart from the exaction of tribute from Badagry in the late eighteenth and perhaps also the early nineteenth centuries.[16] The kingdom thus consisted of the main island of Eko, the tiny adjacent island of Iddo, several large and many small villages on the nearby mainland, and (if Kosoko's claim in his treaty of 1863 with the British may be believed) overlordship of the sandy waste lying between the lagoon and the sea as far east as Palma.[17] Nor did Lagos seek to command the sea: the bar across the entrance to the lagoon was particularly dreaded, and European traders of the eighteenth century and perhaps earlier hired Fanti canoemen from the Gold Coast to communicate with the shore as the local people were unwilling to venture over the surf. The bar equally deterred European exploration; 'the river is shut off by heavens-high breakers, and the land is therefore unapproachable', a Dutch trading official reported in 1716.[18] On the lagoon, however, the Lagosians navigated long distances in trade and war, sometimes as far afield as the Benin River, and in the late eighteenth century maintained a large fleet of war canoes which gave them standing among the local powers.[19]

The government of the Lagos kingdom in pre-colonial times has hitherto been little studied or described. But if Peter Lloyd's distinction between 'tribally structured' and 'highly centralised' authoritarian monarchies[20] is adopted, Lagos apparently inclined towards the second of these types since the Oba, although no autocrat, was much more than a mere 'arbiter between the chiefs', nor does he seem to have been invested with quite the same aura of sacred but somewhat remote kingship which characterised monarchies of the 'tribal' type elsewhere among the Yoruba. The government may have developed in this way only in the late eighteenth century as a result of the increasing wealth and consequently increasing political and military power which accrued to the Oba from the slave trade – from, as Lloyd would say, 'the exploitation of newly available resources'. Probably, however, this feature in the monarchy was more deeply rooted, deriving from the establishment of the dynasty by an outside power, Benin, and from the influence of the Benin kingship itself, which is classed by Lloyd as a centralised political structure 'markedly contrasting with that of the Yoruba states'. Other factors of which the Oba could take advantage in increasing or maintaining his authority were the proliferation of chiefs to an extent disproportionate to the size of the kingdom and his power to add to the number of the war chiefs and (less often exercised) of the Ogalade class.

The kingship was hereditary, passing usually from a dead Oba to the eldest of his sons born while he was on the throne, although this system of primogeniture (which was practised also in Benin) could be set aside when a suitable candidate was lacking in favour of younger sons or even brothers of a former Oba. The choice of a new ruler was made by two of the chiefs, the Eletu Odibo and the Ashogbon, in consultation with the Ifa oracle.[21] The crown was not, as in all the major and many of the lesser Yoruba kingships, held to derive from Ife. Instead, the connection with Benin was recognised in the customs of taking the body of a dead king (after severing the head) to Benin for burial and at the same time of seeking the approval of the Oba of Benin for the coronation of a successor. These customs were discontinued during the first part of the nineteenth century, being replaced by ceremonies which included obeisance to the Oba of Benin but were performed at Enu Owa in the heart of Lagos town.[22] In addition an annual tribute was paid by Lagos to Benin. It is said that during the civil war in the kingdom in 1845, officials were sent from Benin to Lagos in an attempt to collect it, and the British Administrator of Lagos was told in 1869 by the 'ambassadors of the King of Benin' that the exiled Oba Kosoko continued to pay tribute down to 1862.[23]

Buttressing, limiting and sometimes rivalling the monarchy were the chiefs (*oloye*) of the kingdom. The three classes of senior chiefs, whose titles were all hereditary within their extended families (or 'descent groups'), were collectively known from their head-dress (resembling that worn by the Oba) as the White Caps or *Onifila funfun*. They comprised, first, the Idejo, representing the original owners of the land.[24] Among these the most prominent were the Oloto, who maintained a semi-independence as ruler of Oto, the northern side of Iddo island, and of a part of the mainland;[25] the Aromire, or 'friend of the waters', protector and patron of the fishers on the lagoon,[26] and the Olumegbon, who had the right and duty of investing the other Idejo with their white caps and whose title – meaning 'God knows the elder' – seems to imply a claim to seniority among them.[27] The next group was that of the Akarigbere, said to descend from the warriors of the Benin army which conquered Lagos and who were in any case closely associated with the ruling dynasty, as opposed to the Idejo, above whom they claimed to rank.[28] Though they were often referred to as the 'Kingmakers', it was only the first of their order, the powerful Eletu Odibo, who performed such a role. The original function of this chief was to represent the Oba of Benin at the court of Lagos and thus to act as chief minister to the Oba. The third group of White Caps was the Ogalade, sometimes described as the Oba's physicians or as a priestly caste and headed by the influential Obanikoro, who claimed that his ancestor had been sent by the Oba of Benin specifically to look after the ruler of Lagos. Each of these grades now comprises sixteen chieftaincies, a number associated with the sixteen principal Odu or signs of the Ifa divination system, but there is some indication that in the past the number of chiefs was smaller.[29] There was also a rather more numerous fourth class consisting of the war captains, the Abagbon or Ogagun, some of whose titles were probably already hereditary in the mid-nineteenth century and whose leader, the Ashogbon, exercised considerable influence in civil as well as military affairs. It was indeed the Ashogbon who, with the Eletu Odibo, conducted the consultation of the Ifa oracle which preceded the naming of a new ruler. There was also an important female chief, the Erelu, who headed the market women.[30] Seniority among all these chiefs depended in some matters on their titles and offices and otherwise on the respective dates of their installation, the Iwoye (or Iwuye) ceremony.

The extent to which these chiefs were associated in the central government of the small kingdom is uncertain, but as in other Yoruba states they constituted a council. By the mid-nineteenth century all members of the four classes were probably eligible to attend this council, the Ajo Oloye, in which they represented the interests not only of their individual offices but also of their own families and quarters of the town and of settlements outside Lagos town of which they were the patrons. The council met every nine days, after the return of traders from the markets at Ejinrin and Badagry, under the Oba's presidency and in his palace, the Iga. This may have been preceded (as it is today) by a separate meeting of the chiefs, the Ijoko Oloye, under the presidency and in the palace of one of the senior chiefs. Though there was no official inner or smaller council in Lagos, such as existed in some other Yoruba kingdoms, the Oba seems on occasions to have consulted formally with the leaders of each of the four chieftaincy orders and he was in any case free to ask the advice of any chief he chose.[31] He relied especially on the Akarigbere group under their leader the Eletu Odibo, and it has been claimed that originally only this class of chiefs constituted the Oba's council.[32]

In addition to the chiefs, the Ifa priesthood and the officials of the various societies characteristic of Yoruba urban life had their parts to play in the conduct of affairs. Prominent among the societies in the nineteenth century was the Oshugbo, representing the community's ancestors and equivalent among the Awori and Ijebu to the society known elsewhere in Yorubaland as the Ogboni.

The people of Lagos lived for the most part crowded into Isale Eko at the western end of the island. The population, which at the end of the eighteenth century was estimated at about 5000, had risen to some 20,000 by the early nineteenth century.[33] By this time there were probably large numbers of Egun

(Gun or Popo) 'emigrants' who had been absorbed into the original Awori, while a few 'liberated Africans' from Sierra Leone may already have begun to arrive. There was also a considerable population of domestic slaves. Many were doubtless Yoruba from the interior while the presence of Mahi from the hinterland of Dahomey and of Hausa was noted at the beginning of the nineteenth century; indeed, accounts of Lagos down to the end of the century describe the majority of the population as being of slave origin.[34] These Lagosians, like most other West Africans, lived in extended families inhabiting groups of buildings known as compounds (*agbole* – a 'flock of houses'). The compound heads, the Arota, were much venerated, and fitted into the mosaic of chiefly jurisdiction which covered the community. Manual labour, even fishing and farming, was largely performed by the women, while the role of the men, as was usual among the Yoruba, was to govern, to defend the community, and to hunt, though their help was given in such heavy tasks as clearing waste land to be brought under cultivation.

There is some evidence that the dwellings in early Lagos were circular in form, but by the middle of the nineteenth century the typical house was rectangular or square, single-storied, with mud walls some 18 inches thick and sometimes whitewashed; to Sir Richard Burton (on a visit in 1861) they seemed to be 'all roof, a monstrous thatch'.[35] Suitable clay was scarce and bamboo houses were also built, though these were soon subject to the depredations of white ants. In the rains, flooding was a constant menace, and even garden walls had to be thatched to prevent their being washed away. These thatched roofs were vulnerable to the fires which frequently broke out during the dry season, especially when the harmattan wind was blowing. Only the Oba's palace, the Iga Iduganran, was covered with tiles, said to have been presented to Oba Akinshemoyin by Portuguese slave traders; roofing with tiles, as will be seen in a later chapter,[36] was regarded as a royal privilege. In Kosoko's reign the palace was further improved by the addition of plate-glass windows and marble paving to the ground floor.

Captain John Adams, who visited the coast between 1786 and 1800, gives a valuable if somewhat forbidding account of Lagos which, though well known, merits repetition here as the first known description of the town. Lagos

> is built on a bank or island, which appears to have been raised from Cradoo lake, by the eddies, after the sea and periodical rains had broken down the boundary which separated it from the ocean. The island is of inconsiderable size, about four miles from the sea, and a foot only above the level of the lake at high water, which is so shallow that boats of only ten to fifteen tons burden can approach the town. . . .
>
> The necessaries of life are there extremely abundant and cheap, and are brought chiefly from the country or northern margin of Cradoo lake, which communicates with Jaboo, a very fertile kingdom, and inhabited by an agricultural and manufacturing people.

The horrid custom of impaling alive a young female to propitiate the favour of the goddess presiding over the rainy season . . . is practised here annually. . . . One was impaled while I was at Lagos, but of course I did not witness the ceremony. I passed by where her lifeless body still remained on the stake a few days afterwards.

Male dogs are banished to the towns opposite to Lagos, for, if any are caught there, they are immediately strangled, split and trimmed like sheep, and hung up at some great man's door, where rows of the putrid carcasses of their canine brethren are to be seen. They are fetiche, and intended to countervail the machinations of the evil spirit.

At the eastern extremity of the town there are a few large trees, which are covered with the heads of malefactors. The skulls are nailed to the trunks and large limbs and present a very appalling spectacle.

The town swarms with water rats from the lake, which burrow in the ground and are so audacious that they, not infrequently, make their appearance under the dinner table of Europeans before the cloth is removed.

Adams describes the mouth of the river as very dangerous. Many boats belonging to English vessels had been lost there. The French, more prudently, landed their goods in canoes on the beach to the east (the present Bar or Victoria Beach) and paid for porterage to the town. They also preferred to 'warp the fresh water for the use of their vessels through the surf' rather than send boats across the bar for it.[37]

It was the Atlantic slave trade which transformed Lagos from an obscure dependency of Benin into a place of wealth and importance. Despite Pacheco's reference in the early sixteenth century to the sale of slaves from the region north of Lagos, 'for twelve or fifteen brass bracelets each', this trade seems not to have developed at Lagos itself until the 1760s.[38] There is no firm evidence as to the trade of Lagos before this time, but as a central point in a network of inland waterways the island was well situated for the exchange of the products of the surrounding country; fish was probably sent inland and Benin is said to have obtained quantities of sea-salt from the Lagos region.[39] According to tradition it was Oba Akinshemoyin, reigning from 1760 to c. 1775, who established the slave trade in Lagos when he invited a group of Portuguese (probably including Brazilians), whose acquaintance he had made during his exile at Apa in the reign of his predecessor, Oba Gabaro, to set up their business at his capital. In Brazil itself a slave trader and former slave, João de Oliveira, claimed to have opened Lagos, as well as Porto Novo, to the trade.[40] The demand for slaves for the American market was at its height between about the years 1650 and 1850, while on the Slave Coast itself – between the Gold Coast and the Niger Delta – the trade was shifting gradually eastwards from Whydah, where it had reached its peak about 1716.[41] This process was accelerated by the European wars arising from the French Revolution and by the anti-slavery measures of the revolutionary government in Paris. These prevented French ships from trading on the coast and so drew the supply of slaves to Lagos. Another factor was the decline in the power of the Oyo kingdom, which after about 1800 was no longer able to protect its trade route to Porto Novo from Dahomean attack.[42] Thus the slave market of Lagos was soon thriving, eclipsing not only the trade to the west but also that of the Benin River,[43] and stimulating an increased demand for slaves in the Yoruba hinterland.

As elsewhere in West Africa, the capture and movement of the slave cargoes to the waiting ships of the European traders was retained in the hands of the local inhabitants. Captain John Adams wrote that 'An active traffic in slaves' was carried on at Lagos, particularly after the desertion of Ardra (near the modern Porto Novo) by the French traders. He adds:

> It has always been the policy of the Lagos people, like those of Bonny, to be themselves the traders and not brokers. They therefore go in their canoes to Ardrah and Badagry, and to the towns situated at the NE extremity of Cradoo lake, where they purchase slaves, Jaboo cloth, and such articles as are required for domestic consumption.[44]

According to the American seaman Robert Adams, Hausa merchants were continually to be met with in Lagos at this time,[45] who must have been participating in the active trade of the town. Another contemporary observer, T. E. Bowdich, heard that slaves were generally taken for part of their journey to Lagos (presumably the last part) by water, and for this traffic special canoes were built, 'superior in size and convenience to those of the coast . . . covered in, with a distinct apartment for the trader and his wives' and each capable of transporting a hundred slaves. He had also heard that the European traders at Lagos had 'once meditated forcing a passage up the river in armed boats, and a vessel of 18 guns was got over the bar, and anchored close to Lagos town; but the project was abandoned as too perilous'. This episode, if authentic, presumably took place in or about the first decade of the nineteenth century and was designed to circumvent the middlemen controlling the last stages of the slaves' journey. Bowdich adds that 'about nine years ago [that is, about 1808] the King of Hio [Oyo] entirely conquered the Mahees, and upwards of 20,000 of them were brought for sale to Lagos'.[46]

The trade at Lagos reached its height in the 1820s, despite the abolition acts passed by many European countries and by the United States in the first two decades of the century, and in 1825 the town was bombarded by a passing British ship engaged in anti-slaving operations.[47] At this time by far the largest single importing country was Brazil, with Cuba coming a poor second; in return, large quantities of Brazilian tobacco were sold by the Portuguese.[48] The majority of the slaves who were shipped from Lagos were Yoruba from the interior, probably now mostly Egba rather than the Ijebu who had apparently furnished the largest supply in earlier days. But Egun, Nupe and Edo or Bini were also among their number.[49] Many were captives taken in the wars now ravaging the Yoruba country. It was at this time that the young Samuel Ajayi Crowther, an Oyo, and Joseph Wright, an Egba, passed through Lagos as slave captives, though happily destined soon to be released by the Royal Navy and landed in Freetown. Their narratives of the experience are useful sources for the historian, giving a vivid though naturally jaundiced account of their journeys in captivity. Wright was scathing about the Lagosians, who, he tells us, 'are very cruel people. They would sell the children of their own bosom. May God almighty make bare his holy arm in sending the gospel to this benighted land.'[50] Crowther, fittingly for a future bishop, was more moderate in his judgement. He describes how, since there was no way of escape other than by water, he was allowed to go where he pleased during his stay in Lagos, and he noticed that 'One part of the town was occupied by the Portuguese and Spaniards, who had come to buy slaves'. The language spoken there seemed to him only 'a faint shadow' of his own, so different was the local dialect from the Oyo tongue.[51]

The slave trade was still flourishing at Lagos in the early 1840s. William Marsh, a repatriate agent of the C.M.S., saw many slaves in chains in June 1845 at Lagos and also at Isheri on the Ogun, where they were being sold to traders from Lagos.[52] It was under the rule of Oba Akitoye that Domingo Martinez, whom D. A. Ross calls 'the most notorious Brazilian in the Bight of Benin', was said to have made a fortune from slaving of from one to two million dollars. When Martinez returned to the Bight in 1846, after a two-year visit to Brazil, he found that Akitoye, the previous Oba of Lagos, had been replaced by Kosoko, who patronised a different set of slave dealers, and it was probably for this reason that he re-established himself at Porto Novo rather than Lagos.[53] Meanwhile Akitoye, somewhat paradoxically, came to be proclaimed by the Anglican missionaries at Badagry as a martyr to his opposition to the slave trade and in 1851 he was restored to his throne in this character by the efforts of the Royal Navy.

The development of overseas trade on an increasing scale, the ensuing prosperity, and the settlement of European slave traders in their midst constituted a considerable disturbance in the traditional pattern of life of the Lagosians. The growing consequence and wealth of the kingdom enabled it to play a part in the wider politics of the coast. Thus Ologun Kutere, the Oba whom Captain John Adams had met during his visit and who occupied the throne between c. 1775/80 and c. 1800/5,[54] was able by making substantial presents to persuade the king of Dahomey to abandon a threatened invasion of Badagry.[55] On the other hand the same developments contributed to the internal dissensions which arose in subsequent reigns and which eventually were to provide occasion and pretext for the British intervention of 1851. One writer, J. F. A. Ajayi, asserts that Oba Akinshemoyin had granted a 'monopoly of external trade' to his Portuguese and Brazilian friends and that this became 'the central political issue' in Lagos, creating parties favourable and hostile to the postulated monopoly and so bringing about the dynastic troubles which beset the monarchy from the beginning of the nineteenth century.[56] The evidence for this is mainly inferential, and it remains no more than an attractive hypothesis.

Towards the middle of the nineteenth century there appeared even more powerful portents of change on the Slave Coast. These were, first, the emigrants coming in search of their homeland from the colony of 'liberated Africans' in Sierra Leone; then the Christian missionaries who followed in their wake, and lastly the palm-oil merchants, the 'legitimate' trading rivals of the slavers. It was not until after the establishment of British authority in Lagos in 1851-2 that any of these three groups attained prominence there, but from then onwards all were growing rapidly in importance in the town and its affairs. Despite their initial and indeed continued dependence on the new regime, all represented powerful forces pursuing their own separate objectives, often in alliance with or looking for support towards the officers of the British Government, at other times antagonistic to that government's policies and actions.

Sierra Leone, whence came the first 'emigrants', had been founded at the end of the eighteenth century as a private venture by members of the anti-slavery movement in England to provide liberated slaves with a home on their own continent. Laws passed in England in 1807 and 1811 effectively prevented British subjects from again engaging in the slave trade and in 1808 the Royal Navy had begun their patrols on the West Coast – the Preventive Squadron – with the object of suppressing the Atlantic trade.[57] In 1808 the struggling settlement at Sierra Leone was taken over as a British colony to serve as a base for the anti-slavery patrols and as a place where the freed human cargoes of captured slaving vessels could be landed and absorbed into this new and experimental community. Thenceforth Freetown and the colony area became the focus of Christian and humanitarian efforts to combat the slave trade and, through the gospel and through education, to improve the lot of the African. The population continued to grow as more and more liberated slaves were landed. The largest element seems to have been the Yoruba-speakers, known in Sierra Leone as 'Aku'. Under the stimulus of Western education, religion and commerce an Anglo-African society evolved. Within this there developed in the late 1830s a movement for return to the lands whence had come the immediate forbears of the more recent inhabitants and the remoter ancestors of the original settlers in the colony. This movement arose partly for economic reasons – to extend already successful commercial enterprises or to seek better trading opportunities – partly to spread and share the light of the Christian gospel with its attendant advantages, and partly from a desire to return to what still counted for many as their homeland. Another possible cause lay in the suspicion and unease engendered by a well-meant scheme of the Colonial Office in London to relieve labour shortage in the West Indies by recruiting indentured labour for the Caribbean in Freetown.[58]

The first recorded emigrants left Sierra Leone in 1839 and, according to the *Memoirs* of the Reverend Henry Townsend, landed in Lagos. They were shortly followed by another group, who met a hostile reception in the great slaving port, complaining later in Abeokuta that the Lagosians had robbed them of all but their clothes before they allowed them to continue their journey inland.[59] Despite this setback, the movement continued, but it was now directed towards Badagry, whence the emigrants made their way inland to the friendlier town of Abeokuta, so that by 1850 there were estimated to be some 3000 of them living in the Egba capital (founded some twenty years before). Thereafter until 1852 the emigrants avoided Lagos, where the slave trade still boomed and political conditions were disturbed, and where, moreover, few had family ties, the Lagosians having been dealers in captives from the hinterland rather than themselves providing raw material for the trade.

Most of, perhaps all, the early emigrants from Sierra Leone were Christians, usually of the first or second generation. Their parish priests and the mission societies were at first unenthusiastic about the movement of return to the Nigerian homeland,[60] but as the emigration continued, undeterred by the unhappy experience in Lagos of the group referred to above and by the failure of the Niger Expedition of 1841, and as requests arrived from the emigrants for spiritual ministrations, this changed. The first Christian missionary to reach Yorubaland was a Wesleyan Methodist, the Reverend T. B. Freeman, a mulatto of English birth and nationality, who paid exploratory vists from Cape Coast to Badagry and Abeokuta at the end of 1842. He was closely followed by the agent of the Anglican Church Missionary Society – the C.M.S. – the Reverend Henry Townsend, who reached Abeokuta from Badagry in January 1843, having made the passage from Sierra Leone in the *Wilberforce*, a former slaving vessel bought by three young Yoruba for the purpose of transporting their fellow Aku to their own country. Both Freeman and Townsend received warm welcomes from the local authorities as well as from the emigrants and both set up the nuclei of mission stations. From the first, Abeokuta seemed to hold out great promise, but the death in 1845 of Shodeke, the friendly Balogun (captain) of the Egba, caused the C.M.S. to establish their base at Badagry. Here the missionaries became involved in the troubled politics of Lagos since Akitoye, the deposed Oba, was in exile in the town.

Not until March 1852 did a Christian missionary reach Lagos itself. He had been narrowly preceded there by the advance guard of the legitimate traders – the 'palm oil ruffians' as they are often, and rather unfairly, called – for as early as 1850 the London firm of Thomas Hutton & Co. was taking steps towards opening up legitimate trade in Lagos.[61] Hardly had the town been taken by the British when others followed, establishing their 'factories' or trade stations along the shore of the Lagos river or harbour. All this was in accordance with the humanitarian aim to fill the vacuum left by the abolition of the slave trade with an alternative, legitimate trade. As matters turned out, the legitimate trade was to consist, so far as exports from West Africa were concerned, very largely of palm products. At first the trade in this had been a small-scale improvisation by the merchant houses of Liverpool, deprived by legislation of their trade in slaves and still anxious to profit from their African connections, but it rapidly grew in importance. Palm oil was in demand as a lubricant for the machines of the British Industrial Revolution and was a principal constituent of soap, which was being increasingly used. The extent of this demand has been exaggerated by the protagonists of 'counter-colonial' economic theories about the Abolitionist movement (to which reference is made again in the next chapter),[62] and it had the unhappy effect of increasing domestic slavery since cheap labour was now needed on a growing scale for the harvesting of the palm-trees, the processing of the oil and above all its transport from the interior by head porterage. But to the humanitarians the development of the trade seemed a providential instrument in their long and heroic fight against the traffic in human lives, and it cannot be wondered at if at times they exaggerated its potentialities in their arguments to induce action by the British Government.

Dynastic troubles

The rift in the royal house of Lagos, which provided the British with pretext and opportunity for their intervention there, was of long standing. It stemmed from the succession to the throne on the death of Oba Ologun Kutere, probably between 1800 and 1805,[63] of Adele, a younger son of the Oba, who was preferred to his elder brother Oshinlokun (or Eshilokun). Although there seems to have been no irregularity about this since all sons born to a reigning Oba were competent to succeed him if chosen by the Kingmakers and the Ifa oracle, Oshinlokun and his adherents stirred up opposition to the new ruler, on one occasion with the help of the neighbouring Ijebu. According to Ajayi's thesis, this strife reflected differences over the conduct of the slave trade, Oshinlokun being supported by those in favour of the Portuguese and Brazilian monopoly', which stemmed from the time of Akinshemoyin, and Adele wishing to introduce 'a more open policy of trade'. There seems no trace of this in traditional accounts, though Law has drawn attention to a suggestion made subsequently by Adele to the British traveller Hugh Clapperton at Badagry in 1825 – probably not very seriously – that the British should help him take Lagos while he in return might collaborate in suppressing the slave trade. Losi, on the other hand, implies that as the reign went on Adele lost his earlier popularity with his people as a result partly of his children's introduction of the unbecoming Egun masquerade into the palace and partly of the freedon with which he allowed his subjects to adopt the Islamic faith which was now penetrating southern Yorubaland.[64] At some point Adele was forcibly prevented by the recalcitrants from taking his father's remains to Berin for burial, and it was apparently soon after this that he was supplanted by Oshinlokun, an event which according to Law's calculations probably took place in 1820 or 1821. The ex-Oba, accompanied by the slaves whom he had inherited from his father, including many Hausa Muslims, now sought refuge in Badagry, where at the invitation of the local chiefs he assumed the headship of the town.[65]

Badagry lies some thirty-five miles to the west of Lagos. Although harbourless and separated from the coast by a narrow lagoon and a strip of land a mile or so wide, it had grown during the eighteenth century into one of the major slaving ports of the coast, ships anchoring, as usually at Lagos, in the open roadstead opposite the town. It seems to have been founded about 1736 by Egun refugees driven eastwards by the Fon of Dahomey, and soon became an outlet for the trade of Oyo and the commerce of the Egbado in the hinterland. Despite the lack of farmland and the consequent dependence of the town on food supplies from the interior, the population grew as more Egun and the local Yoruba (Awori and Egbado) were attracted there, and Portuguese, French, Dutch and English slave traders built their barracoons, or slave warehouses, along the nearby shore.[66] Unlike the Yoruba towns it had no king, although the chief called the Akran was sometimes regarded as senior to the rest. It seems at about the mid-eighteenth century to have been tributary to, or even considered as part of, the kingdom of Oyo, but in the last decade of the century, as has been seen above, it was for a time tributary to Lagos. Adele apparently remained in exile there for some twelve to fourteen years, during which he unsuccessfully attempted on more than one occasion[67] to recover Lagos. He did succeed in helping the people of Badagry (by magic, according to Losi) to repel a Dahomean attack and he gave aid to the Egba in their first (and unsuccessful) siege of Otta and again in the Owiwi War against Ibadan. Adele was the king whom the English explorers Clapperton and Richard Lander met when they landed at Badagry in 1825, and he was still in exile there when Richard and John Lander visited the town in 1830 at the beginning of their famous journey which settled the course and termination of the Niger. This latter visit came at a time when peace had only recently been concluded in a war between Lagos and Porto Novo; according to the Landers, 'This distracted country is ever at war with her neighbours, and consequently is always in a state of agitation and poverty.'[68] Within a few years of the Landers' visit — dates between 1832 and 1835 have been suggested by Law — Oshinlokun's son and successor, the unpopular Oba Idewu Ojulari, took his life (in the traditional account) at the behest of the Oba of Benin, to whom his subjects had appealed, and Adele was recalled to his former throne. Law claims that this represented not only the victory of Adele's branch of the royal dynasty over that of Oshinlokun 'but also the restoration of Benin authority over Lagos and the establishment of Egba influence there in place of that of Ijebu and Ibadan' towns which had been allied with Idewu in the tortuous diplomacy of thes years.⁶⁹ The first part of this conclusion may be somewhat overstated since it is doubtful whether Benin was able to exercise any close control over so distant a state as Lagos at this time, but the persistence of Egba interest in and influence upon the affairs of Lagos during the consular period there forms a theme of some prominence in later chapters of this book.

The various sources agree that Adele's second reign at Lagos, which ended with his death, lasted only two years, and he was succeeded at some time in the 1830s by his son Oluwole. But Oluwole's accession passed over a young and vigorous prince who, as the younger son of Oshinlokun, claimed to be the senior member of the royal house. This was Kosoko, who now put himself at the head of a faction which attempted to depose Oluwole. The failure of this armed rising, known as the Ogun Ewe Koko ('leaves of the coco-yam war') from a rebel song,⁷⁰ forced Kosoko and his followers to flee from Lagos, some going to Epe on the eastern lagoon and the rest scattering to other towns. Kosoko himself went down the western lagoon to Porto Novo and later to Whydah. In both places he came to know well the Portuguese and Brazilian slave dealers settled on this part of the coast, and he adopted their trade When Oluwole lost his life in an explosion of gunpowder in the palace in 1841, Kosoko would have succeeded to the throne, according to Losi,⁷¹ had the chiefs responsible for nominating the new Oba known his whereabouts. In the event, they chose Akitoye, younger brother of both Oshilokun and Adele and thus uncle to the last two Obas and to Kosoko. The new king, 'a soft, charming, rather naive character' in Ajayi's description,⁷² overruled his chiefs' advice, especially that of the Eletu Odibo, the senior chief and Kosoko's implacable enemy, in attempting a reconciliation with his nephew. Kosoko was recalled to Lagos with his followers and installed as chief of Ereko, a part of Lagos island, where he was allowed to form his own court. He quickly set about rebuilding his position in the town, finding his strongest support among the war chiefs and apparently also among the small Muslim community in the town. In disgust at this development, the Eletu Odibo left Lagos and removed to Badagry. After some time, however, Akitoye determined to recall his minister, presumably needing his support. This precipitated a rising by Kosoko and his party in July 1845.⁷³ In the course of this the Oba's enemies soon gained the upper hand and were able to surround Isale Eko, including the palace area. This rising, named the Ogun Olomiro, or 'salt-water war', from the brackish water in the wells where the Lagosians were forced to drink during the siege, is said to have lasted about three weeks. Finally, Akitoye, accepting defeat, managed to escape up the lagoon to the north and was allowed by Oshodi Tapa, Kosoko's war captain, to pass by the Agboyi creek into the Ogun River and so to reach Abeokuta, where he was accorded temporary asylum.

Resistance continued in Lagos for some three days after the Oba's flight, but Kosoko was then able to enter the Iga and to assume with that act the long-coveted title of Oba. He at once recognised the escape of Akitoye as a threat and after accepting (Losi tells us) Tapa's explanation that the ex-Oba had thrown his pursuers into a 'trance', sent messages to Abeokuta demanding Akitoye's head. The chiefs who dominated the Egba government had no intention of harming the royal exile, whose claim on them as son of a woman from the Owu quarter of Abeokuta they accepted and whom they regarded as a useful ally. His presence, however, occasioned disputes between the leaders of the Ogboni society, who, rather than the kings of this federated town, constituted the civil government, and the Ologun, or war chiefs, who were prepared to surrender him to Kosoko.[74] In the event, in March 1845, Akitoye was provided by the Egba with an escort to Badagry and here, in the traditional town of refuge for the Lagosians, he managed to re-establish his cause. His followers rallied to him from Lagos, he became the protégé of the resident European missionaries and traders, and he was assured of diplomatic and military support from the Egba. Hostilities were resumed across the lagoon, but at this point the course of events was interrupted. Akitoye turned for help in regaining his throne first to the missionaries and then through them to Consul John Beecroft, the official representative of the power whose cruisers had long been patrolling the coast and whose intervention on the African shore was now to lead, step by step, towards the creation of southern Nigeria.

2

The Reduction of Lagos

The roots of intervention

The consequences of the violent irruption of the British into the affairs of Lagos at the end of 1851 were so far-reaching and of such importance as to set the historian searching for causes, even for a single grand cause, of a magnitude comparable to those consequences. This may in part account for the unsatisfactory and unconvincing nature of many of the explanations adduced, first by contemporaries and participants, then by historians of colonial times, and last by the sometimes more objective historians of the post-colonial school. The objects of intervention stated in 1851 were the same as those given for the establishment of the consulate of the Bights of Benin and Biafra: to extirpate the 'abominable traffic' in slaves for which Lagos had become notorious and to foster the legitimate trade of the Yoruba hinterland. This twofold explanation sufficed for the historians of colonial Nigeria; it was not merely acceptable on sentimental grounds but also seemed to fit the evidence as to the motives and methods of those who authorised and carried out the intervention.[1] The mid-twentieth century, however, produced a generation suspicious and wary of the colonial thesis in all its aspects, who reinterpreted the intervention as being actuated by British self-interest, and especially by the desire to protect and expand British commerce in West Africa.[2] Both these explanations contain much that is true and important, and indeed they supplement rather than contradict each other to a greater extent than the protagonists of the counter-colonialist thesis understand. But both are inadequate, and for the same broad reason: that they attempt an explanation in monocausal terms, thereby over-simplifying a situation of some complexity and obscuring the fact that the event under analysis, like most events in history, was the consequence o interaction between different causes and between different motives, sometimes conflicting, sometimes complementary.

It is necessary to ask, first, how the British were brought to intervene at Lagos, and then, in subsequent chapters of this book, how, after fierce initial resistance to their presence, they were able to maintain themselves ashore with only the barest reserve of force. The answers to these questions must be sought in both the British, or metropolitan, and the local situations. It is also necessary to identify the separate links in the causal chain, tracing the means by which one event led to another, often independently of and sometimes contrary to the intentions of the actors. For there is no short cut in historical explanation: the 'model' or the 'covering law', especially when derived *a priori* from events outside those under analysis, cannot replace the establishment of a coherent narrative and the identification, examination and classification of particular causes in a particular situation. In the present instance, these causes readily arrange themselves as external — those prompting the actions of the British — and internal or local, and the former will be examined first.

The natural advantages of Lagos as a centre of commerce were clear to its early visitors. G. A. Robertson, for example, wrote in 1819 that 'Lagos is one of the most desirable places on this coast for an European settlement, as it lies between the great branches of the Niger and the Western trade. ... The inhabitants are already disposed to habits of industry. ....'[3] Thus suggestions that Great Britain should intervene officially at Lagos had been reaching London for several years before Queen Victoria's Government authorised the action which was taken at the end of 1851. They came from three sources: the Anglican missionaries, who were in touch with Akitoye at Badagry, the European and other traders, and the Egba, whose capital at Abeokuta was now coming to be the focus of missionary ambition in West Africa. For all these, use of the port of Lagos and freedom of movement for trade on the 'roads' (or bush tracks) and rivers, especially the Ogun, leading from the lagoon into the hinterland, were an important interest. The earliest suggestion (leaving aside Oba Adele's feeler to Clapperton in 1825) seems to be that made by Henry Townsend of the C.M.S., who on his return to Badagry from a visit to Abeokuta in 1844 advised the taking of Lagos and support for the Egba in their resistance to the encroaching Dahomeans. Next there is a letter addressed by the 'British Residents at Badagry to the Governor of Cape Coast or any of Her Majesty's Naval Officers on the West Coast of Africa' on 20 August 1845, for dispatch to the first passing ship, which transmitted a promise by Oba Akitoye to give up the slave trade and admit the English to Lagos in return for help against Kosoko, described as a vile slave trader who aimed at 'nothing less than the entire extirpation of the English'. On the same day Townsend wrote in similar terms to the headquarters of his society in London.[4]

Conditions in Dahomey itself were already causing anxiety to the British Government. Several fruitless efforts were made during the 1840s to persuade King Ghezo to enter into an anti-slaving agreement, and when a consulate for the two Bights was set up in 1849, based on Fernando Po, a vice-consul, John Duncan, was posted to the Dahomean port of Whydah. At the beginning of 1850 Palmerston, the Foreign Secretary in Russell's administration and a strong and consistent opponent of the slave trade, was visited at the Foreign Office by a deputation from the C.M.S., and at about the same time he received a persuasive letter from the merchant Thomas Hutton. Both stressed the need to keep open Abeokuta's communications with the coast and to end the slave trade at Lagos, described as the 'natural port' of Abeokuta. Ever responsive to such appeals, Palmerston passed on these views to Beecroft, his new consul, adding that the C.M.S. had told him of 'a chief friendly to the English' who had been expelled from Lagos. He also mentioned reports that numerous liberated slaves had been kidnapped after reaching Abeokuta and sold in the Lagos market. The consul was to investigate these matters and remonstrate with the Lagos authorities.[5] Beecroft does not seem to have visited Lagos to carry out these instructions but in July 1850, after an abortive mission to the King of Dahomey, he wrote to the foreign secretary recommending that Whydah should be blockaded and that an anti-slaving treaty should be made with Akitoye, who would then be replaced on his throne, thus releasing the Abeokutans 'from the jeopardy that they are continually in of the fear of the King of Dahomey'.[6] In August he passed on to Palmerston a pathetically worded appeal for help from the Egba chiefs:"All the world from the feet of the edge of the sea, they are the enemies of the Egbas ... as Lagos, Porto Novo, and Dahomey. They desire to close the road that we may not hold intercourse with our friends the English.'[7]

The British Government were more disposed to heed such appeals than they would have been in the 1840s after the disillusionment caused by the Niger Expedition of 1841 or in the 1860s when the expense of the West African territories was beginning to weigh on them. Already three small colonies were in existence down the West Coast: on the Gambia, at Sierra Leone, and on the Gold Coast. Official opinion concurred with the humanitarian thesis that the Preventive or Anti-Slavery Squadron alone could not hope to extinguish the trade despite the increasing efficiency which resulted from the gradual introduction of steam vessels, and the need for land bases, especially on the Slave Coast itself, and for forceful action by land was admitted. For a few months in 1843 a small detachment of troops from the Gold Coast Corps had been stationed at Badagry, and now the consulate for the Bights provided if not a base at least a foothold. The effectiveness of action on land had been demonstrated in the brisk measures taken in 1840 by the Hon. Joseph Denman, commander of the armed schooner H.M.S. *Wanderer*, against the large and notorious slaving base at the mouth of the Gallinas River. 'For the first time a definite step had been taken to strike at the root of the trade.' Christopher Lloyd writes. 'Instead of hanging about the coast on the chance of capturing a slaver as she entered or left harbour, the barracoons themselves had been destroyed', and an export of some 12,000 to 15,000 slaves yearly had been decisively checked.[8] But action of this kind so alarmed the local traders that, as the merchants and the Free Trade Members of Parliament were quick to point out, it was as discouraging to the growth of legitimate trading as to slaving, and more positive steps were needed if the situation was to be even contained. It was here that Akitoye's troubles provided so attractive a solution, and the scheme to restore him to the throne of Lagos, first propounded by his missionary patrons, gained a vigorous adherent in John Beecroft, Her Majesty's energetic consul and forwarder of her interests in the Bights, who in turn persuaded his superior, Lord Palmerston, of its feasibility.[9]

Oba Akitoye's approach to the British authorities on the coast for protection and help in regaining his throne is sufficiently explained by self-interest. As early as March 1846 he had made an unsuccessful attack by land and lagoon on Lagos with the Egba as allies. The missionaries strengthened his case by representing him in the role of an enthusiastic opponent of the slave trade.[10] But there is no evidence for this before his deposition,[11] whereas his connection with the well-known slaver Domingo Martinez, who had backed his expedition in 1846 and was to do so again in 1848, suggests the reverse.[12] The point is of no great importance in the present context. What is clear is that his rival Kosoko was both in possession of Lagos and co-operating with the Portuguese slave traders based there, so that the ex-Oba would naturally conclude that his best policy was to win the support of the anti-slaving forces by adopting or at least professing their views. At Abeokuta and again at Badagry he had the opportunity for this, and his cause was taken up with particular enthusiasm by the Anglican missionaries who, as has been seen above, were not slow in offering advice to the British Government as to the steps which should be taken to eradicate the slave trade.

Meanwhile, in 1850–1 there were encouraging signs of a diminution of the trade on the Bights and especially at Lagos. A great advance occurred when in 1850 the Brazilian Parliament at Rio passed a drastic act which within three years closed what had been by far the largest market for slaves. This was the direct result of pressure by the British Government and the Royal Navy, culminating in Palmerston's enforcement of the Aberdeen Act of 1845 under which British cruisers were empowered to arrest Brazilian slavers, either loaded or unloaded, north or south of the line and even in Brazilian waters. Towards the end of 1850 the missionaries at Abeokuta sent reports that the price of slaves at Lagos had fallen from $60 a head to $45, presumably as a result of the Brazilian situation, and that the trade was 'spoiled', while the last ship to reach Bahia with a legal cargo of slaves was the *Relampago*, which left Lagos in 1851 at the end of Kosoko's reign there.[13] But even as the Brazilian trade ceased, the increasing demand in Europe and elsewhere for sugar and cotton was leading to a revival of slave exports to Cuba and also to an increased export to the southern United States. Once again the price of slaves rose, reaching new records. This enabled the humanitarians in the House of Commons, backed by the missionaries and enjoying Palmerston's support, to defeat a resolution tabled by Sir William Hutt to discontinue the Naval Squadron.

Early in January 1851 Consul Beecroft paid a visit to Badagry, going by sea on board H.M.S. *Jackal*. From the C.M.S. station, where he was the guest of the agent, the Reverend C. A. Gollmer, he wrote privately to Lord Stanle at the Foreign Office. After apologising for not having 'yet got into the system of writing so much', he went on to say that he had heard that Lagos was in consternation, presumably over his visit to Badagry, and that 'it is ten thousand pities that it was [sic] not under the British, it would do more to shake the Slave Trade here than anything else.'[14] The next day he had a talk with Akitoye, whom he pronounced 'a quite prudent man to all appearances'. The ex-Oba maintained a large number of followers at Badagry, all kept under arms, but nevertheless Beecroft did not think his position in the town to be secure since a considerable part of the population supported Kosoko, with whom they kept in communication.

From Badagry Beecroft went inland to Abeokuta, where he inspected the defences, concluding that they would be 'of very little utility against an invading enemy' – a view in which he was soon proved wrong when a fierce Dahomean attack in March 1851 was repulsed by the Abeokutans in a battle fought mainly along the walls. On his return to Badagry the consul was presented by Akitoye with a formal request, which had been drafted by Gollmer, for British protection. He replied by persuading the ex-Oba to come aboard the *Jackal* and accompany him first to the Benin River and then to Fernando Po, the seat of the consulate.[15] Three days after reporting this, Beecroft sent a second dispatch to the Foreign Office (written under the stress of fever) in which he urged that Lagos should be taken under British protection. Recognising that this would require the use of force, he recommended that an attack should be mounted from Badagry: 'you go down the lagoon, sans ceremonie you may command it being an island. . . . Lagos ought not to be allowed to escape, place the right person there all is well'.[16] The consul then suggested to the commander of the Squadron that he should take immediate action against Lagos, to which Commodore Fanshawe replied that he must await specific instructions from the Admiralty for any such action.[17]

In the meantime a decisive step had been taken in London cowards intervention. On 20 February 1851 Palmerston signed a dispatch authorising Beecroft to conclude a treaty for the abolition of the slave trade with the ruler of Lagos, and on the following day he instructed him further to represent to the king 'that the British Government is resolved to put an end to the African Slave Trade, and has the means and power to do so'. The consul was to tell Kosoko that 'Great Britain is a strong power both by sea and by land, that her friendship is worth having, and that her displeasure it is well to avoid'. If the Oba showed a disposition to refuse this advice, he was to be reminded 'that Lagos is near the sea and that on the sea are the ships and cannon of England, and also that he does not hold his authority without a competitor'.[18] Robert Gavin concludes that these instructions were 'ambiguous', reflecting a division in the British Caoinet,[19] but when the consul received them five months later,[20] he did not doubt that he held in his hands an instrument whereby the problem of Lagos could be resolved.

Beecroft's decision to remove Akitoye from Badagry soon became justified by the violent civil war which broke out there in mid-June between the ex-Oba's supporters in the town, led by the Mewu, an exiled chief from Porto Novo who also controlled Anowo, a town tributary to Badagry on the road to Abeokuta, and the majority of the Badagry chiefs, who were backing Kosoko. Many buildings were set on fire, including the factory of the English trader Hutton, where an English member of the staff was killed, and two large compounds belonging to Sierra Leonean 'emigrants'. The fighting ended in the flight of the Badagrian chiefs to neighbouring villages, from which they mounted a counter-attack a week later. By now, however, the pro-Akitoye party had been joined by some 600 or more Egba warriors led by twenty of the Abeokuta war chiefs,[21] and the supporters of Kosoko were again forced to retreat to their canoes.[22] The following month two determined attempts were made to regain the town by Kosoko's forces from Lagos, though the Oba himself does not seem to have been present with his troops. Gollmer, in charge of the C.M.S. base, wrote that in the first of these waterborne actions, 'There were about 100 large canoes, containing 10–25 men each', which opened fire on the town from their swivel guns and muskets. The Lagosians ultimately withdrew without effecting a landing, but returned to the attack later in the month. On the second occasion the engagement lasted about five hours during which, Gollmer says, the attackers 'loaded their swivels and guns, pulled inshore, fired continuously and quickly returned to reload, and so they continued'. Once again, however, they did not succeed in landing.[23]

By now the damage done at Badagry, presumably mostly in the first battle, had been considerable and the town was largely ruined. When the American Baptist missionary T. J. Bowen had landed there in August 1850, he had estimated the population at 10,000. He returned in November 1851 to find 'the site of this once populous town now covered with fields of India corn' and only about 1000 people living there in rude shelters.[24]

News of events at Badagry reached the British Government from naval and missionary as well as consular sources. The Bashorun, or commander of the Abeokutan army, prompted by Gollmer, the C.M.S. agent, wrote in early July to Captain L. T. Jones, the senior Royal Navy officer on the coast, to stress that despite the defeat of Kosoko's supporters in Badagry and the repulse in March of the Dahomeans at Abeokuta, the situation was still serious for the friends of the British. 'At present Badagry is the only medium of communication between the English and Abeokuta', he wrote, but 'If Lagos is destroyed and Akitoye restored, we should have little to fear.'[25] Palmerston reacted strongly. He had recently interviewed Crowther, sent to London by the C.M.S. with the aim of setting out the case for British support to the Egba and the unrestricted use of the river Ogun, and he now sent a request, in September, to the

Admiralty that the Dahomean coast should be blockaded and that Captain H. W. Bruce, the commodore (or commander-in-chief) of the naval forces, should consider sending an expedition against Lagos,[26] while in October Beecroft was authorised by the Foreign Secretary to supply the Badagrians with muskets and ammunition to the value of £200.[27]

The Admiralty acceded without delay, though also without enthusiasm, to the foreign secretary's requests. Instructions were given for a blockade of Whydah and the rest of the so-called Dahomean coast from 1 January 1852, and Bruce was given leave to proceed at Lagos according to his 'own discretion and judgement', with authority to hire a small steamer for the operation if he thought it necessary.[28] It had taken time to induce the Admiralty to reach this measure of co-operation. As another writer has recently pointed out, the extent to which the activities of the Naval Squadron were decided by the Admiralty and by the Foreign Office remained an open question,[29] and despite the success of Denman's exploit in the Gallinas, naval officers were reluctant to commit their forces ashore. Bruce took a lukewarm view of plans by Palmerston and Beecroft for action at Lagos, and he drew the attention of the Admiralty to an article of an Anglo-French convention of May 1845 which stipulated that no part of the coast should be occupied without the consent of the other party – a legalism of which little notice seems to have been taken elsewhere.[30] His reluctance to extend his commitments was shared by the Admiralty, who warned him that he was 'not to keep possession of Lagos, nor to remain there beyond what is absolutely necessary'.[31] But before any of these instructions could be put into effect, they had been overtaken by the action taken against Lagos at the end of November.

In acknowledging Palmerston's two crucial dispatches of the previous February, Beecroft wrote in September that he was postponing a visit to Lagos 'until the rainy season subsides, which will be in November'.[32] Adhering to this programme, the consul, accompanied by Akitoye (who had with him a small suite of five persons), arrived off Lagos in H.M.S. *Bloodhound* on 13 November. Commander Wilmot of the sloop *Harlequin* reported that he had already been ashore to visit Kosoko, who had received him politely. Beecroft then steamed along the coast to Badagry, where he and Akitoye landed briefly on 15 November, the ex-Oba being greeted there, according to the consul, 'with demonstrations of boundless joy'. On 18 November the *Bloodhound* was back in the Lagos roads, but a fierce storm delayed the opening of negotiations. The political climate was as inauspicious as the weather, for a messenger had come from the town to say that if the British party crossed the bar in more than one boat they would be fired on. Eventually, however, Kosoko agreed to allow two boats to enter the river under a flag of truce, and on 20 November Beecroft's party was rowed to the Iga, where it was received by the Oba and his chiefs.[33]

The British representatives at the ensuing palaver consisted of the consul, Commander A. P. E. Wilmot, Commander Gardner of H.M.S. *Waterwitch*, and Lieutenant R. Patey from the *Bloodhound*; there is no confirmation in official accounts of the picturesque tradition that Akitoye, disguised in European clothes, was also present.[34] They opened the discussion by pointing out the advantages to the Oba of peace, but this, they said, depended on his seeking the friendship of the English and on the total abolition of 'Foreign Slavery' – that is, the export of slaves – to which the large majority of chiefs on the coast had already agreed. These proposals met a stony reception; in the words of the British note of the conference, they were 'declined with the remark that the friendship of the English was not wanted',[35] and the British returned to their boats.

Akitoye must have been relieved, although, knowing Kosoko's pride and determination, little surprised, at his rival's outright rejection of the terms put to him at the conference. Beecroft's equally unrecorded reaction may well have been less of disappointment at failure than of satisfaction that the opportunity had at last come to take decisive measures against this obstinate refuge of the slave trade. At any rate he lost no time in writing to Commander T. G. Forbes of H.M.S. *Philomel*, at that time the senior officer in the Bights Division, that having 'used every available means . . . to make a treaty' with Kosoko, he had no alternative now but to ask the Royal Navy for 'a sufficient force to compel him to make a Treaty or dethrone him and replace the rightful heir Akitoye'. It was necessary, he added, to act speedily since 'war' – presumably the expected attack by Kosoko and the Dahomeans on Badagry – was likely to break out at any time and because the bar was relatively easy to cross at this season.[36] The following day, 23 November, Forbes had a meeting with Beecroft – presumably at sea – and after the consul had shown him Palmerston's dispatches of the previous February as authority for taking action against Lagos, they decided to collect as large a force as possible and to enter the river.[37]

Thus Great Britain was committed to action against Lagos. Robert Gavin writes that Beecroft had 'dug up an old despatch of 20th February 1851' to justify the subsequent proceedings.[38] This is a misrepresentation. At a time when communications between London and distant diplomatic posts took months in transmission, instructions of this kind were conceived as giving authority for courses of action in wide terms and extending over a considerable period. Moreover, from Beecroft's point of view these dispatches were far from being 'dug up' but were instead of current reference, having reached him only two months before,[39] and their import was corroborated by the Admiralty instructions of October,[40] apparently still on their way to the scene of action. Two months later, on receipt of news of the unsuccessful operations in November, a new foreign secretary was to contend that Beecroft had exceeded his instructions, chiding him that 'if the Chief of Lagos refused to abandon the slave trade, you were to remind him of British power, but not directed immediately to begin hostilities'.[41] Granville had now replaced Palmerston at the Foreign Office, and there was less disposition in Downing Street to encourage or sanction forward action of this kind. Nevertheless, the dispatch ended by commending Beecroft's zeal. At Lagos, meantime, the die had been cast and an end had been made to the long and tangled causal sequence by the decision of two men, prompted by a third: Beecroft the consul and former trader, Forbes the naval officer, and Akitoye, claimant to the throne of Lagos, ally of the Egba, and the hope of the British missionaries and humanitarians.

Aggression repulsed and rewarded

There were two battles of Lagos, the first in late November 1851, ending in the defeat and withdrawal of the attacking force, and the second a month later, ending in the flight of Kosoko, leaving his ruined capital to Akitoye. Descriptions of these engagements have been given in a number of recent works,[42] so that no more than an outline of events is called for here. One initial problem confronting the British officers, omitted from these accounts, must be mentioned. This is the lack of information available to them about both the bar and the channel beyond it. As has been seen in the last chapter, the hazards of the former were such that many, perhaps most, trading vessels preferred to remain rocking uncomfortably in the roads and communicating with the shore by canoes hired, with their crews, from the Gold Coast. Almost certainly to naval vessel, as opposed to ships' boats, had previously crossed into the river, where the depth of water was unknown. Thus the decision to use the paddle-steamer H.M.S. *Bloodhound* in the assault constituted a considerable risk, even though she was of relatively shallow draught, and a passage through the bar was surveyed beforehand by Thomas Earl, Master of the *Harlequin*.

The first attack was launched on 25 November by a force which had been hastily collected by Forbes after his interview with Beecroft. It consisted of 306 officers and men, sailors and marines, conveyed in H.M.S. *Bloodhound*, and twenty-one boats towed behind the steamer; they were preceded by a naval gig flying a white flag on board which were the consul and Commander Vilmot. After successfully navigating the bar, the *Bloodhound* with her attendant boats entered the channel leading to Lagos island and the lagoon. As she did so she was met by musket fire from outposts which were apparently on both sides of the river.[43] At first, according to the consul, the expedition's leaders were disposed to regard this firing as being unauthorised by Kosoko. But after the threats made to him, the Oba was not disposed to allow this armed force to approach his shores with impunity, and it could well be argued that the British were misusing their white flag. In any case the fire did not cease as the flotilla drew nearer, and it soon became (as Beecroft rather plaintively writes) 'so galling as to render the Flag of Truce nugatory'. The *Bloodhound* continued to navigate these little-known waters without returning the fire until she reached a point a the north end of the island opposite the town, which now at last was visible to those on board – to whom it must have looked, as it did to Burton in 1861. 'as if a hole had been hollowed out in the original mangrove forest'.⁴⁴ But here the steamer grounded, and as she did so she came under heavy cannon fire from the shore. The British waited a further twenty minutes without firing, then hauled down their white flag and began to retaliate. But their position as an immovable sitting target was uncomfortable and soon their casualties began to mount. After about an hour of this, it was decided to attempt a landing in order to capture the battery, which was the mainstay of the defence. Despite inadequate covering fire from the badly positioned *Bloodhound*, the landing party got ashore, but there they met with such stiff resistance that they were unable to do more than set fire to a number of buildings. 'The mud walls and very narrow streets afforded so great an advantage to the enemy who were swarming in vast numbers and proved themselves such good marksmen', Beecroft wrote, 'that it was thought advisable to recall the people to the boats.' The *Bloodhound* was successfully refloated and darkness brought an end to the firing. On the British side two officers had been killed and two officers and ten men wounded. The following morning Forbes ordered the expedition to withdraw. Beecroft wrote that he feared an outbreak of fever if a longer stay was made in the river, but this seems merely an attempt to disguise the fact that the expedition had met with a disastrous failure.

The news of the British defeat spread fast. At Badagry the firing had been clearly heard. The American missionary Bowen, who was in the half-ruined town, reports that 'Before nine o'clock . . . the negotiation commenced: bang-boom. . . . "The English", I said, "are abolishing the slave trade." ' But as the sound of gunfire continued unabated, he became alarmed and hurriedly left for Abeokuta, where a few days afterwards he heard how matters had been concluded.⁴⁵

Beecroft's impetuousness, aided by Forbes's underestimate of the capacity of Kosoko and the Lagosians to resist an attack, had resulted in humiliation for the British. The situation could not be left unmended. The consul now turned, as he should have done earlier, to Bruce, the commodore of the Squadron, for advice and support. He also wrote to the Oba of Benin, whose influence at Lagos he evidently overestimated. In his letter to the Oba he declared that Kosoko, by opening fire on a flag of truce, had made war on England and that the English would now acknowledge no other ruler at Lagos than Akitoye. He threatened that if Kosoko did not surrender his sovereignty 'before the end of the month' (he was writing on 4 December) 'Lagos will be totally destroyed by fire and not one house will be left between that and Jaboo'.⁴⁶ There is no record of this letter ever having reached Benin, and in any case the British did not wait for the expiry of their oblique and rather ill-considered ultimatum. Meanwhile, during the night of 30 November, a party from H.M.S.s *Harlequin* and *Volcano* had gone ashore by moonlight and succeeded in setting fire to a group of slave barracoons at the eastern entrance of the river (presumably near the western end of the present Bar Beach).

By the time that Bruce reached Lagos, on 18 December, he had received the orders of the previous October from the Admiralty giving him full discretion in acting against Lagos, and after discussion with the consul and the naval officers in the area, he agreed to help mount a second attack. At his suggestion, Beecroft first returned briefly to Badagry, where he had landed Akitoye after the failure of the action in November, and arranged with the ex-Oba that some 630 of his armed followers should make their way along the shore in order to support the seaborne attack on Lagos. Beecroft then again took Akitoye on board and on 21 December was back in the Lagos roadstead, where a second and larger force of ships and men were assembling under the command of Captain L. T. Jones of H.M.S. *Samson*.

At Lagos Kosoko was using the interval in the fighting to reinforce his defences, already shown to be unexpectedly strong. These defences seem to have been wholly based on shore fortifications, no important part being allotted to the war canoes, which must have been judged no match for the more stable and heavily armed naval boats of the British. Along the south-western shore facing the river, where the Marina runs now, a continuous trench was dug and an earthen wall thrown up; batteries of guns, of which there were over forty pieces, one whose barrel was over ten feet in length, were placed at key points. A stout stockade two miles long covered the batteries and those weak places in the defences where the depth of water allowed enemy boats to approach the shore.[47] According to Burton, defences were also erected on the west bank of the river at 'Takpa's Point', presumably the most southerly of three small promontories beyond the bar.[48] Inspecting these fortifications after the battle, Beecroft remarked that 'Had an Engineer from Woolwich been on the spot it could not have been better planned'. Probably Kosoko had the benefit of advice from his Portuguese friends in preparing for the British attack, as Forbes told Bruce, but the art of fortification must have been familiar to him since most Yoruba towns were protected by mud walls and outer ditches, often with elaborately contrived gates.[49] The army manning these defences at Lagos was afterwards estimated by the attackers at some 5000 warriors, all armed with muskets.

On 22 December Akitoye's flag was seen flying at the western entrance to the river, signalling the arrival of his small army from Badagry. The troops reported that on their march towards Lagos they had been attacked by adherents of Kosoko at the village of 'Ageedoo' (Ajido, a few miles east of Badagry), and had driven off their assailants and destroyed the village. Two days later, on Christmas Eve 1851, Captain Jones led H.M.S.s *Bloodhound* and *Teazer* (the latter being a screw steamer) over the bar, accompanied by a fotilla of boats from these and from other ships remaining in the roadstead, and by the consul's iron galley, the *Victoria*, which had been fitted with twelve-pourd and twenty-four-pound rockets. Christmas Day was spent at rest in the river, despite attempts at harassing fire from the shore. On the 26th the attack went in, directed at the north end of the island where the Iga was situated and where the water was believed to be deep enough to allow the boats to approach close inshore. The hazards of the river as well as of the bar were now better known, a second survey having been made by the Master of the *Harlequin* with two assistants.[50] Yet both the *Bloodhound* and *Teazer* soon went aground, the former (piloted by the African John Johns) near her destination at the north of the island and the other further south. Thus both the two ships and the men in

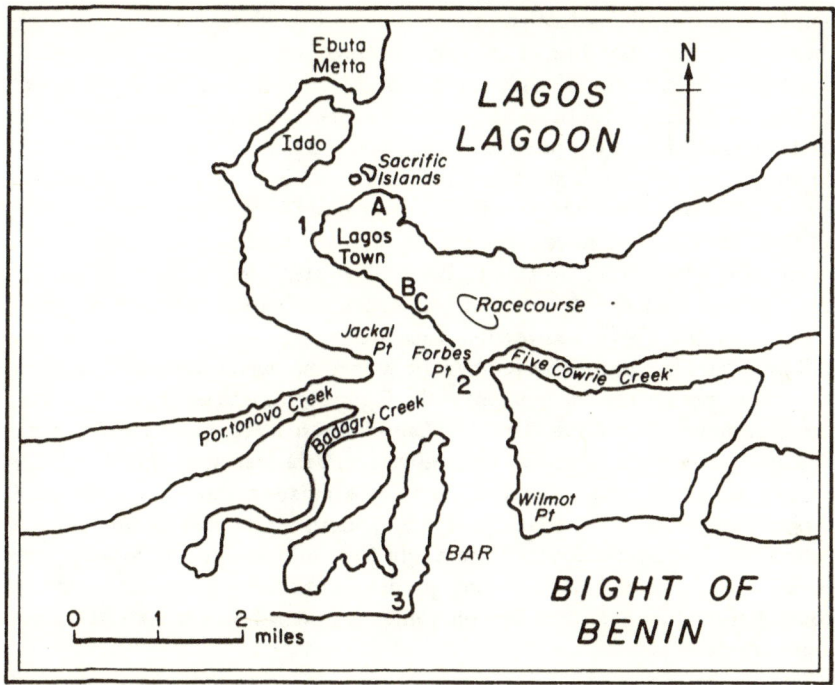

Key

A King's palace or Iga Idunganran
B C.M.S. compound
C British Consulate
1 Where H.M.S. *Bloodhound* went aground, 1851
2 Where H.M.S. *Teazer* went aground, 1851
3 Probable point where Akitoye's men assembled, 1851

Lagos and Lagos River, based on the surveys of 1851 and 1859

the boats were exposed to heavy fire. At this point Captain Lyster (of H.M.S. *Penelope*) led a force of some 200 men in boats to an unstaked part of the beach where they succeeded in landing and spiking a shore battery of two twelve-pounders. But the party was strongly counter-attacked by a much larger force and was soon forced to retreat to their boats, suffering many casuabies and leaving two men in the hands of the enemy. During the afternoon other landing parties were organised with the aim of silencing the enemy's guns, but they met with varying success and when night fell the battle was still undecided.

At daylight on 27 December the *Teazer*, now refloated, moved up with her attendant boats to join the *Bloodhound* at the north of the island, and the ships, including the *Victoria* with her rockets, now opened up an intensive bombardment of the palace and the town. During the course of this lasting almost the whole day, one of the rockets scored a hit on the Oba's powder-magazine, which exploded with a great roar. Meanwhile, the British attempted no further landings. But the artillery and the rockets had done their work, and after the explosion of the powder-magazine firing from the town begin to die down. By sunset all was quiet, and refugees could be seen putting off for the mainland in canoes piled high with their household goods. The next morning, 28 December, all remained 'serene and quiet, not a solitary sound of a gun'. Then came news: 'after breakfast', Beecroft wrote, 'the Second Chief of the small village opposite[51] came on board, and informed me that we were conquerors, the Town was totally evacuated'.

The victory had been achieved by superior fire-power, as was indicated in the Yoruba names for the engagement – the Ogun Agidingbi or Ogun Anoyaya, the 'Booming' or 'Boiling Battle'.[52] Lagosian casualties are unknown, while British casualties amounted to two officers and thirteen men killed and five officers and seventy men wounded. Had Kosoko made greater use of his fleet of war canoes, with their swivel guns and cannon, rather than relying almost entirely on his static defences,[53] he might have inflicted greater losses on the enemy and prevented their landing parties from reaching the shore, but he could hardly have affected the outcome, almost wholly the result of the bombardment.

In the evening of 28 December Beecroft went on shore and inspected Kosoko's defences. The following day Akitoye was ferried across the river with his followers and left to master the situation in the almost deserted town. He learnt that Kosoko with his leading chiefs and warriors had fled down the eastern lagoon to take refuge on the Ijebu (northern) shore. The remaining chiefs signified acceptance of Akitoye as their king, and the Oba was thus enabled to repossess the throne and palace. On 30 December the Royal Navy dismantled the Lagos batteries, spiking the guns and dumping most of them at sea,[54] and on the last day of 1851 Beecroft with Captain Jones, Lieutenant Patey and an officer of the Marines visited the restored Oba and obtained his signature to a treaty for the supression of the slave trade. But now Captain Bruce arrived on the scene and a more solemn undertaking between Akitoye and his protectors was arranged. This took place on 1 January 1852 on board H.M.S. *Penelope* in the Lagos roads. The treaty (reproduced as Appendix A) was in the form of the usual printed draft treaty providing for the abolition of the slave trade, to which three articles were added: these forebade human sacrifice (VII), promised protection to Christian missionaries and their converts (VIII), and provided for the adhesion of the French Government if it so wished (IX) (which it never did). It was signed by Bruce and Beecroft on behalf of Queen Victoria's Government and by Akitoye and two of his chiefs. A salute was fired by the ship's guns, wine and biscuits were served, and thus opened the consular era at Lagos.

Intervention analysed

The reduction of Lagos was the culmination of three separate but interlocking causal sequences. The first of these, indigenous or Lagosian, arose from the politics of the island kingdom, while the two others were British, arising from the humanitarian drive to abolish the slave trade and from the less altruistic desire to extend political, commercial and religious interests. The first, the African element in the explanation, has been either minimised or almost entirely ignored alike by 'colonial' and 'anti-colonial' historians, and yet it is important. The dispute over the throne of Lagos and the growth of hostile factions around the two claimants, backed by external alliances, provided a pretext and more for British intervention. The British naval and consular presence on the coast offered an opportunity which the party in eclipse, that of Akitoye, could not overlook. It could be argued that this local situation was irrelevant, or of only minor relevance, to the fact of intervention, which would have taken place even had Lagos been a united kingdom. But such speculation is illegitimate in historical writing, and it postulates, moreover, a passivity on the part of the indigenous inhabitants which goes beyond what is credible.

The contemporary official explanation, accepted by the 'colonial' school, ascribing intervention to Britain's humanitarian concern to eradicate the obstinately lingering slave trade, has much force. Abolition had called for a tremendous effort by those who supported the movement, and long after the British trade had been ended it continued to exact sacrifices from the British nation and to generate its own arguments for political and other forms of action. Nor was the leadership in the later stages confined to the humanitarian group; in particular, Palmerston, a key figure in both intervention at and the subsequent annexation of Lagos, devoted much of his energies to the prosecution of the war against the slave trade. Closely aligned with the negative aim of abolition, but coming in second and not first place, was the positive aim of its substitution by legitimate trade. Once it had been accepted in London that the fulfilment of these aims required action at Lagos, it became the role of those on the coast to translate the general permission given by Whitehall into an appropriate form. The Royal Navy, often reluctant to extend its operations, especially on land, had first to be assured of the need for intervention and of official sanction and encouragement. Meanwhile the consul was supported, and sometimes hurried forward, by the missionaries, zealous for the extension of their spiritual and ecclesiastical kingdoms, and by the traders, eager to build up their trade and to outflank competitiors, legitimate or illegitimate.

Later historians have viewed the contemporary and 'colonialist' explanation of intervention at Lagos with fashionable scepticism. Ajayi writes:

> it is at best only a half-truth to say that Lagos was bombarded in 1851 because it was a 'notorious slave depot'. The anxiety of Britain to intervene in Lagos was not just the philanthropic desire to destroy the slave trading activities of the Portuguese and Brazilians there, but also the economic desire to control the trade of Lagos from which they had hitherto been excluded and from where they hoped to exploit the resources of the vast country stretching to and beyond the Niger.[55]

His conclusion is that 'there was a strong commercial interest in Eritain's struggle against the slave trade',[56] but he refrains from any attempt to compare the relative weights of the humanitarian and commercial motives, except perhaps by implication. Gavin goes considerably further, and writes that 'Slave trade suppression was for Palmerston a means to an end; the end being the expansion of British commerce with Africa'.[57] There seems little justification for this assessment. The relative unimportance of British trade with Africa both at this time and subsequently throughout the nineteenth century – a fact remarked by most recent writers about the partition of the continent towards the end of the century – does not bear it out nor does it tally with what is known of the career of Palmerston, or indeed of others engaged in the long, tedious and costly fight against the slave trade. Yet it was clearly realised that commerce and the stimulation of commerce had an important and necessary part to play in the eradication of the trade, and furthermore it was a natural responsibility of any British government to ensure not only that other countries should not obstruct the campaign against the trade but also that they should not take commercial advantage of Britain's self-abnegation. That the internal slave trade continued to exist and even to grow during the century, partly as a result of the measures taken to replace the external trade, was unfortunate and unforeseen, but it remained a separate issue and one which does not affect the argument.

An American scholar, Earl Phillips, reacted vigorously against this economic interpretation in his doctoral thesis of 1966. He writes that, 'the arguments put forward by modern African scholars that this British interference in native affairs was dictated by economic considerations falls far short of the mark' and indeed in some cases is evidence of an 'obsessive psychological barrier' which prevents an objective appraisal of British motives. More generally, he considers it 'unfortunate that the commonly accepted explanation for the expansion of European influence and power into the lesser developed areas of the world in the nineteenth century is based on economic theories', an approach which obscures 'the plethora of causes which underlay this complex historical movement'.[58]

The place of motive, public and private, cannot be overlooked in any account of human affairs. But this is an element of exceptional complexity in any form of explanation and the historian's advantage of hindsight does not always serve, and may sometimes hinder, his reading of what was intended by the actors in the events under analysis; statements about motive, moreover, are peculiarly difficult to substantiate. As regards the British intervention at Lagos, it can at least be said that the motives of those concerned with such action, and competent to authorise and carry it out, eventually coincided sufficiently to overcome countervailing factors. But the primary concern of the historian must be with events, acts and situations, and here again the problem is complex. What is required to explain the events at Lagos in 1851 is not merely an analysis but also a description of the dynastic dispute there and of the different policies and actions of the British Government, their officials, the Anglican missionaries, and the commercial houses, as these all developed from day to day and year to year. Intervention – the battles of November and December – occurred at the point of intersection of several separate causal forces. It is necessary to go further, and to ask whether any of these forces can be seen to have predominated over the others. The answer which seems to emerge from the preceding narrative is that the struggle of the British against the slave trade, pursued with much greater vigour and persistence than by any other nation, was the foremost, though certainly not the single, cause of their violent irruption into the affairs of Lagos at the end of 1851.

3

Before Campbell

Following the flag: traders, missionaries and 'emigrants'

The defence of Lagos in November and December 1851 was one of the most determined attempts by Africans to resist the conquest of their continent by the European invaders of the nineteenth century.[1] Its failure gave the British a new foothold on the West Coast which in the high days of imperialism during the last two decades of the century was to provide a base for rapid and vast expansion. But as the island kingdom lay ruined and conquered in January 1852 these days were as yet far off. When news reached London of the defeat of the November expedition, Palmerston was no longer at the Foreign Office to defend the actions of the Queen's officers on the coast, having been dismissed in December 1851 for his premature approval of Louis-Napoleon's *coup d'état* in France, and Granville's reaction showed some irritation and uneasiness. But the success in December stifled criticism in Whitehall. On 23 February 1852, Malmesbury, the foreign secretary in Derby's new government (Palmerston having achieved his 'tit for tat with John Russell' two days before), wrote to congratulate the consul whose 'professional and local knowledge ... perseverance and activity' had doubtless been of great service to Commodore Bruce, and to approve the treaty which had been signed with Akitoye.[2]

A semi-official pamphlet was issued to counter possible doubts about the legality of the action taken at Lagos. After alluding to the persistence of the slave trade, despite the good news from Brazil, and to the work of the missionaries among the Yoruba repatriates at Abeokuta, the author cited the Swiss jurist Emmerich de Vattel in questioning 'whether, on the general principle of the law of nations, such places as Lagos can be deemed to possess rights as States or be entitled to the observances of international law'. The pamphlet concluded that 'As a nest of piracy and plunder, the destruction of Lagos was a duty owing by civilized nations to themselves', and that apart from such general considerations, 'the conduct of Lagos towards English subjects created in itself an unquestionable cause of war'.[3] The reasoning was not impeccable, but there was little public interest either in England or abroad in events at Lagos.⁴ Meantime, the intervention was being energetically followed up by the Royal Navy. During the first two and a half months of 1852, Bruce's officers, Wilmot and Forbes, obtained a series of twelve anti-slaving treaties with states along the coast and in the hinterland. These included Abeokuta (5 January 1852), Dahomey (13 January), Porto Novo (17 January), Ijebu (25 February), and Badagry (18 March). The treaty with the Ijebu was signed at Lagos by six chiefs sent from the capital, Ijebu Ode, who additionally gave a verbal promise to Wilmot that they would 'put (Kosoko) on one side and even . . . give him up soon'.⁵ On the conclusion of the treaties the naval authorities announced the lifting of their coastal blockade, which had already occasioned a protest by the commodore of the French naval patrol.⁶

In Lagos itself the quiet after the storm was an uneasy one. The slavers were undoubtedly in retreat, but many were finding a refuge with Kosoko at Epe only some thirty miles down the eastern lagoon or at Porto Novo some fifty miles to the west. Lagos could now become a functioning part of that system of informal rule represented by the consulate for the Bights of Benin and Biafra. Consul Beecroft himself, however, the mainstay and indeed the originator of the system, soon left for his headquarters on the Spanish island of Fernando Po in the eastern Bight. From here he could keep watch on the Niger Delta, the centre of the palm oil-trade,⁷ where just two years later he was to bring about the deposition of King Pepple of Bonny with very much less trouble than that of Kosoko had cost him.⁸ He seems to have visited Lagos on only one further occasion. Thus there was at first no intention to follow the reduction of Lagos by the establishment of a continuing British presence ashore. In these circumstances authority had to be supplied there by a weakened and beset monarchy, Oba Akitoye reigning precariously from the Iga Idunganran over a burnt and partly depopulated town, and by the over-extended Preventive Squadron of the Royal Navy, whose twenty vessels (in 1852) were responsible for patrolling hundreds of miles of coastline and whose captains, though they often spent days and sometimes even weeks in the Lagos roads, were naturally reluctant to cross the bar. But already some of those who had left the town during the fighting were returning, and Akitoye's position was strengtheneed by his formal reconciliation, arranged by Commander Wilmot, with Ajenia and Akinpelu Possu, the two war chiefs who had been leading supporters of Kosoko.⁹

The difficulties and dangers of the situation at Lagos were not immediately apparent in the aftermath of the British victory, but there was no delay in appreciation of the importance of the town as a centre for communication with the interior. Its harbour had been proved accessible to vessels drawing up to ten or eleven feet of water, and the lagoons and rivers held the promise of inland navigation for vast though still unknown distances. Within a few months the African Steamship Company of Liverpool began its mail service down the coast as far as Fernando Po, calling regularly at Lagos. Almost at once the standard-bearers of change began to appear. In the van were the traders, seeking to tap the market in palm oil. The Sardinian subject Giambattista Scala, who arrived in February 1852, claimed to have been the first though the Hungarian adventurer Amadie, said to have been 'Secretary' to Domingo Martinez, came the same month. William McCoskry, agent for the firm of Hutton, Legresley representing Banner Brothers, and J. Sandeman of Steward & Douglas, who had all been prospecting the market at Badagry, also paid exploratory visits about this time, while in March 1852 there arrived from Whydah the German Lorenz Diedrichsen, who the following year sold his business to the Hamburg firm of O'Swald & Co., represented by Hermann Grote. Though profits were not as high as in the slave trade, they were encouraging enough, a ton (300 gallons) of palm oil selling in Liverpool for about £40, some two or three times its cost in Lagos. Thus the merchant community continued to grow and to enjoy a modest prosperity, and its ranks were soon increased by Sierra Leonean and Brazilian 'emigrants'.[10]

'The basis of the oil market', C. W. Newbury writes, 'was credit and cowries'.[11] Most of the European traders gave out the goods which they received from their principals to the local middlemen, generally Sierra Leoneans, and after an interval — perhaps as long as six months — received in return consignments of oil. Messrs O'Swald, however, were already importing cowries from Zanzibar, and after their arrival in Lagos their regular supplies of these, the most widely used currency on the West Coast, gave them a monopoly which enabled their agents to deal directly with the oil suppliers.[12] It was also necessary for the traders to regulate their relations with the local authorities and in particular to provide the Oba with the traditional revenue based on exports from and imports into his territories. To this end a commercial agreement was made on 28 February 1852 between Akitoye and his chiefs and a group of European merchants. This provided that a customs duty of 3 per cent *ad valorem* should be paid to the Oba on imports and of 2 per cent on exports. In return the Oba was to afford protection to the merchants and their goods, allowing them to build their warehouses and piers 'on the eastern point entering the river, and as far as the passage' — now called Five Cowry Creek — 'which divides Lagos from the sea'. The Oba was to be responsible for any stoppage of trade and would compensate this by payments of oil. He also agreed to impound the property of Lagosian traders who defaulted on their debts to merchants from whom they had taken credit and to sell this for the creditor's benefit. The last clause established a mixed committee of four under the Oba's presidency to adjudicate in trading disputes.[13] The treaty remained the basis of trade relations within Lagos for two years, until the practical difficulty of determining the value on which payments to the Oba were to be made led to the negotiation of a revised treaty with Akitoye's successor.

The *Memoirs* of Giambattista Scala, though romanticised and often in-

Cruiser's boats about to board a slaver
From the *Church Missionary Intelligencer*, volume VII, 1856

Shipping slaves through the surf
From the *Church Missionary Intelligencer*, volume VII, 1856.

On the 'road' from Lagos to Abeokuta
From the *Church Missionary Intelligencer*, volume IV, 1853

The Lagos steamer fetching the mail

accurate in detail, give an interesting picture of conditions in Lagos at this time.[14] In November 1851 Scala, a Ligurian trading on his own account, who at an earlier stage of his career may have been concerned in slaving activities,[15] had been in Bahia. Here he hired the Sardinian brig *Felicità* (commanded by Captain Reggio), loaded it with a miscellaneous cargo, and sailed across the Atlantic. After putting in at Accra and Keta he arrived on 10 February 1852 off Lagos, where he found H.M.S. *Harlequin* in the roads. Wilmot, commander of the naval brig, listened sympathetically to Scala's request to enter the harbour but tried to dissuade him from doing so, saying that the town was in a state of anarchy and that a counter-attack by Kosoko, the deposed Oba, was expected. However, Akitoye and two of his chiefs[16] were visiting the *Harlequin* at this time, and as they showed interest in Scala's proposals Wilmot withdrew his opposition. The next day the *Felicità* crossed the bar under the protection of three armed boats from the *Harlequin*, and Scala, after receiving a friendly, even exuberant, welcome from a large crowd which had rushed to the beach, unloaded his cargo of 150 barrels of rum, 1000 rolls of tobacco, foodstuffs and manufactured goods. Scala describes the town at this time as still 'a shapeless mass of ruins' inhabited by only some 5000 or 6000, mostly the aged or very young, of the previous population of about 22,000. But trade began briskly enough and on 3 March he was able to load the *Felicità* with a cargo of palm oil which he consigned to a London firm, he himself remaining in Lagos. Gradually the former inhabitants returned, and as they rebuilt their houses — not a lengthy or difficult operation — the town began to assume a more cheerful and animated appearance.

Like the traders, the Christian missionaries lost little time in establishing themselves under the new regime at Lagos. The Anglicans realized the importance of the island, not so much for the sake of its population, who were far from numerous when compared with great inland towns like Abeokuta and Ibadan,[17] but from the point of view of missionary strategy. 'The possession of Lagos throws open the interior, and affords peculiar facilities for the encouragement of lawful trade, and the development of the industrial energies of the people', as one of the Church Missionary Society's publications put it in 1853. Suppression of the African slave trade was not enough: 'We want their institutions changed'.[18] More particularly, Lagos was 'the port of Abeokuta', since it commanded the outlet of the river Ogun to the lagoon and thence to the sea, and it was on the Egba of Abeokuta, through whose territories the Ogun flowed, that missionary hopes centred for a Christian Commonwealth in Africa.[19] Although it was hardly possible that the event 'should escape misrepresentation', the taking of Lagos seemed to the missionaries 'God's interposition for the good of Africa'.[20]

Between February and March 1852 the Reverend C. A. Gollmer paid an exploratory visit to Lagos, and the success of this reconnaissance led him in the following June to remove the C.M.S. base from Badagry, where only few converts had been made, to Lagos. During this first visit Gollmer obtained from the pliant Oba Akitoye a generous grant of land for the purposes of the mission. This grant, soon to be the subject of much contention first with the traders and then with the consul, comprised five separate plots: (1) at Oke Faji on the Lagos river, nearly opposite the mouth of the Badagry Creek, now the site of Christ Church Cathedral and Bishopscourt; (2) an area to the north, identified by a group of breadfruit trees — where slaves had formerly been kept and where St Paul's Church now stands in Broad Street; (3) 'Lima's place', evidently so-called from the residence of Kosoko's Portuguese aide, at first used as a cotton store and later given up by the mission; (4) another waterside plot, at Ebute Ero on the north side of the island, where Holy Trinity Church no stands, and (5) a plot behind the Oba's palace, the Iga. The grant was 'without any condition and free of expense and without any limit of time'. Like other grants of land by the Oba during this period it seems to have been made without the public and express participation of the Idejo chiefs of the town, who in theory and to an undefined extent in fact were the owners of the land, though presumably these chiefs were consulted by the Oba in council.[21]

The first Christian services at Lagos of which there is record took place in the courtyard of the Oba's palace in the morning and afternoon of 11 January 1852, Akitoye himself being present at the second. They were conducted by James White, a 'native catechist' born of Yoruba parents in Sierra Leone, who had been sent from Badagry by Gollmer to prepare the ground at Lagos.[22] White was full of confidence, natural or apostolic, and before long did not hesitate to rebuke Akitoye for pagan observances and failure to attend service. By May 1852 he claimed to have opened a school attended by twelve boys.[23] When Gollmer arrived to take up permanent residence in Lagos in June, his quarters were in 'a large deserted slave barracoon', but by October he was able to move into the partly completed mission house at Oke Faji on the waterfront. This building, said to have been prefabricated in Sierra Leone, was christened by the Lagosians the Ile Alapako, or 'house of planks', and was not finally replaced until 1960. Responsibility for evangelisation on the north-east side of the island was assigned to White, while Gollmer, assisted by J. B. Coker and Samuel Pearce, both Sierra Leoneans, preached and ministered at different points — a favourite spot being under a large tree — on the south and west where the emigrants and Europeans were settling. Despite the interest in Christianity shown, spasmodically, by the Oba and by a few chiefs, the bulk of the regular congregations was made up of Sierra Leonean 'emigrants', and it was not until January 1853 that White recorded the conversion of the first Lagosian Christian, an old man named Adeduju.[24] Meanwhile, the Wesleyan Methodists had also set up a mission and school, though the work was thrown into disarray after just over a year by the sudden death in June 1853 of John Martin, their first missionary agent.[25]

With the traders and the missionaries came the emigrants (who should more correctly but less familiarly be called 'immigrants' or 'repatriates'). As Gollmer remarked in 1853, the Sierra Leoneans were arriving 'almost by every mail'.[26] Many now stayed in Lagos, rather than making their way inland to Abeokuta and elsewhere, and soon their community, amounting to several thousand and estimated in 1865 at about one-fifth of the total population, constituted an influential section of the town. They were known, by a contraction of the words 'Sierra Leonean', as 'Saro' and their leading men were the 'Daddies'. As immigrants, without rights to farm the land or fish the waters, they took naturally to trade in order to support themselves, and soon occupied an important place in the commercial organisation of Lagos. A few of the more enterprising emerged as competitors of the much larger European concerns, but the majority were content to co-operate with the Europeans as middlemen. As Mrs J. H. Kopytoff points out, the 'breaking of bulk' was an important and intricate feature of the palm-oil trade since the oil was produced in very small amounts by innumerable farmers in the interior, and the producers demanded only very small quantities of the goods which they were taking in exchange. 'The trade between Lagos and the hinterland was carried out then not in three stages − exporter, middleman, producer − consumer − but involved numerous middlemen in the chain of trade to and from the coast.'[27] Many of the Saro made their homes among the European merchants in the waterside area, though their principal settlement was on the western point of the island known as Olowogbowo ('the creditor claims his money from the debtor' seems to be the meaning of this place-name).

At the same time as the coming of the Sierra Leoneans, another immigration was taking place into Lagos, that of the Brazilians or 'Amaro' (possibly a contraction from 'America'[28]; these were mostly Yoruba who had taken advantage of the relatively favourable manumission laws in Brazil to emancipate themselves. Merging into this group were a number of 'emigrants', again mostly Yoruba, from Cuba. It is not known when the first Amaro reached Lagos, but a few probably came in the 1840s and there is a tradition that during his reign Kosoko sent his chief Oshodi Tapa to Brazil to arrange for the return of former Lagosians there. By 1852 the district behind Oke Faji where the C.M.S. obtained their land from Akitoye was already known as Brazilian Town, Popo Aguda (Portuguese Street) or Popo 'Maro, and in 1862 the number of the community was estimated as 3000. Many of the Amaro had adopted Roman Catholicism in the New World, and in April 1853 the evangelical Gollmer was lamenting that 'a Roman Catholic cross, some eight feet high', had been set up by 'white and black Portuguese and Brazilians' not fifty yards from where he planned his church.[29] They also brought with them from America artisan skills and crafts which they found an opportunity to practise in Lagos. For this reason, and probably also because of their smaller financial resources, they engaged in trade to a lesser extent and on a smaller scale than the Saro. Their monument remains, however, in the tradition of classical building and baroque plaster decoration which they founded in Lagos[30] (the traces of which a Philistine generation is now busily eradicating).

Apart from difficulties in their encounters with the traditional religious practices of the Awori, the Christian missionaries in Lagos met competition from Islam. This had been established in the town probably in the eighteenth century and seems to have received support from Kosoko. In his flight the ex-Oba was accompanied by a number of prominent Muslims, including the Imam, but the community left in Lagos was soon increased by Muslims from among both the Sierra Leoneans and (to a much lesser extent) the Brazilians.[31]

Kosoko at Epe

To all these new elements in Lagos, as to the restored monarchy of Akitoye, the presence of Kosoko on the eastern lagoon constituted a serious threat. On his flight from Lagos Kosoko had sought refuge first in villages along the shore[32] and then, with the permission of the Awujale, ruler of the kingdom of Ijebu Ode, had settled at Epe on the north shore of the lagoon. This town, which is mentioned several times in Osifekunde's account of eastern Yorubaland, had presumably originated as a settlement of fishermen and perhaps also of boat-builders, and it may be surmised that it was one of those waterside towns on which were based the war canoes which Osifekunde described as forming an important arm of the military forces of the Ijebu.[33] Its position was of some strategic importance since it commanded the narrows which connect the main Lagos lagoon with the Leke lagoon further east, from which waterways lead to Benin and the delta of the Niger.

There was a precedent for Kosoko's flight to Epe in that after the Ewe Koko war against Oba Oluwole, some fourteen or fifteen years before, a number of his followers, including chiefs Dada Antonio and Osho Akanbi, had taken refuge there, using it as a base for raiding Lagos. In 1852 Kosoko was quickly able to build up an independent state at Epe in opposition to Lagos. He had been accompanied by some three or four hundred warriors,[34] several prominent Lagosians, including at least one holder of a major chieftancy (the Oloto), and his leading 'caboceer' Oshodi Tapa, a Nupe from the Niger and former slave in Oshinlokun's court. He was soon joined by a group of European slave traders, his old associates, including the Portuguese Lima who acted as one of his two secretaries (the other being a 'Brazilian' repatriate) and who was also his 'chief engineer and artillerist'.[35] He also extended his authority southwards from Epe to the strip of land between the lagoon and the Atlantic, from Leke and Palma (or Orimedu)[36] on the east as far as Langbassa in the direction of Lagos;[37] as already mentioned, one report claims that he continued to pay tribute to the Oba of Benin for this area, as for the Kingdom of Lagos, until his return to Lagos in 1862. This territorial base enabled him to engage again in the export trade, probably in slaves but also in palm oil and other products from Ijebu, so that Palma, despite its lack of a harbour, became a thriving little port.

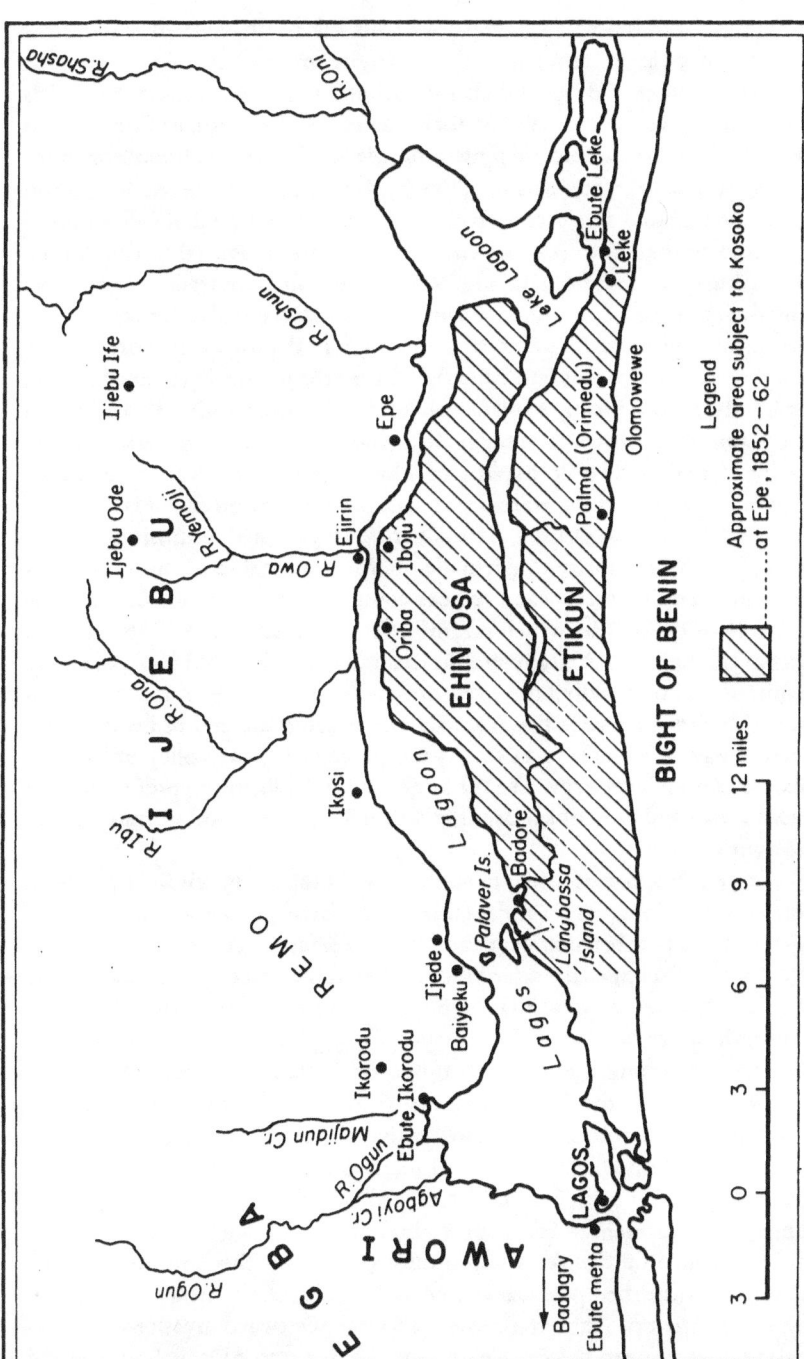

Lagos and Epe; Kosoko's kingdom in exile

Though Kosoko seems to have looked on the south-western part of his coastal territory as a remnant of his Lagos patrimony, Epe belonged indisputably to Ijebu Ode, as did also Palma and Leke (though the Awujale's authority must have been somewhat distant there).[38] The attitude of the Ijebu to this intrusion into their land presents a problem. Neither tradition nor other sources suggest that the occupation of Epe by the Lagosians and their acquisition of the remoter coastal area were resisted or even resented by them. Writing to Commander Forbes, Awujale Anikilaya claimed to be neutral in the dispute between Akitoye and Kosoko, saying 'We want nothing but trade, and we have nothing but commercial intercourse with Kosoko'. It seemed to him that it was the British who protected Kosoko by allowing him the use of the ports of Ape (Epe) and Olomowewe (beyond Palma).[39] Given the proximity of Epe to Ijebu, this is hardly a convincing explanation of the Ijebu attitude. According to tradition among Lagosian descendants in Epe, that town had been deserted before the arrival of Kosoko because of a local dispute, and Kosoko is said to have given presents — coral, state umbrellas, palm wine and four Hausa slaves were among the items — to the Awujale, first to gain his permission to settle there and then his authority to persuade the former inhabitants to return. It is also remembered that there was a remote connection between Kosoko and the royal family of Ijebu Ode, which might have eased relations.[40] Moreover, the support of the Egba for Akitoye would naturally lead their old rivals the Ijebu to favour Kosoko. Finally, the government of Ijebu Ode may have been weakened at this time since the Awujale was nearing the end of his life; he is believed to have died later in 1852. Ayantuga describes the policy of the new Awujale, Fidipote, with regard to the Lagos quarrel as being to profit from the increased trade which Kosoko brought to his kingdom without making any alliance with him.[41]

But the most important factor in explaining Kosoko's success in establishing himself almost at once as an independent territorial power was his military strength. He is remembered in Lagos and Epe as a leader of courage, strength and energy — a Yoruba appellation (*oriki*) describes him as 'an elephant shaking the forest' — and his career shows that he inspired loyalty in his followers. He had been brought up to warfare and was especially experienced in the naval form which obtained among the lagoon peoples. As Archibald Dalzel noted in the eighteenth century,[42] the Oba of Lagos was master of many war canoes, and when Kosoko escaped to Epe he seems to have taken a large part of this fleet with him. He and his chiefs also owned many domestic slaves. Thus from the first days of his exile he disposed of forces sufficient to impress the Awujale and his subjects and to menace his former kingdom.

The emergence of Kosoko's autonomous state and the hostility between Lagos and Epe disturbed political and economic conditions around the eastern lagoon to an extent probably unknown since the westward invasions of Benin two hundred years or so before. Apart from the threat to Akitoye's regime and to the political, missionary and commercial interests now established at Lagos, the westbound trade of Kosoko's neighbours to the east, the Mahin or Ilaje,[43] and, more important still, the trade of the Egba down the Ogun to Lagos were interrupted. The Egba in particular were alarmed by Kosoko's growing power and by reports of his alliances with the Ijebu and other neighbouring states. In May 1852 the Reverend Henry Townsend of the C.M.S., who had become an influential figure at Abeokuta, passed on a warning to Commodore Bruce from the Egba chiefs that Kosoko was intending to attack Lagos in about three months' time. According to the chiefs, Kosoko was 'drawing into league with himself the Jebus, the Dahomeans, the small Towns near Lagos that were formerly in his interest, and a part of the Benin people'. He was confident of success, 'the guns having all been removed from Lagos'. The chiefs went on to complain that these disturbed conditions prevented them from cultivating their farms – a plea well calculated to win missionary sympathy – and that the presence of the Ijebu on the left bank of the Ogun made it unsafe for them to use that highway.[44]

Bruce, with all the Royal Navy's suspicion of entanglements ashore, was unenthusiastic about undertaking new commitments. He had already warned Wilmot against displaying the Union Jack in Lagos, 'As it is not convenient for H.M.'s Government to acquire new territorial possessions in Africa'.[45] He replied reassuringly to the Egba, but in July put the question to the Admiralty as to whether he would be justified in using force to prevent Kosoko from regaining his kingdom. The Admiralty referred this to the Foreign Office, where a resigned answer in the affirmative was given on 30 August and notified to Beecroft for his information: 'his Lordship is still of the opinion that the Commander in Chief of H.M.'s Ships on the West Coast of Africa should be authorized, if necessary, to use Force in order to prevent Kosoko from regaining his usurped authority at Lagos'. The minutes on this correspondence indicate the reluctance and distaste, mingled with fatalism, with which Derby's 'Who? Who?' ministry viewed the commitments entered into at Lagos by their predecessors and their energetic agents on the coast. On the Townsend and Egba correspondence Malmesbury wrote: 'Having put Akitoye on the throne we must maintain him there for the present at all events and follow out our policy.' On Bruce's letter, Stanley minuted with querulous realism: 'We are installed against our will in a quasi-protectorate of Lagos, having turned out this very Kosoko and put in an anti-slaving chief. There is nothing to do now but to go through with the policy thus forced on us.' 'Approved without a doubt', added Malmesbury.[46]

The vice-consulate

Recognition of the growing importance of Lagos came slower in official circles in distant Whitehall than among the missionaries, humanitarians and traders, but gradually the problem of maintaining the British position there, gained at some cost, was appreciated. By now the consulate had become established in the eastern half of the area, the Bight of Biafra, as a form of government, and almost immediately after the reduction of Lagos, Bruce had recommended to the Admiralty that consuls be placed there and at Whydah, though adding unrealistically that they should be 'strictly forbidden to interfere in the political concerns of the countries in which they are residing'.[47] Remote as it was from any situation envisaged by the reformers of the British consular system in 1825,[48] the system of 'informal empire' run by consuls was well adapted to circumstances, and when in June 1852 Beecroft asked permission to transfer temporarily to Lagos Louis Frazer, his vice-consul at Whydah, the foreign secretary promptly agreed, adding that the Government were aware of the need to appoint an agent at Lagos and that it was no longer desirable to keep a representative at Whydah.[49] In November 1852 Beecroft, accompanied by Frazer, landed at Lagos from H.M.S. *Penelope*, and after breakfast at Gollmer's 'mansion' on the waterfront was escorted by Oba Akitoye in person and a fleet of fifty or sixty canoes to the Iga. Here Beecroft presented the new vice-consul to the Oba and his council of chiefs with some state, and Akitoye agreed to allow Frazer to occupy quarters in his palace until he could erect a building for himself. Beecroft and Frazer then left for Fernando Po, where the latter was to spend a few days preparing his baggage before returning to Lagos, entering upon his duties there the following month.[50]

This first representative of the British Government to reside in Lagos emerges from the consular correspondence as a somewhat unsatisfactory and shadowy, even shady, figure, and yet with some consistency of policy. When he was appointed to Whydah at the end of 1850, it was made clear to him that he would be subordinate to Beecroft, whose jurisdiction stretched as far west as Cape St Paul on the Gold Coast. He accordingly wrote to Beecroft expressing admiration in fulsome terms for the consul whom he saw as 'carrying out a new light among the Darkies'. He professed an interest in zoology, but less innocently was intimate with the Portuguese and Brazilian slavers, and he was later reproved by Consul Campbell for himself holding four young Africans 'in servitude'. Bruce had found him 'wanting in tact and knowledge of the African character' and he had quickly upset the King of Dahomey by being 'very overbearing in his communications'. This caused Malmesbury to minute that he ought to be removed. But as sometimes happens in government service, his removal was to a more important post, where at Lagos Oba Akitoye soon complained of his arrogant manner.[51]

Clearly Louis Frazer was inadequate for the post which – as Lugard's unlikely forerunner – had fallen to him, and he was unable to provide leadership or even to put up an appearance of impartiality. In the hot, damp climate of Lagos jealousies and rivalries luxuriated, while the threat from Kosoko across the lagoon seemed to exacerbate rather than to reconcile the different factions. The European community, who depended more than most on co-operation between themselves, found it especially difficult to work together. This soon appeared in the allegations made by the merchants that the C.M.S. in the grant made to Gollmer in March 1852 had obtained from the Oba an unfairly large share of the available land, especially on the waterfront, where most of the Europeans preferred to live as it was pleasanter, cooler and (they believed) healthier than elsewhere in or near the town. These complaints were first raised by Messrs Forster and Smith, copies of whose letters were passed by the Foreign Office to Beecroft and Frazer in December 1852. An attempt to settle the matter by Commander White, one of the Squadron officers, broke down, according to White, because of the personal hostility to Gollmer of both J. G. Sandeman, Forster & Smith's agent, and of Vice-Consul Frazer. Sandeman widened the grounds of complaint by accusing the missionaries of encouraging their Egba friends to make war on their neighbours; Gollmer, he wrote, was 'head of the war department. Frazer, whose background, like that of most of the West Coast consuls in the nineteenth century, seems to have been a commercial one, continued to support Sandeman, and he made matters worse by administering a somewhat gratuitous rebuke to Gollmer for flying the Union Jack on the C.M.S. canoe.[52]

A yet more serious difference arose between Frazer and the Royal Navy as a result of the expedition to Badagry in ships' boats which he persuaded Commander Heseltine to make with him at the end of 1852. The object was to restore 'by a little patient palavering' (in Frazer's words) the Wawu and other chiefs who had been forced to leave Badagry during the disturbances of June 1851. This also entailed persuading the Mewu, the Porto Novan chief there who, like Akitoye, had won the favour of the missionaries,[53] to leave the town. The expedition, which had continued to Porto Novo and thence to Ado, then under siege by the Egba, failed to achieve these ends and instead brought down on Frazer the wrath of the commander-in-chief, who wrote plainly to him that he could not 'sanction any further interference on the part of Her Majesty's Naval Officers on a similar occasion'. It also deepened the ill-feeling between the missionaries and the merchants, the former blaming Sandeman in particular for influencing the vice-consul against Akitoye's supporters in Badagry and against the Egba. Frazer gamely but impertinently kept up the correspondence, refusing to accept the rebuke or acknowledge the commodore's seniority and denouncing 'the machinations of the missionaries' until the exasperated Bruce broke off relations and denounced the vice-consul in a thunderous dispatch to the Admiralty as a man who attempted to fulfil his consular duties 'by attaching himself to a party cause' – that of the traders.[54] Yet in truth, by attempting to bring about the free flow of trade from the interior and along the lagoons to Lagos, Frazer was anticipating a policy which was to be applied so far as they were able by all his successors, who encountered similar obstacles.

Criticism of the missionaries' land-hunger soon involved criticism of Oba

Akitoye as their protégé and this in turn revealed the continued existence in Lagos of support for Kosoko. Akitoye had cause for suspecting in particular chiefs Ajenia and Possu, and in April 1853, according to Gollmer, at a meeting with thirty-five of his chiefs, he threatened to punish Ajenia's followers as 'proved disturbers of the peace'.[55] In the same month Frazer forwarded to the Foreign Office complaints by 'caboceer Tappa' that his men were being harassed by Akitoye's followers when visiting Lagos peaceably from Epe.[56] Frazer next reported Possu's allegation that despite his having returned to Lagos with the permission of the English, he was being plotted against by the other Lagos chiefs and by Madame Tinubu, the redoubtable trader and niece to Akitoye, who, after helping to build up the Oba's cause in Badagry, had followed him to the capital. Frazer also sent on a copy of a letter from Townsend at Abeokuta to Gollmer, repeating warnings from the Egba chiefs of Kosoko's hostile intentions, but he expressed greater anxiety about the behaviour of Oba Akitoye, who was 'always causing commotions' and making complaints, instigated in this by Townsend and Gollmer. Akitoye reciprocated in a letter to Bruce which attacked Frazer and asked for his removal.[57]

Frazer's final error in his career at Lagos was his involvement in what can be called 'the Amadie affair'. At the end of May 1853 Akitoye had been strengthened by the arrival of a force of Egba warriors sent by his allies the chiefs of Abeokuta.[58] About the same time his former associate Domingo Martinez sent to him a party of twenty slaves whom he claimed to have intercepted on their way from Lagos to the coast at Aghwey where they were to be shipped. Martinez's motives for this action remain mysterious but probably it was prompted by trade rivalry. Inquiries established in any case that the slaves had been bought and dispatched by two Lagos dealers, Ojo Martins, a local 'Brazilian', and Amadie, the Hungarian merchant who had been a signatory to the commercial agreement of February 1852. Akitoye turned for advice to Commander C. G. Phillips of H.M.S. *Polyphemus*, who reminded him that under Article v of the treaty of January 1852 it was his duty to expel any foreigner who engaged in the slave trade. Fortified by this and by the presence of the Egba troops, Akitoye gave orders that Amadie should be arrested and conveyed to Badagry. He also ordered the arrest of an unnamed third man, his 'own subject', who, he said, had been implicated in the attempted slaving and who now escaped by putting himself under the protection of Chief Ajenia.

Amadie's arrest was a somewhat dramatic affair and caused a good deal of indignation among the expatriate merchant community. It became known almost at once as his calls for help as he was being taken a prisoner down the river in one of Akitoye's canoes at about ten o'clock in the night were heard by his friend Conto in his house on the waterfront. Conto, realising that he could count on the vice-consul's sympathies, alerted Frazer, who at once sent a canoe in pursuit, but in the darkness of a rainy night Amadie and his guards could not be followed further than the mouth of the Badagry creek. The following day

Frazer protested energetically to Phillips about the abduction of Amadie, stressing the alarm which this treatment of a white man was causing to the other Europeans and describing the affair as 'a combination betwixt Akitoye and the Portuguese'. Phillips passed on the matter to his commander-in-chief, to whom he sent copies of Frazer's excited letters, and these in turn reached the Admiralty and then the Foreign Office.[59] But though the Navy tended to treat this shore-based quarrel with lofty calm, the repercussions were considerable. Ajenia's refusal to give up the 'third man' worsened the delicate relations between the Oba and Kosoko's former supporter to the extent that, according to Scala,[60] Akitoye ordered the arrest of Ajenia himself and of Possu, his fellow war captain. Both Consul Benjamin Campbell and Scala saw the affair as responsible for the dangerous situation which arose in Lagos in the following two months.

With regard to the slave trade, Frazer reported complacently soon after his arrival that it 'seems to have been entirely abolished in the Bight of Benin; it is never, even, spoken of'.[61] In June 1853 he sent a general account of Lagos trade to the Foreign Office.[62] The chief exports were palm oil and ivory, nearly all the former being shipped to England. Imports were roll tobacco and rum from Bahia, the larger cowries ('blue shells' – *Cypraea annulus*) from Zanzibar, which were the monopoly of the Hamburgers, cloth, and other items in small quantities. The problem was to find shipping: 'there has been, all along, more oil than ships'. Then, again taking up the role of spokesman for the merchants, he added that 'if Accatory [Akitoye] would only remain quiet and leave the roads open, the trade would be immense. At this moment the two principal roads to Porto Novo and Jaboo are shut. There are forests of palm trees in all directions, that no one dare enter in consequence of the unsettled state of the country.'

The closing of the 'roads' and waterways to traffic as a result of the political disturbances among the inland kingdoms had an almost immediately damaging effect on the economy of Lagos since it was by these routes that palm oil travelled from the producing areas; Lagos, moreover, was becoming more than ever dependent on staple foods grown on farmland beyond her boundaries. This issue of the roads was to persist throughout the consular and early colonial periods at Lagos and eventually was to provide the pretext, and something more than the pretext, for the expedition against Ijebu Ode in 1892 which began the last, short phase in the expansion of the Lagos Protectorate. Frazer had diagnosed the issue, but he was hardly the man to cope with this or the other problems of Lagos. In February 1853 Lord Wodehouse at the Foreign Office informed Beecroft that the Government had decided to suppress the vice-consulate at Whydah, which had been unoccupied since Frazer's departure, and to appoint a permanent consul at Lagos, a post for which Mr Benjamin Campbell, 'a gentleman long resident on the coast of Africa', had been chosen on the recommendation of Bruce (now rear-admiral). The consular district was to be divided, Campbell's western share, the consulate for the Bight of Benin, being defined as stretching from Cape St Paul, at the eastern extremity of the Gold Coast, to Cape Formosa at the southern tip of the Niger Delta. Beecroft and Campbell were directed to keep up 'an unreserved and friendly communication and co-operation', and it was made clear that the new arrangement was being introduced not from any dissatisfaction with Beecroft but because of 'the altered state of affairs at Lagos'. A letter of appointment told Campbell that his salary was fixed at £500 a year, with permission to trade (of which he seems not to have availed himself) and an initial allowance of £170 for his kit. Copies of the treaty with Lagos of 1 January 1852 and the anti-slave treaties with neighbouring states were also sent to him, with the observation that 'It will be your duty to watch over the due execution of these Treaties. . . . ' At the same time Frazer was told that there was no further call for his services and he was to return to England as soon as convenient to himself and his successor; his passage would be paid provided it was not delayed.[63]

Campbell was trading and acting as magistrate on the Isle de Los (off the Guinea coast, north of Sierra Leone), and presumably the winding up of his business required time. In May 1853 Frazer complained to the foreign secretary of Campbell's delay in arriving at his post, he himself being impatient to return to England, having parted, he grumbled, from his rainy season gear.[64] He still had two months to wait, but on 21 July 1853 Campbell at last landed in Lagos from Sierra Leone. The same day he was presented to Oba Akitoye and his chiefs by Commander Gardner R.N. Frazer was present at the ceremony and later handed over his papers to the new consul.[65] Benjamin Campbell assumed office at Lagos.

4

To the Palaver Islands

Benjamin Campbell

Although as early as August 1852 Lord Stanley in the Foreign Office had referred to Lagos as a 'quasi-protectorate', it was Benjamin Campbell's tenure of the consulate for the Bight of Benin between July 1853 and his death in April 1859 which established this character, making a counterpart to Beecroft's 'informal empire' (in K. O. Dike's phrase) in the Niger Delta to the east and laying the foundation for the colony and protectorate of Lagos which were to follow. Campbell must rank then among the creators of Nigeria. Although he may seem a somewhat obscure figure to sustain this role, he was well known in his day to the officers of the Royal Navy and to the traders and supercargoes on the coast, and he owed his appointment to the patronage of Admiral Bruce, commodore of the Preventive Squadron; certainly he would have been known by name, if not personally, to Beecroft. He had first been employed by the British trading firm of Macaulay & Babington in Sierra Leone, had worked for the Liberated Africans' Department in Freetown and sat on the Governor's Council there, and had then set up as a trader on his own account in the Rio Nunez in the 1830s. During this time, although he had a wife living in Britain, he formed attachments to at least three women of mixed descent: Fanny Potts, later wife of W. H. Pratt, a prominent 'recaptive' in Sierra Leone; a daughter of Mrs Isabella Lightburn, a notorious participant in the slave trade, and lastly Mrs Elizabeth Skelton, widow of another trader. Despite the connection with Miss Lightburn, which was to form the basis of charges made against him by French officials towards the end of his career in Lagos, he was said to have co-operated wholeheartedly in the anti-slaving activities of the Royal Navy, as well as in the prevention of smuggling in the rivers of Sierra Leone and its vicinity.[1]

By the time he came to Lagos, Campbell had served for some twenty years on the West Coast. He was a man of fifty-two or fifty-three and in good health, which he attributed, at least when writing to the Foreign Office, to his avoidance of 'excesses'.[2] Nor was consular work entirely new to him as for a time in 1852 he had taken charge of the French post in Sierra Leone while the consul there was on leave.³ But the anxieties of his exacting office at Lagos were to wear him down and his correspondence from there contains frequent references to attacks of the usual West Coast complaints of dysentery and fever. He seems to have been without family when he arrived in Lagos – whether he lived as a bachelor or not remains a mystery – but in 1858 a daughter of his by Fanny Potts came to Lagos as the wife of a Sierra Leonean, Walter Lewis, who was destined to make a successful career there.⁴ That he was of above average height appears from his remark that when he visited the Benin river on H.M.S. *Minx* in 1856 he was forced to live on deck as the clearance was so low,⁵ but no more personal account of him survives.⁶ Presumably he was of Scottish birth or at least descent, and until and unless more is discoverable it is perhaps permissible to picture him as a dour, Conradian figure, isolated by the need to hold the balance between the different factions which struggled for influence in his small remote world of Lagos. Certainly he was a man of strong personality and of decided, though far from immutable, views. These views he put before the foreign secretary with such prolixity that Lord Clarendon minuted on one occasion that Campbell wrote 'at such interminable length that I have not time to read him'.⁷

Apart from the many political troubles which beset him, Campbell had a good deal to put up with in inconvenience and discomfort at his post. On arrival he found no office or house prepared for him, and at first he was obliged to live in the C.M.S. compound with Gollmer, who (for a short time) saw in him 'a blessed instrument in the hand of God for the good of the country'.⁸ It is hard to imagine how two such strong-willed men of such different outlooks succeeded even for a day in living under one roof. Eventually separate consular premises were acquired, but as these amounted to a mud-built 'hovel' (the word used by a naval officer who stayed there), 'not elevated more than a foot from the ground', and were in any case crowded by Campbell's clerk, servants, and boatmen, they were hardly suitable. In mid-1854 the consul hired two rooms in the upper part of the 'storey house' erected by Sandeman, the local British merchant, but this was only a temporary expedient and he begged Lord Clarendon to provide him 'with a tent' and some 'camp stools' if no more could be done for him.⁹

Politically, the main challenge to the British consulate at Lagos under Campbell came from the exiled Kosoko in his base at Epe down the eastern lagoon. Though the period is rich in notable characters, it is Campbell and Kosoko who between them dominate the history of these years, during which relations between Lagos and Epe posed a problem which the consul was never able to solve. The object of the present chapter is to follow these relations through their changing phases of war and diplomacy down to the Treaty of Epe in September 1854. Apart from the intrinsic importance of the topic in the history of Lagos, it should serve to throw light on the political and economic relations of the lagoon people and on their warfare, to illustrate the beginnings of official contact between the Yoruba and the British, and to give an insight into Yoruba methods of diplomacy as well as the somewhat makeshift diplomacy practised by the British at this time in Africa.

The great lagoon on which both Lagos and Epe are situated, known in Yoruba by the generic term *Osa*,[10] forms a part of the vast system of rivers and lagoons which provides a sheltered waterway roughly parallel with the coast from west of Porto Novo to the eastern delta of the Niger, a distance of some five hundred miles. At Lagos a channel enters the sea, while to the north and east numerous rivers — notably the Ogun, the Oni, the Oshun and the Shasha — discharge their waters into the lagoon. In most places the depth of the lagoon is little more than three feet and there are many sandbanks, but in the Lagos River on the west there is a depth of twenty to thirty feet, which made possible the development of the harbour, and a channel some twenty feet deep runs through the lagoon eastwards to Epe and beyond.[11]

For many generations the lagoon had provided a livelihood for the Awori and Ijebu fishermen whose villages clustered on its shores. It was also a highway for trade, warfare and conquest. As was seen in the first chapter, many of the slaves reaching the Lagos market were brought by water, and the palm oil which came to replace the slaves as a commodity similarly travelled by canoe down the rivers and across the lagoon.[12] Many other commodities were also transported in this way, and numerous lagoonside markets grew up, among which Ikorodu and Ikosi were prominent. Apart from their trading canoes, the kingdoms and towns around the lagoon maintained fleets of war canoes, as did Lagos. These were generally larger than the trading canoes (except for the slave transports). Warfare on the lagoons was evidently as frequent an occurrence among the southern Yoruba as the land wars of the interior, and it took a form which can be designated as 'naval' since the canoes served not only as transports, enabling a swift and silent approach to an enemy position, but also as fighting units which engaged in battles on the water.[13] Before the introduction of firearms these battles seem to have been fought at fairly close quarters with throwing spears and clubs as the principal weapons,[14] but in the late eighteenth century muskets came into use for canoe as well as land warfare and cannon were also mounted in the canoes, sometimes on swivels. Combat thus took place over greater distances, as happened in the battle at Badagry in 1851. Lagoon strategy included the blockade, as carried out by the Lagos war fleet operating against Badagry in 1784, while a favourite tactic was for canoes to lie concealed in the long grasses of the marshy shores in order to ambush the enemy.

The study of relations between Lagos and Epe in the consular period is a study of diplomacy at least as much as of warfare. On the British side, responsibility for negotiations with local authorities on the West Coast of Africa and in the interior was for much of the nineteenth century entrusted to trading (or extrading) consuls, naval officers, and sometimes even merchants and missionaries. The methods of these amateur diplomatists, ignorant of the finesse of chancelleries and of the niceties of the *Règlement*, were usually rough and ready, and often went far beyond the scanty instructions and intentions of Whitehall. But to the Yoruba diplomacy was a fine and familiar art. Their numerous kingdoms negotiated both among themselves and with their neighbours, and this international intercourse was conducted along recognised lines and according to a strict and practical protocol.[15] Officials such as the *ilari* of the Alafin of Oyo, usually described as 'messengers', fulfilled the functions of travelling envoys, and regular diplomatic contacts were maintained between Oyo and Dahomey.[16] The Yoruba word *ajele*, for the resident representative abroad of a kingdom or power (such as Ibadan), was adopted with some appropriateness to describe the British consuls.[17] In the present study the principal figures are Kosoko and Campbell, but negotiations were conducted between them by such varied intermediaries as chiefs, naval officers, missionaries, traders, and household slaves.

Kosoko attacks

On his arrival Campbell found Lagos in an ugly state of tension between the adherents of Akitoye and of Kosoko. The latter's party had greatly increased in strength with the return to the town of those who had fled during the British bombardment, including the Portuguese and Brazilian slavers. Indignation had been aroused by the Oba's handling of the Amadie affair, and in Campbell's view it was this which now led Chiefs Ajenia and Possu to return openly to allegiance to Kosoko. Campbell estimated that the armed retainers of these and other discontented and pro-Kosoko chiefs amounted to over a thousand, while another thousand would be likely to join them from the Muslim community, the majority of whom supported Kosoko, and from among the followers of the Portuguese.

At this point the situation was exacerbated by the inopportune arrival of two English trading vessels, the *Lydia* (Liverpool) and the *Hope* (Bristol), whose masters proceeded to offer for sale supplies of muskets and gunpowder, the bulk of which was bought by the Portuguese dealers and resold to Kosoko's party. Campbell, learning that Akitoye had before his arrival forbidden the import of arms, issued rebukes to the ships' masters in terms which caused an unsympathetic official in Downing Street to minute that he was forgetting that 'he was only a consul and not a governor'. In his dispatch reporting these events Campbell added that he was deprived at this time – July 1853 – of any support from the Royal Navy since there were no cruisers at present on the bar, H.M.S. *Spray* having recently anchored but left again without communicating with the town. As Frazer had apparently sailed a few days earlier, presumably on the mail boat, the new consul was left alone to face a situation of great danger and delicacy, but a postscript to the despatch added that H.M.S.s *Spray* and *Waterwitch* were now off the town.[18]

Though serious, the situation was not enough to daunt a man of Campbell's character and experience. While the captain of the *Lydia* busily wrote off denunciations of Campbell, with whom he associated also Gollmer, to his principals in London — 'The fact is, the trade will be ruined if the whites meddle with all the native wars', he told them[19] — the consul arranged a rocket signal with the naval vessels by which he could summon their help in an emergency. He also held meetings with the Oba and with the leaders of the opposition party to urge calm and the maintenance of peace. But on 5 August 1853, when he had been barely two weeks at his post, the growing tension erupted into violence.

Hostilities[20] in the town began soon after daybreak, when Akitoye's supporters, either in the belief that Kosoko's war fleet had already set out from Epe or perhaps encouraged by the presence of the Royal Navy to try conclusions with the opposition, opened fire on the compounds of Ajenia, Possu and other known adherents of Kosoko. Firing continued for much of the day and into the night. According to White, the C.M.S. catechist, the pro-Kosoko forces, joined by many deserters from Akitoye, had launched attacks against three objectives: the Oba's palace, the C.M.S. headquarters at Oke Faji, and the compound of the Ashogbon, the leading war chief. Meanwhile, hundreds of refugees crowded into the mission compound, where both Campbell and Gollmer were living, and a guard was mounted there by a detachment of the Oba's warriors. During the night, three boats of H.M.S. *Waterwitch*, the only cruiser now off the town, arrived at the mission compound on the waterfront, the crew having sighted a rocket sent up during the evening. Campbell had no knowledge of the firing of this signal, and apparently had not yet judged it necessary to call on the Navy for help; in his report he surmised vaguely that the rocket had been let off by some Portuguese 'for purposes of their own'. But the arrival of the naval force was opportune, and at daybreak on 6 August the consul, accompanied by Gardner, the commander of the *Waterwitch*, and White of the C.M.S. as interpreter, succeeded in arranging a cease-fire.[21]

Campbell was persuaded that the opposition in the town was actuated not so much by hostility towards Akitoye as by indignation over the machinations of Madame Tinubu, and he next obtained a promise from the Oba to send away this great trader and undoubted trouble-maker.[22] He was also suspicious of the part played by Gollmer who, as he told the Foreign Office in a dispatch written two years later, seemed to have used his influence with Akitoye to persuade him to open the attack and who had been very active behind the scenes up to the time that the wounded began to be brought into the mission-house, at which point he 'took to his sofa, declaring he was suffering from fever and lumbago'. It was subsequently suggested by Campbell and Gardner that Gollmer had persuaded the Oba to take advantage of the arrival of the armed boats to put down his rebellious chiefs.[23]

But the crisis was not over. On 11 August there appeared on the lagoon off Lagos a flotilla of Kosoko's war canoes, armed with cannon and containing an army estimated at 1500 men, led by Kosoko in person. Campbell opened a parley with this fleet through the Hamburg merchant Grote, but the next day, learning that two more British cruisers had arrived off the bar, he broke off communications. Kosoko had meanwhile landed a considerable force on the south side of the island, and by the evening of 12 August this was within a quarter of a mile of the mission compound, into which refugees continued to flock.[24] During the night the consul remained on watch with Gardner, three other naval officers, and four European merchants. But by now Commodore Bruce, having sighted the flag of distress hoisted by the consul, was sending help. Though the night (of 12/13 August) was moonless, eight well-armed boats of the Royal Navy succeeded in crossing the bar safely. They arrived just as a group comprising the largest of the Epe canoes, eighty feet in length,[25] with Kosoko himself on board accompanied by Tapa and Lima, made an unopposed landing at Possu's compound on the north shore, only about half a mile from the Oba's palace. This force, unaware of the arrival of the armed boats from the British men-of-war, now prepared to attack the mission-house, presumably in concert with the force to the south, as soon as day should break. They were forestalled by a burst of fire from the British naval force, under Commander Phillips of H.M.S. *Polyphemus*. Only a few shots were sent into the compound, but Kosoko was sufficiently alarmed to call off his attack. In the darkness he and many of his warriors escaped, but others (probably those on the south shore), hotly pursued by Akitoye's men, were killed or drowned as they struggled to reach their canoes. Thus ended the engagement known to the Lagosians as the Ija Afasegbojo – 'the wonderful war' (literally, if enigmatically, 'fighting like one who collects rain water in a sieve').

Owing to the unpreparedness of Lagos (for which Newbury[26] with some justice blames Frazer, now well on his way to the safety of England) and the weakness of Akitoye's regime, Kosoko had come near to success. His failure to take the town on this occasion can be attributed to the timely arrival of the ships of the Royal Navy, to the thwarting by Akitoye (perhaps advised by Gollmer, as the consul suspected) of any attempt at a rising by his – Kosoko's – adherents within the town to coincide with the attack from Epe, and to the dispersal of his forces in landings on both the north and south shores. But the troubles of Lagos were still far from solution. Possu and Ajenia had escaped and were now at Epe in full support of the ex-Oba there. There were rumours that Kosoko was sending presents to win over the chiefs of Ijebu and Abeokuta, who were gradually overcoming their political differences with each other.[27] Trade was disrupted, foodstuffs at Lagos doubling in price. Campbell tried to counter Kosoko's diplomacy by warning the Egba against the 'wicked and turbulent men' at Epe and, in a letter which could not be delivered, threatened the Awujale that if he did not expel Kosoko, the English queen might be forced into 'carrying war into the country of her friend the King of Jaboo'.[28] The consul followed this a week later by a letter to Kosoko and his chiefs in which he told them that though the British would never allow Kosoko to return as king of Lagos, they 'had no wish to harm or disturb him, wherever he may sit down and make his peaceable trade'. This conciliatory approach seems likely to have been prompted by the merchants, already inclining towards support for Kosoko. Its inconsistency with the consul's letters to Abeokuta and Ijebu Ode went unremarked in the Foreign Office. It elicited a swift reply (in Portuguese) in which Kosoko claimed that he had come to Lagos only to rescue Ajenia and Possu. He disarmingly asked, 'When I can be accused of being a criminal, who is innocent?' Finally, having learnt of Akitoye's sudden death, he begged that he and his followers might be allowed to return to 'our dear country'.[29]

The death of Akitoye apparently took place on the night of 2 September[30] and was announced early the next morning to Gollmer, who gave the news to Campbell. Although the consul on his arrival at Lagos had found the king infirm and prevented by rheumatism from walking, this was unexpected, and there was a report that Akitoye had been poisoned, either by his enemies or, distracted as he was by political anxieties, by his own hand.[31] Campbell relates how he first questioned the chiefs and learnt that they considered the legitimate heir to be Dosunmu (Docemo), Akitoye's eldest son, and how only then did he reveal to them the Oba's death. Once again Kosoko's claims to the throne were set aside, and Dosunmu was informed of his accession, the news being given to him in his canoe as he followed his trade as a fisherman on the lagoon (and while 'singing a barcarolle', adds the romantic Scala).[32] The numerous and complicated ceremonies to be performed by the Oba-elect and the appropriate chiefs and officers of the court were carried out in the recesses of the palace with unusual haste, and the following day Dosunmu was formally acknowledged as Oba of Lagos, receiving a salute of twenty-one guns from the boats of the Royal Navy.

Dosunmu, a man of about thirty years, had ascended his throne at a time of crisis. Despite the reverse in August, Kosoko was growing in strength. Ajenia and Possu, with their followers, were important accessions, and Kosoko now gave refuge at Epe to more Portuguese and Brazilian traders who, after having successfully defied the orders of the enfeebled Akitoye, were now forced by the new Oba, at the instance of the consul and missionaries, to leave the town. Soon the Epe were mounting piratical attacks on the trading canoes crossing the lagoon, even, according to the consul, on those of the Ijebu, and food supplies to Lagos were being interrupted. Early in September the American missionary Bowen was fearing a repetition of Kosoko's attack and reported that his canoes were blocking river communications with Abeokuta. Thus Dosunmu welcomed the arrival of a further force of Egba warriors, numbering two thousand or more, sent to him by the chiefs of Abeokuta despite Kosoko's attempts to buy over their support.³³ But the Oba's Egba allies had omitted to provide funds for this force, whose members, after exhausting the cowries given them by the Lagos merchants, took to kidnapping the local people, until Campbell, at the suggestion of Bruce, expended over £100 in presents to the Egba troops and also to the 'Issoes' (living west of Badagry), who 'in their small canoes and fighting with spears', were convoying the Egba traders across the lagoon and visiting Epe to obtain intelligence for the consul.³⁴

In early September a combined British and Lagosian expedition was launched against Epe. It was commanded by Phillips, whose omission to consult the consul about the operation illustrates the odd lack of liaison between the British naval and civilian authorities. Seven boats, containing some ninety sailors and marines and accompanied by sixty canoes with 1000 of Dosunmu's warriors, left Lagos. They returned after an absence of two days and a night, having gone only about halfway to their objective and accomplished no more than the burning of four villages and the capture of seven small canoes, at the cost of one marine slightly wounded. Campbell's ensuing complaint against Phillips to the Foreign Office was answered in a letter to the Admiralty from Bruce, who inconsistently explained that Phillips had run short of ammunition and that it had never been supposed that so small a force could have attacked Epe with any chance of success since the town (Bruce erroneously supposed) was a mile from the shore, and also was 'entrenched and stockaded' (this proved true) and 'filled with armed men to the number of 3,000 or 4,000'. No officer, Bruce concluded, could be 'braver and more zealous' than the impugned Phillips.³⁵

The débâcle of the Phillips expedition must have encouraged Kosoko considerably, and his war canoes continued to take the initiative in hostilities on the lagoon. On 15 September they captured three canoes carrying nineteen persons near Ikorodu. A week later they attacked a group of Egba canoes making their way north from Lagos towards the Ogun. The Egba returned the fire, but then (in Gollmer's account to the C.M.S.) 'by strategem, another division of the enemy's canoes hiding in the bush, and firing upon them in the back, proved too much, and eight canoes with about eighteen people, were taken', while the rest returned hastily to Lagos.³⁶ In the following month a second expedition from Lagos was organised, this time on a larger scale but again under Phillips's command. On 10 October, nine boats from H.M.S.s *Polyphemus*, *Waterwitch* and *Alecto*, carrying 120 officers and men, left Lagos across the lagoon. The next day they were joined by a fleet of canoes containing Lagosian and Egba warriors. After burning the 'slave market' at 'Hedjenna',³⁷ they passed into the narrow part of the lagoon and approached Epe. Phillips's report describes the town as being 'masked' by forest, but three landing places could be seen. At the first, by the market, the enemy was strongly entrenched. Beyond this was a belt of trees and then a beach protected by a stockade which extended into the water, while a third beach further east was similarly fortified.

As the flotilla drew near the shore, it encountered heavy firing from the market which drove back an attempted landing by the Egba. It was now sunset, and the boats retired out of range and anchored for the night. At 7 a.m. on the twelfth the attack was resumed with the firing of shells and rockets. Phillips's plan was to make the main landing at the market with a diversionary landing on the western beach, but this failed because (according to his report) the Egba ignored his signal to advance and the few Lagos warriors who obeyed were quickly repulsed. At 10 a.m. the commander decided that the expedition was 'wasting powder and losing lives without prospect of doing much further mischief'. He thereupon called in the boats and began the return. Two sailors had been killed, one was severely wounded, and one marine slightly wounded. Lagos and Egba casualties were not reported. The result was all the more disappointing since Campbell's informants subsequently alleged that Kosoko, Tapa, Ajenia and Possu decamped from Epe early on the twelfth, leaving men in the trenches to cover their withdrawal, so that had the force remained a further day the town would probably have fallen.[38]

These failures led to recriminations between the Lagos and the Egba as well as between the consul and the Royal Navy. To accusations that they had refused to land and engage the enemy, the Egba replied by complaining that being 'interior peoples and unused to canoe warfare and canoe paddling', they had been tricked into accepting the most rickety canoes. But they then offered to make an attack by land on the slave baracoons on the coast at Olomowewe ('Jebu of the Charts').[39] They set out on 22 October, marching along the beach – or, more probably, along the track immediately behind the beach. About ten miles from their destination, they were attacked by some six hundred of Kosoko's men, but drove them back. In this encounter they claimed to have killed five European slave traders who fired at them with their pistols; these included the well-known Signor Conto, Amadie's friend. Lima was also present, but escaped into the bush. On reaching the baracoons, the Egba found them deserted, but after the younger soldiers had raided the stores and made themselves drunk, a retreat was ordered. Meanwhile, the *Polyphemus* had proceeded by sea to Olomowewe and had found there – but apparently failed to apprehend – the schooner *Deslandes* from Jersey and two Sardinian vessels, the property of the slavers.[40]

The raid on Olomowewe was the only bright feature in a critical situation. Campbell reported home that, though Oba Dosunmu 'by his firmness, moderation, good sense and active energy, gives promise of maintaining peace and order', Lagos was so harassed by the depredations from Epe that external trade had ceased, other than that with the Egba, whose canoes had now to be convoyed across the lagoon from 'Aboney creek' (the Agboye, or western arm of the Ogun estuary).[41] Then, on successive nights in early December, Kosoko's men, who had been lying in wait near the Agboyi creek, fell upon two Egba 'caravans' (or trading parties) carrying palm oil on the path to

Abeokúta, and captured about three hundred men and women. These ambushes, which took place at Ebute Metta, only a mile or two from the Oba's palace across the water, caused great alarm. Arrangements were made for the Egba warriors at Lagos to escort future caravans for ten miles up the Abeokuta road, while Campbell urged the Egba to send a chief and an additional hundred or hundred and fifty trusty soldiers to Lagos. The consul also did his best to persuade the reluctant British naval officers to give protection to the canoes crossing the lagoon, but they found such service, he said, 'infra dig'.[42] He told the Foreign Office that the slave trade in the Bight was again on the increase, a reference probably to shippings from Palma and its neighbourhood, and suggested a renewal of the blockade: a measure opposed by the naval commander on the grounds that it would discourage legitimate trade and that Campbell's information was unreliable.[43] In England, meanwhile, press criticism of the British action at Lagos in August roused the organ of the Church Missionary Society to ask indignantly: 'Shall Kosoko be permitted to possess himself of Lagos, as the Muscovite Czar has possessed himself of the Danubian principalities?'[44]

Resort to diplomacy: a time of conferences

At this point – between writing his dispatch of 20 December 1853 about the kidnapping of the Egba and the first week of January 1854 – Campbell changed his policy from one of encouraging and forwarding attempts to overthrow Kosoko by force to one of conciliation and pacification, offering support for Kosoko in return for his recognition of Dosunmu as Oba of Lagos (though the basis of agreement was broadened as negotiations proceeded). In this he was turning decisively from the policies advocated by the missionaries to those which appealed to the traders, whose interests were directed more to the restoration of trade through the port of Lagos than to the suppression of the slave trade, though the latter remained a consideration with them since slaving tended to drive out legitimate trade. Doubtless Campbell as an ex-trader himself had all along felt some sympathy for the commercial point of view. Moreover, his change of course met with the approbation of the commander-in-chief of the naval squadron. The Navy had already shown reluctance to become more deeply involved in hostilities against Epe and was understandably impatient at being required to prop up one ruler against another. Apart from these considerations, it was now clear that the consul did not command the resources in men, money or armaments to intervene decisively against the 'pirates', and thus Campbell's projects of appeasement and 'co-existence' reflected his assessment of the balance of power on the lagoon.

The implementation of the new policy provided a problem in diplomacy. Campbell wasted no time. Having obtained Bruce's support, he set off down the coast on 7 January 1854 on board H.M.S. *Pluto* to 'the port of Jabu', by which Palma is meant. On arrival the consul, who had been suffering intermittently from fever for a month, was too ill to land through the surf, so Lieutenant Norman Bedingfeld,[45] commanding the *Pluto*, took his place and held an interview ashore with Tapa, Kosoko's representative. Bedingfeld, who had established friendly relations with Tapa on a visit to Epe in February 1852, succeeded in obtaining an invitation for the consul to visit Kosoko. A week later, on 13 January, Campbell, accompanied by Bedingfeld again and by the assistant-surgeon of the *Pluto*, crossed the lagoon to Epe where they arrived the next day. They were welcomed on the beach by Tapa and by two Portuguese merchants, Lima and Pedro. They walked through the town, noting the well-sited trenches and earthen ramparts, and in the evening were served a 'well-dressed dinner' in Tapa's house before returning to their boats. On 16 January Campbell was again ill, so Bedingfeld went ashore and made a number of proposals to Tapa. These, discussed in an 'orderly palaver',[46] stated that if Kosoko relinquished his claim to the Lagos throne, ceased to harass the people of Lagos, and abjured the slave trade, the British would allow him to continue to use 'Jaboo' (Palma) as his seaport, guarantee him against molestation from Lagos, and treat him as any other friendly African chief. These proposals were well received, with the exception of the first. On their side, Tapa and the chiefs suggested that a conference should be held between them and Dosunmu's chiefs at some place midway between Lagos and Epe. This recognised that the next step must be to try to secure Dosunmu's participation. With this purpose in view, Campbell took leave of Tapa on 17 January (on this occasion it was Bedingfeld who was too feverish to go ashore) and the British party regained Lagos the following evening.[47]

Campbell next reported to the Foreign Office that he had 'with some difficulty prevailed on King Dosunmu to send some of his Caboceers' (that is, his chiefs) to meet those of Epe. He gave no account of the meeting at which this had been achieved, but the matter was so speedily settled that on 27 January the consul again set out across the lagoon to continue his negotiations. He was accompanied by Bedingfeld with four other officers from the *Pluto*, by Dr E. G. Irving, a former naval officer and now a medical missionary and political adviser to the C.M.S., and two Lagos merchants, one being J. G. Sandeman and the other the unnamed 'agent for the mail packets', by whom Scala is probably meant.[48] The party travelled in six boats, including two paddle-box boats[49] from the *Pluto*, one carrying a brass gun and the other a rocket tube. With the tide in their favour they took about three hours to reach the group of three uninhabited islands now marked on maps as the 'Palaver Islands', which lie near the centre of the lagoon at the point where it narrows to a distance of about two miles, the Yoruba names being 'Agbekin' for the largest (some third of a mile in length) and most northerly and 'Arekin' for the two smaller ones.[50] Here they anchored for the night and were joined by seven Lagos chiefs, each in his own canoe with his attendants. During supper, which was served to all in the consul's boat, a canoe approached from Epe under a white flag, and greetings were exchanged. Early the following morning (28 January), the Epe messengers returned with the news that Kosoko's chiefs were nearby but were nervous at the presence of the armed boats. Bedingfeld and Irving set out to reassure them, and soon returned with Tapa, described by Irving as 'a corpulent, good-natured-expressioned man', attended by servants holding his sword and coloured umbrella. A breakfast party followed, and (to quote Irving again) 'Kosoko's fleet now hove in sight, to the number of between sixty and seventy large canoes, containing from thirty to forty men each; many with small iron guns in the bows, each having the white flag and sticks, and presenting a very gay and striking effect.' After some discussion it was decided to land for the conference on the island of Agbekin.[51] An approach was cut through the thick reeds which fringed the shore, and a conference place prepared in the shade of a great tree whose branches were draped with trailing plants. The consul's party was seated in the centre, with the Lagos and Epe chiefs on either side on mats and under their umbrellas. The Epe delegation was led by Possu: 'tall and stout', according to Irving, 'with large features, expressing sensuality, sullen moroseness, suspicion and vindictiveness'. He was accompanied by Tapa and one White Cap chief, the Onisiwo (an Idejo). The Lagos party was headed by four White Cap chiefs and included the Olumegbon, the Eletu, and the captain of the Egba force at Lagos.[52]

When Tapa and Possu had consented to 'do homage' (by which Irving presumably meant greeting by prostration) to the White Caps from Lagos, the proceedings opened at about noon. It soon appeared that there was a 'universal desire for peace', and speakers on both sides regretted that the country should be divided and trade halted 'because two kings' sons chose to quarrel'. The delegates then placed their interests in the consul's hands; Tapa added that the Epe chiefs wanted to 'come home' to Lagos and he suggested that Kosoko could return as a 'private person'. Campbell replied that two kings could not live in one town – a maxim not in accord with contemporary Yoruba practice[53] – and that Lagos already had a king, Dosunmu, whom they meant to keep. The first objective should be to open the lagoon and punish kidnapping. The meeting agreed that these measures were necessary and should be adopted until the two delegations could consult with Dosunmu and Kosoko respectively. The conference ended at about 4 p.m. with the splitting of kola, the serving of refreshments, and a demonstration by the English of an airgun and a Colt revolver.

Irving ended his account of the conference (much more detailed and picturesque than that given by the consul) with an analysis of the reasons which had led the representatives of Kosoko to take their unexpectedly conciliatory attitude. According to his information, the chiefs at Epe were losing heart as they came to realise the determination of the English to uphold Dosunmu. He had heard that at the previous meeting at Epe all the chiefs except Possu had advised Kosoko to accept the consul's terms, and that Kosoko was being pressed to reach a settlement by his Ijebu hosts, who had gone so far as to suggest that he should otherwise 'go to sleep' — a euphemism for taking poison. There is no confirmation of these reports, and it is necessary to add to this probably biased assessment that Kosoko's ready appreciation of the importance of winning over the consul and his method of setting about this illustrate his qualities as a politician and diplomatist. The measure of his achievement was not lost on Oba Dosunmu, who was so much disturbed by the news from the conference that Irving and Gollmer 'endeavoured to cheer him up, by assuring him that the English are not going to desert him'. Irving adds that Dosunmu was 'afraid of being poisoned, as he says his father was by Ajinnia, Pellu [Possu], and Tappa'.

In his report written the day after his return from the Palaver Islands, Campbell was optimistic about his understanding with Kosoko. Already — presumably as a result of the earlier meeting at Epe — navigation on the lagoon was free from interference by Kosoko's war canoes, some of the markets on the Ijebu (that is, the northern) shore were open, and the prices of essential articles at Lagos had fallen by a third. But this happy state of affairs was short-lived. By May Campbell was complaining of Dosunmu's refusal to allow trade canoes to come from Epe to Lagos. For this he blamed Gollmer, alleging that the missionary had 'a hatred almost demoniacal' towards Kosoko and had 'insinuated to the king and his chiefs that it was the intention of the Admiral [Bruce] and [the consul] to bring Kosoko back to Lagos'.[54] Three months later he reported that Kosoko still kept his word not to disturb the Lagos trade, despite 'very strong provocation' from Dosunmu, who maintained his ban on direct trade between Lagos and Epe. According to the consul's informants (evidently the merchants), Kosoko's followers at Epe 'comprised the best portion of the former population of Lagos being for the most part industrious and honest traders'. There was no truth, he continued, in Gollmer's assertion that the Ijebu were 'angry with the English because they hang Kosoko on their neck to trouble them', for Kosoko had taken refuge at Epe with the full consent of the Awujale. To a letter from Gollmer and Gerst complaining that they, with some other C.M.S. agents, had been maltreated by Kosoko's friends at Ikorodu, Campbell retorted that as 'Foreigners born' (they were Germans) these two missionaries had no claim to his protection. He also alleged to the foreign secretary that Gollmer was spending much of his time intriguing and 'in carrying on a rather extensive trade in palm oil and ivory within the missionary compound, and he may be seen, on what are called Egba market days, jacket and waistcoat off, shirt sleeves tucked up, with his usual active energy running here and there, gauging a huge cask of palm oil, weighing a tooth of ivory, counting out cowrie shells, opening merchandise, sending his trusty messengers Pearce and George Williams to the King and chiefs, and receiving messages from the king'.[55]

Campbell considered himself bound by the agreement reached at the January conference on the Palaver Islands to support Kosoko's plea to be allowed to trade with Lagos. He pointed out to Dosunmu that his continued refusal to allow this would lead the merchants and supercargoes now trading at Lagos to deal direct with Kosoko at Palma, reducing the shipments of palm oil from Lagos; Kosoko's large fleet of war canoes would also enable him to monopolise trade from Ijebu. But Dosunmu maintained his stand, stiffened (the consul wrote) by the 'secret influence' of Gollmer and the 'open opposition' of the still unbanished Madame Tinubu. Meanwhile, Kosoko and the Epe chiefs confined themselves to sending an occasional unarmed canoe to the consulate to ask whether permission to trade had yet been granted. These visits were so much resented by the Oba's party that on one occasion the Epe messengers found themselves threatened by armed men from the palace. Campbell gave them his protection, accompanying them in his boat across the lagoon for five miles, but then wrote to Kosoko warning him against further visits. Both he and Kosoko were losing patience, and at length the consul, justifying himself by a rumour that Kosoko was preparing again to resort to force in order to return home, determined to reach a settlement. An opportunity was now afforded him by the visit to Lagos of the senior officer of the Bights Division, Commander Thomas Miller, with two naval vessels, H.M.S.s *Crane* and *Minx*.[56]

The treaty of Epe

On or about 26 September 1854 the naval steam vessel *Minx* crossed the bar into the Lagos river and anchored off the consulate. On the twenty-seventh she was boarded by Consul Campbell, accompanied by Commander Miller, three other naval officers, three Lagos merchants – Scala the Sardinian, W. R. Hansen a Fanti from the Gold Coast, and 'Josi Pedro Da Cousta Roy', presumably a Portuguese – and S. B. Williams, a Sierra Leonean repatriate trader who was employed by the consul as interpreter.[57] From Lagos the *Minx* proceeded to Agbekin island, whence the consul sent a message inviting Tapa to another conference there. Tapa replied by asking the British to continue to Epe, where Kosoko himself was ready to see them, to which Campbell and Miller agreed. On arrival at Epe the consul's party was met by Tapa and taken to Kosoko's compound, where they were cordially welcomed by the former Oba. Campbell then proposed a 'solemn engagement' between Kosoko and the British on the terms already outlined in previous meetings, with the additional incentive for Kosoko of an annual compensatory payment. This was well received, and the meeting then adjourned for dinner, after which the British returned to the *Minx* for the night.

The following day, 28 September, the British landed again, armed with the 'solemn engagement' fairly written out. A full-scale palaver was held during which the articles of the engagement were interpreted first into Portuguese, which many on the Epe side spoke fluently, and then into 'the country language' – Awori Yoruba. On each article a well-conducted discussion was held, causing Campbell to remark in his report on the acute understanding of the issues which was displayed by the Epe. Finally, 'Kosoko rose to put his mark to the paper, expressing the hope that he would be allowed to die in Lagos and not in exile' (a peculiarly dreadful fate for a Yoruba prince); he then called on his chiefs to subscribe similarly to the agreement. After both sides had signed, Campbell gave a promise (apparently verbal) that on his return he would 'insist' that Dosunmu and his chiefs should allow the Epe canoes to trade freely with the merchants at Lagos; he made no reference to any possibility of Kosoko's ever being allowed to return there.[58]

The treaty of Epe[59] consisted of seven articles. Under the first, third and fourth, Kosoko and his chiefs pledged themselves to abstain from any attempt to regain possession of Lagos, to abjure the slave trade, to protect merchants and traders who wished to live among them for legitimate trade, and to assist the consul in reopening the markets on the 'Jaboo shore'. In the second article Campbell and Miller agreed to recognise Palma as Kosoko's port, while under the sixth Campbell engaged that his Government should pay to Kosoko for life an annual sum of 2000 heads of cowries or 1000 dollars[60] at his option. Article V laid down that an export duty should be levied on Kosoko's behalf of one head of cowries for every puncheon of palm oil and two strings of cowries a pound on all ivory exported from Palma. (This to some extent protected the market at Lagos by checking competition at Palma, though the duty levied at Lagos on palm oil remained double that stipulated for Palma.) The last article provided that the agreement should enter into immediate force and be binding until annulled by the British Government. The signatories were Kosoko and fifteen of his chiefs on the Epe side and Campbell and Miller for the British, the rest of the consul's party acting as witnesses.

In announcing the signature of the treaty to the foreign secretary, Campbell wrote that he felt 'great confidence' in its being faithfully observed and leading to a considerable increase of trade. He attributed Kosoko's 'present pacific disposition' and readiness to sign the treaty to the removal of the 'evil influence' of Lima, who, after surviving the affray at Olomowewe with the Egba, had lately died of dysentery at Epe. He added that he had learnt from one of Kosoko's leading men, himself an Egba, that the captives taken at Ebute Metta had all been redeemed by their relatives; none had been sold as slaves on the Benin River, as had been reported.[61] On 15 January 1855 a Foreign Office official minuted on Campbell's dispatch: 'This is a bad precedent but I think upon the whole the Treaty should be applied', and the consul was told on 23 February that though the amount of compensation in Article VI was 'much larger than H.M.'s Government have ever engaged to pay under similar circumstances', the treaty was approved.[62]

Though the point was not commented upon in Whitehall, Campbell's omission, or inability, to associate Oba Dosunmu and his chiefs with the treaty augured ill for its success. It could be argued that there was no reason for Dosunmu to be included in the arrangements whereby Kosoko was to give up the slave trade and the British to recognise his position at Epe and Palma, territory to which Dosunmu made no claim. But the treaty was intended as an instrument for the pacification of the lagoon, and Kosoko's renunciation of the Lagos throne was its first, and probably in the consul's view its most important, clause. Moreover, Campbell had taken trouble to ensure the participation of Dosunmu's representatives in the January meeting, as suggested by the Epe chiefs. Between the conference on the Palaver Islands and the visit to Epe which saw the signature of the treaty, the consul's dispatches were preoccupied with his quarrel with the C.M.S. agents, especially Gollmer, and with explanations of his actions in June 1854 at Badagry, and they contain no mention of Dosunmu in connection with peace-making on the eastern lagoon. It must be supposed that in this interval Campbell came to realise that Dosunmu was bound to disapprove of the bargain which he was to propose at Epe, and that he trusted in his ability to deal separately with the Oba on his return.

But trade with Lagos was an important objective for Kosoko, and before signing the treaty he had obtained the consul's promise of support over this. Campbell kept his word, and on his return extracted from the Oba an undertaking that the Epe should be allowed to trade freely at Lagos. At his suggestion a piece of ground was fenced in to serve as a market for the Epe traders and also, on alternate days, for those from Badagry and Porto Novo who were expected to resume their visits.[63] But the consul soon had reason to suspect Dosunmu's good faith. Before the end of the year he was reporting that work on the new market had ceased, and he associated this with the return to the town of a number of slave dealers.[64]

Campbell performed one further service for Kosoko after the conclusion of the treaty. On 27 November he went by sea on board H.M.S. *Scourge*, preceded by H.M.S. *Crane*, to proclaim the formal opening of the port of Palma, which took place on 29 November. Kosoko, attended by all his chiefs, had crossed the lagoon to meet the British party, but the surf was so heavy that only the valiant Tapa and a few war captains came out to the *Scourge*, where they were entertained by a display of 'cutlass exercise' and taken on a tour of the ship. After the visitors had left, the *Scourge* fired a salute, which was answered by volleys of musketry from the shore where an 'English ensign' awarded to Kosoko could be seen flying.[65]

After the treaty

The subsequent history of Lagos–Epe relations down to the end of the consular period must be left for later chapters and can only be briefly indicated here. It should be noted, first, that the Treaty of Epe added little to the security of Dosunmu's throne, whereas it conferred real benefits on Kosoko. Moreover, reports that Kosoko was again preparing to attack Lagos revived after little more than two years and continued down to the end of the period, while his stipend under the treaty does not seem to have ever been paid.[66] From this it may seem that the Treaty of Epe had only an ephemeral effect on the political situation on the lagoon. Yet even apart from its intrinsic interest as the outcome of several months of manœuvring and negotiation, the treaty had some political importance. It was a step towards the general pacification of the lagoon; it gave prestige and stability to the state founded at Epe by Kosoko; finally, it was to lead indirectly to the extension of British authority for some forty miles along the coast and on the eastern lagoon, since it was the colony at Lagos which succeeded to the territory between the lagoon and the sea which had been acquired by Kosoko and recognised by the treaty as within his sphere. Though the harbourless port of Palma could never attract much shipping, its trade had been sufficient to make it worth while for such a firm as Régis Ainé to open an establishment there in 1855.[67] More important than the duties raised at Palma, however, was the fact that title to the eastern coastline enabled the colonial administration to ensure that trade was not diverted from Lagos harbour.

In making the treaty Campbell could not foresee these developments; to him it merely marked a stage in the struggle to establish his authority. His success was the result both of his own qualities and of the dynastic quarrel which allowed him to play off one prince against the other. For his part Kosoko must have congratulated himself on the bargain which he had made at Epe. British recognition of his state entailed a measure of British support, and possession of Palma enabled him to draw off a large part of the export of palm oil from Ijebu. He may have calculated that in a few years he would be rich and strong enough to make a powerful effort to regain his kingdom, for he too could not foresee the decision taken by Palmerston in 1861. In the event the descendants of Akitoye and Dosunmu remained on the Lagos throne, while Kosoko's descendants retained only the chieftancy of Ereko. Their quarrel continued long after the deaths of the principal protagonists. But already the era of the war canoes on the eastern lagoon was drawing to an end, and in the long process of pacification the negotiations and treaty of 1854 had played their part.

5

Mr Consul Campbell

The consul and the slave trade

Benjamin Campbell's first and most pressing problem had been to keep Kosoko at bay and to prevent his recapturing Lagos. In this, with the aid of the Royal Navy, he succeeded, although to the very end of his consulate a threat from Kosoko remained. Beyond this, the broad and long-term aims in Lagos of the British Government during this period were confined to the continuation of the fight against the slave trade and to the encouragement of 'legitimate trade', the latter being a phrase should not be construed as synonymous with the furthering of British commercial interests. Though the Foreign Office accepted from the beginning that support of Akitoye involved the maintenance of a 'quasi-protectorate', Campbell throughout his years as consul received no directive which envisaged any objective other than these two. This failure to define the political aims of the consulate and the consequent lack of precise instruction to Campbell about the nature of his political duties allowed the consul great latitude in his interpretation of these duties, while his official position involved him in many different issues and many different interests in the increasingly complex situation at Lagos. With no force under his command and entirely dependent for support during the dangerous early years on the intermittent visits of vessels of the Royal Navy, he was still able by his personality and character to establish himself and his consulate in a position of considerable influence and even power, while at the same time managing, often only after volumes of explanation, to extract approval for his proceedings from his often hesitant and sometimes unsympathetic masters in Downing Street.

Despite the meagreness of his salary and although he was allowed by the terms of his appointment to engage in trade, Campbell seems to have found it necessary to make a full-time job of his consular duties. Whether he ever learnt the Yoruba language is not known, but at all events he was able from the first to find an interpreter and subordinate staff competent in English from among the Saro. For the first six months he used the C.M.S. catechist James White as interpreter at a salary of £20 a year, subsequently employing in this capacity

S. B. Williams, a prominent emigrant, whose services as intermediary rather than simply interpreter commanded an annual salary of £60 in 1856, increased in 1859 to £90. The consular messenger was J. B. Pearce, also of the C.M.S., earning £10 a year, and Campbell later engaged J. P. Boyle as clerk.[1] The lack of consular premises remained a great problem until in June 1854, after Campbell's pathetic plea for a tent, the Foreign Office agreed to send out a prefabricated frame house – the famous 'corrugated iron coffin or plank-lined morgue, containing a dead consul once a year', seen by Richard Burton in 1861[2] – which was erected, probably in the middle of 1855, on the waterfront to the east of the C.M.S. compound. For this the consul was required to pay £40 a year in rent.[3] For visits to the remoter coastal areas in his jurisdiction Campbell was dependent on the co-operation of the Royal Navy, with whom he seems to have maintained consistently good relations, while for travels on the lagoon and between Lagos island and the mainland he had his own boat, the 'consular barge' as the missionaries more grandly termed it. A pier opposite the consulate provided a convenient landing-place. The original light draught boat which Campbell took over from Frazer[4] was lost at sea in April 1855 'from astern of H.M.S. *Crane*' during the attempt to deliver an important letter from the consul to the ship's commander, and the Foreign Office sanctioned the provision of a new whale-boat of about twenty-eight feet in length, which reached Lagos in July 1855.[5] This in turn was upset on the bar in February 1857 when carrying Campbell on a visit to Commodore Adams, and without mentioning his own experiences on this alarming occasion the consul reported the loss of all the fittings. The Foreign Office, while agreeing to meet the cost of repairs, tried to establish the principle that the upkeep of the boat was the consul's responsibility, withdrawing after Campbell had explained that he used the boat for duty only, there being (he said) no pleasure at Lagos.[6]

The attitude of the foreign secretaries towards their consul at Lagos cannot be judged by the parsimony with which they met all his proposals for expending public funds, which reflected not so much the financial policy of the government as their own general disinclination to embark on the sort of justification which the Treasury required.[7] They seem indeed to have placed increasing confidence in Campbell, despite the accusations against his character and activities which came from several quarters and might have seemed to them disturbingly numerous. These began with allegations by the French Ambassador in London, Count Walewski, that Campbell had wrongly retained certain monies which he had acquired while in charge of the French consulate in Sierra Leone. The correspondence on this matter concluded with the foreign secretary's telling Campbell that he appeared, despite his protestations to the contrary, to owe some £43 to the French Government, a claim which Lord Clarendon recommended 'should be immediately paid'.[8] Rather more serious were the accusations levelled against the consul by the missionaries, mainly to the effect that he was discriminating against them in favour of commercial interests, and by the merchants that he was obstructing their trade and exceeding his authority. More serious still were the allegations, again made by the French Foreign Ministry, that he had been connected with the slave trade while in the Rio Pongas. These clouded the last months of his life, but his answers to the charges read convincingly enough, and the significance of the episode now lies in its revelation of French hostility to the consul's ascendancy in Lagos.

In all but the first of these cases Campbell received the support of the Foreign Office and generally also of the naval officers on the coast. Lagos, to the foreign secretary and his officials, was a remote but not unimportant tropical outpost, and Campbell's dispatches, however prolix, were carefully read (at least by the officials) and his recommendations considered. His proposals for the posting of a salaried vice-consul to assist him at Lagos and for another to reside at 'Quittah' (Keta, west of Whydah) were not sympathetically received,[9] but his recommendation for the appointment of an unpaid vice-consul for Badagry and Porto Novo met with approval and his candidate, McCoskry, was accepted, although in the event the latter continued to spend most of his time in Lagos and was eventually relieved of a post he had never really occupied.[10]

The Foreign Office's interest in the affairs of Lagos and willingness to maintain the consulate there stemmed from the commitment to repression of the slave trade. Reports from the missionaries and, less exuberantly, from the consul, extolling the potential riches of the Yoruba interior, and the rising exports of palm oil contributed in an incalculable but probably not very serious measure to this policy. As the routine patrols of the Preventive Squadron continued at sea, despite the withdrawal of some of the best cruisers on the outbreak of the Crimean War in 1854, so did the consul on land continue to play his part in the campaign for abolition. The vigour and efficacy of these efforts rose and fell, but Campbell shows himself throughout his period as consul to have been a consistent opponent of the trade and a sincere servant of his government's policy.

The consular period at Lagos opened just after the slave trade to Brazil had collapsed. But with the ever-growing demand in Europe for sugar and cotton, the trade to Cuba and to the United States was still flourishing, carried on mainly by ships flying the American flag and taking slaves from around the mouth of the Congo and from the coast south of Dahomey. The situation was aggravated by an acute shortage of labour for the plantations in the tropics. The French were especially affected by this as a result of the abolition in 1848 of slavery in their colonies, and from the early 1850s they had been trying to persuade the British to allow them to recruit contract labour in British India. Their requests had been refused because of the opposition of the Indian authorities, but at the end of 1857, with the support of the Foreign Office, a long-drawn negotiation began for the conclusion of a 'coolie convention' under which they could obtain Indian labour. Meanwhile the government of

Napoleon III had developed a greater interest in the possibility of obtaining labour in West Africa; they were conniving at various means of evading the anti-slavery laws of their own and other countries, and were resentful of any interference with their nationals even when they were deeply implicated in slaving activities. The consular records from Lagos contain many references to actual or attempted slaving from these obstinately persisting areas of the trade, of which only a selection can be mentioned here.

One small part of the system of combatting the trade was the regular lists of vessels suspected of being employed in slaving which the Foreign Office sent out to Campbell and other recipients for communication to the officers of the Squadron whenever opportunity occurred. As these lists were compiled in London mainly from information gathered from far-flung consular posts, such as Havana, they were generally so out of date as to be of little use (the telegraph, still in its infancy, did not reach Lagos until 1886). For his part Campbell kept a sharpish eye on the movements of known or suspected practitioners of the trade in his area. In March 1854 he drew attention to the presence of the American barque *Carrier Pigeon* off Whydah; he felt certain, he wrote, that the casks on board were filled with water (for consumption by a slave cargo) and that palm oil had been only floated on the surface of the casks to conceal this.[11] Early in 1855 he noted the arrival by canoe from Whydah of Louis Lemagnière and a Señor Jambo, who were received by Oba Dosunmu 'in state' and announced plans to set up a trading factory in Lagos. Campbell disclosed first to the Oba, who took little notice, and then to Commander Miller of H.M.S. *Crane* his knowledge of the past slaving activities of the two men and of their local associates, and on Miller's insistence they were ordered by Dosunmu to leave the town, Lemagnière doing so only after an attempt to claim that he had been appointed to the office of French consul. Clarendon defended this action in his reply to subsequent diplomatic protests in London.[12] Similarly, in 1856 Campbell reported the arrival in Lagos of Signor Giuseppe Carrena, a Genoese 'of advanced years' who had formerly traded at Bahia and now wished to establish himself on a remote part of the coast east of Palma, and whom the consul strongly suspected of proposing to engage in shipping slaves sent by Kosoko from Epe.[13]

From 1857 onwards the consul was reporting frequently and unfavourably on the activities of the Marseilles trading firm of Régis Aîné, who were now established at Lagos as well as elsewhere on the coast and whose mail service to the Gabon was subsidised by the imperial French Government. Régis were heavily engaged at this time in shipping 'free emigrants' (contract labour – or disguised slaves) for the Antilles from the coast of Dahomey,[14] and if this continued, Campbell wrote in August 1857, it was likely that the whole Yoruba country would be plunged into war in order to provide sufficient captives to meet the demands of the reviving trade at Whydah. A couple of months later, however, the consul reported that the Régis contract was proving a failure since the slaves bought for $50 a head could not compete in price (presumably in Cuba) with those supplied by the Spanish slavers; the current price on the Coast for a male slave in good condition was almost twice that in the Régis contract.[15] The following year a particularly horrifying case came to light when a party of 'free emigrants', purchased for $10 a head and destined for the island of Bourbon, mutinied on board the *Regina Coeli* at Monrovia, after the alleged murder of three of their number by the ship's cook, and massacred the French crew and twenty seven of their own party. Campbell drew attention to the connivance of the Liberian Government at the presence of the ship, the payment of $6 a head for passports inducing them 'to wink at such undertakings'.[16]

Even more serious than these French evasions was the abuse of the United States flag. In August 1857 Campbell told the Foreign Office that the extent to which the American flag was being used to cover vessels engaged in the Cuban trade, combined with the absence for the last two years of United States cruisers from the coast, led him to suspect that the American Government had political designs on Cuba. The dispatch found its way to Palmerston, then prime minister, who minuted that it should be communicated in confidence to the Spanish Government.[17] Campbell next drew attention to the 'considerable reluctance' shown by officers of the Royal Navy in exercising 'the right of visiting suspicious vessels which hoist the United States flag' and suggested that they should use the authority of the Aberdeen Act to detain vessels with this flag but without proper certificates of registry. His dispatch came to be answered, however, after the fall of Palmerston's Government and he was told that the Law Officers advised against his proposal.[18]

The slaving activities carried on from the coast of West Africa by French and American citizens have to be reconciled with the fact that both the French and the United States navies maintained anti-slavery patrols, the French from 1828 and the Americans from 1842, after the conclusion of the Webster–Ashburton treaty. From the 1840s the French squadron was kept at adequate strength and operated effectively, sending numerous suspects to Senegal or Cayenne, and despite the French failure to ratify the treaty of 1841 between the five great powers, giving reciprocal rights of search and including an equipment clause, the British and French co-operated well enough in anti-slaving patrols until the introduction of recruitment for contract labour in the 1850s.[19] With the Americans, there were many difficulties, and the device of joint cruising, to overcome American reluctance to grant rights of search, was never effective because of the preponderant number of British vessels. Down to the very end of the campaign, many Americans professed to regard British humanitarian concern for the slaves as hypocritical cover for an ambition to monopolise the West African trade.[20] Nevertheless, relations between the navies were cordial enough, and when in August 1854 Commodore Mayo, commander-in-chief of the United States naval force on the coast, paid a visit to Lagos, Campbell greeted him on board his flagship, the frigate *Constitution*, in the company of

Oba Dosunmu and six chiefs. The commodore (rather like the German emperor at Björkö in 1905) happened on this occasion to have by him a written 'proposition'. This provided for the protection of American citizens at Lagos and conferred on them equal rights with the subjects of other powers. It was read out to Dosunmu and the chiefs, who then obligingly made their marks on the document.[21] But in the event American traders do not seem to have appeared at Lagos during the consular period and American cruisers only very rarely visited the area.

By the time that Campbell first took up his post, shipments of slaves from Lagos and its immediate vicinity had virtually ceased. As the Amadie case showed, however, slaves were sometimes sent from there by canoe to Porto Novo and Whydah, and in 1854 Campbell detected 'a decided attempt' to revive the trade at Lagos itself. He attributed this last to the influence over Dosunmu of his sinister relative Madame Tinubu, and to the return of a number of the old Portuguese slavers, including Jambo and Machado, about which he addressed a protest to the king.[22] Except for a rumour heard by Campbell in 1858 that Oba Dosunmu's canoes were capturing slaves, mostly Hausa and Nupe, who had escaped from Whydah,[23] this seems to be the last report directly concerning the trade in Lagos. The consul attributed the general decline there to the increasing trade in palm oil and to the dishonesty of the consignees of slaves in Cuba.[24] In this he seems to forget the efforts of the Royal Navy, but in any case reports of slaving vessels taken in the area had become few.[25]

The area within his consular jurisdiction which occasioned Campbell the greatest anxiety with regard to slaving activities was, as has been noted above, the coast of Dahomey, especially at Whydah. This port had been conquered by Dahomey in 1727, giving that kingdom direct access to the sea and to the slave traders engaged in the Atlantic trade. It was here as well as on Porto Novo beach that Domingo Martinez conducted his operations after his return to Africa in or about 1846.[26] Since 1841, when Régis opened their branch there, Whydah had also become a port for the export of palm oil, but as the career of Martinez and also some of the activities of Régis show, the trades were in certain circumstances compatible. In October 1853 Campbell suggested a renewal of the naval blockade to counter the reviving trade in the Bight of Benin, but Commodore Bruce objected that this would be 'most inexpedient . . . at this moment when the natives are showing so strong a desire for legitimate trade' – this last being a matter on which he was not in fact well informed.[27] In February 1856 the consul was attributing the increase in the shipping of slaves from Whydah to the activities of Martinez and complained of the effect of this on the political situation in the interior and the supply of oil to the Lagos market. He was also concerned about the plight of self-emancipated Africans from 'the Brazils', who embarked on Portuguese ships which landed them not at Lagos, as promised, but at Whydah, where they were liable to be soon re-enslaved.[28] In September the next year Campbell suggested the addition to the Squadron of a couple of sailing vessels with auxiliary steam power applied by screws.[29] Palmerston, however, was more prepared to extend the remedy applied at Lagos, and in mid-1857 he asked for consideration of 'the practicability of occupying and retaining Whydah with a view to put a stop to the Slave Trade which is carried on from thence'.[30] A reconnaissance was carried out by Commander Aplin of H.M.S. *Hecla*, and Campbell, whose observations had been invited, gave the scheme an enthusiastic reception. Forgetful of the casualties and dangers encountered at Lagos in 1851, he wrote: 'No native force whatever can withstand a few charges of shrapnell [sic] and rocket shells', and gave his opinion that the occupation of Whydah, 'in fact making a British Settlement of it', would forever crush the slave trade in the Bight of Benin.[31] In the event, probably as a result of Palmerston's loss of office in February 1858, the project was not pursued.

Consul Campbell's repeated warnings that a revival of the slave trade on the coast disturbed political conditions in the interior was rooted partly in the prevalent but mistaken contemporary interpretation of the Yoruba wars of the period as being actuated merely by the hunt for slaves,[32] but partly also in direct observation of the consequences of the revival. For example, the success of an Ibadan raid northwards towards the Niger in late 1855, returning allegedly with upwards of a thousand captives who were sent via Abeokuta for sale at Whydah, and similar marauding by the Ijaye, had a naturally disturbing effect on the Egba, whose chiefs found warfare of this kind more profitable and exciting than legitimate trade, and in 1856 and 1858 the consul reported, with detectible *Schadenfreude*, a series of raids by the Egba of Abeokuta, the white hope of the missionaries.[33]

As regards the situation at Lagos, the consul admitted the existence of domestic slavery there on a large scale and a complete lack of any condemnation of slave trading. There was no such thing in Lagos as a 'slave abolishing population', he wrote in 1855, and everyone there 'would rejoice to see the slave trade reopen tomorrow', as would the chiefs at Abeokuta. Apart from the chiefs, there were very few 'really free men' in Lagos, and in 1858 he estimated that out of a population in Lagos of some 25,000, about 90 per cent were slaves. The increased cultivation of land in these days of peace was leading to more purchases of predial slaves, 'for no native of free condition will hire himself to another to farm work, such being regarded as exclusively the labour of slaves'. Even the liberated Saro of Lagos and Abeokuta were holders of domestic slaves and on occasions suspected of buying and selling their fellow humans. But Campbell also pointed out that domestic slavery was very different from that on the plantations; the slave had a real hope of redemption and while still a slave was treated as a member of his master's family, eating from the same bowl and looking to his master to provide him with a wife. Cotton cultivation in Africa, as opposed to that in America, tended to loosen rather than tighten the shackles of slavery, owing to the rising value of human labour. He also wrote to

Clarendon to deny a suggestion made to Palmerston by a deputation of merchants in 1857 that Africa had a surplus population ready and eager to emigrate to the West Indies.³⁴

The consul was always ready to provide formal documents of emancipation to slaves who approached him for these, while in the case of those from the distant interior who were returning home he furnished passports. Though he realised that his presence would always be resented by the chiefs, he considered that the 'masses' of Lagos (to use his own word), of whom nine out of ten were still called slaves, were thankful for his presence and protection.³⁵

Trade and politics in Lagos

Though the suppression of the external slave trade was the first consideration with the officials in London and the officers of the naval squadron to whom the consul looked for support, Campbell, as the man on shore on whom fell the brunt of hostility directed against the English in Lagos, was at least equally concerned with the problem of internal security. His negotiations with Kosoko, leading to the Treaty of Epe, had by no means resolved the problem, and had even in one aspect exacerbated it since the consul was now suspected of sympathy with the exiled Oba, so much more vigorous and fit to rule than the apparently pliant and well-disposed Dosunmu.

In early 1855 and again a year later Campbell was apprised of what he took to be serious plots against himself and the European merchant community and also those of the 'repatriates' who supported him – against, in fact, the consular regime itself. He identified the moving spirit in these as being Madame Tinubu. The first of the conspiracies came to its head in January or early February 1855 when, according to Campbell's informants, Tinubu and her associates plotted with a number of Dosunmu's slaves to assassinate the consul as he returned in darkness from a visit to his Hamburger friend Grote. Warned of this, Campbell left his 'country built house' and once again moved with his archives into Sandeman's house on the waterside. Meanwhile, the expulsion of Lemagnière and other slavers, on the orders of Commander Miller, had heightened feelings against the British and their allies, and one of the latter, a Brazilian repatriate named Antonio Martins ('in credit with the merchants and doing an extensive business, being known to be friendly disposed towards the English'), was shot at in his premises on the waterside and narrowly escaped being hit. Campbell thereupon ordered some of the Sierra Leoneans to make inquiry into the affair. He was given a confused report – that a party among the conspirators wanted to replace Dosunmu on the throne by a son of Oba Adele, that others aimed to restore Kosoko – but armed with this he demanded the execution of Martins's assailant and the banishment of Madame Tinubu. Neither of these demands was met, but the consul was told that an 'instigator' of the crime had been executed, and had to rest content with this.³⁶

The second plot was on similar lines. It was timed for March 1856, during Campbell's absence on a visit to the Benin River. William McCoskry, who was acting in Campbell's place, learnt of the matter from Savage, a Sierra Leonean trader, and held an investigation in the presence of the king, who had apparently heard from his own sources that something was afoot and sent off his valuables in a canoe to the consulate. In the event, the arrival of three cruisers off the bar dampened down the local excitement. But two months later Madame Tinubu's followers became involved in a battle with those of the Oba, and Dosunmu, roused from 'his usual apathy', ordered the arrest of Badu, Tinubu's Muslim husband. Tinubu thereupon burst into the royal council and demanded Badu's release. The harassed king called for the consul's support and five boats were sent across the bar from H.M.S. *Childers*. At this point Tinubu disappeared, leaving her followers to attempt to bribe the Oba to call off his measures, but Campbell insisted on the boats remaining in the river until she emerged from her hiding place in the house of Turner, another Sierra Leonean trader, and crossed to the mainland with her people. Tinubu waited five days on her farm at Ebute Metta in the hope that the situation would change, and then returned to Abeokuta, her original home, where she was able again to play a considerable role and was later awarded the title of Iyalode ('Lady') of the Egba. Many of the traders in Lagos who had suffered from her attempt to monopolise commerce between the Egba and the Europeans were delighted to see her go, but it is unlikely that those to whom she owed some £5000 in palm oil were as willing as Campbell supposed to write off this debt.[37]

These occurrences confirmed the precariousness of the British at Lagos and their unpopularity with traditional society there. Campbell's resources were few; his consulate was run on a shoestring, and even his modest proposal to expend £1200 over five years in presents to the chiefs with whom anti-slaving treaties were made did not meet with the approval of the Foreign Office.[38] After his years on the coast the consul was thoroughly at home there, yet he seems to have been cut off from all but formal contacts with the indigenous leadership at Lagos. His African associates were chosen from the 'emigrant' community, as was natural for a man with his family associations, and he showed little sympathy with or understanding of local customs and ways of life. He was particularly insensitive, for example, to the protests made by Dosunmu against the roofing of Scala's new storehouse with 'crooked old-fashioned tiles' of a locally made type reserved for use on the royal apartments, rebuking the king for his 'silly objection' which must be due either to superstition or 'frivolous pride', while Dosunmu for his part was provoked into accusing the consul of undue partiality to Scala.[39] More important than such squabbles was the revival of the threat from Epe, where Kosoko still conducted affairs with his 'for an African unusual but ill-directed energy'. In October 1856 Campbell told the foreign secretary that the ex-Oba, 'who has hitherto observed his Treaty engagement with scrupulous fidelity', was now planning to move to Ado, attacking Lagos *en route*, and the following month there was a new rumour: that Kosoko wanted to occupy Otta, thereby cutting land communications between Lagos and Abeokuta.⁴⁰

Though nothing came of these reports, Campbell's changed attitude to Kosoko caused a rift between him and an influential section of the merchants, three of whom (McCoskry and Sandeman, previously his close associates, and Hansen) accused him in a letter to Commodore Adams of acting provocatively towards Kosoko. The burden of the charges was that he had caused one of Kosoko's canoes passing near Lagos on its way from Epe to Porto Novo to be 'ransacked under the pretence that it might contain munitions of war'. He countered by accusing McCoskry and a Hamburg merchant, Peter Diederichsen, of having paid a clandestine visit to Kosoko at Epe in violation of Dosunmu's interdiction of trade between Epe and Lagos. McCoskry indignantly wrote to the commodore that he was 'no subject of the King of Lagos' and did not need permission from him or the consul for his movements, and he denied making any secret about his trip. Campbell, who had happened to see the canoe setting off from the gallery of his house ('the sun had just set and the clock had struck six'), produced evidence that the merchants had passed through the creek during the night, and he received support in his quarrel with McCoskry from the Oba, from a number of 'emigrant' merchants, and from the Royal Navy. Adams replied to McCoskry that Dosunmu considered his visit to Epe 'at the present time, both hostile and offensive', and told him that 'The Chief who permits you to reside in his Territory has a perfect right to order you to quit it when your conduct becomes obnoxious to him'. Such measures were not in the event invoked and the two merchants at length agreed to pay the fines imposed on them by the Oba.⁴¹

Though he enjoyed the confidence and on most occasions (as in the affair just described) the support of the Navy, whose officers often spent several days ashore putting up at the consulate, for the greater part of his time as consul Campbell was conscious of his lack of continuous visible means to enforce his authority. In June 1856, alluding to an earlier recommendation by Admiral Bruce that two or three iron steam vessels should be specially built for service in the Bight of Benin and on its lagoons and rivers, he pointed out the advantages which stationing an armed steamer inside the bar would bring. Anticipating naval objections, he added that the prophylactic use of quinine against fever, as demonstrated in the Niger Expedition of 1854 and in the recent visit of H.M.S. *Bloodhound* to the Benin River, mitigated the hazards of such service for the white sailors. A minute by Palmerston the following November approved the suggestion, which was taken up with the Admiralty. In January 1857 Campbell was told that H.M.S. *Drake* had been allotted to Lagos. In the meantime the *Minx* had spent some time in the river during the last months of 1856 and her presence, Campbell considered, had curbed Kosoko's hostile ambitions.⁴² In the event the *Drake* was sent to China and its place was taken by H.M.S. *Brune*, a steam gunboat of just over five feet draught, which arrived in Lagos (after an attempt by the Navy to divert her for service in Sierra Leone) in December 1857. Oba Dosunmu was shown over the vessel at her anchorage off the consulate, and a gun and a rocket were fired for his edification.[43] Thus from this time British interests at Lagos were assured of the support of a small but permanent force.

In the intervals between these alarms and quarrels, Campbell had the satisfaction of being able to tell the Foreign Office that tranquillity prevailed at Lagos and trade was growing. His first trading report was not sent until January 1857. In it he wrote that Dutch and Spanish vessels and one Sardinian had traded at Lagos, as well as numerous British. The major export from Lagos and from the Bight of Benin as a whole was palm oil, other items being ivory, cotton, and cotton fabrics, the last being destined for Brazil. The proceeds of the palm-oil cargoes were 'doubtless converted into Manchester and Glasgow fabrics, without which no Foreigners can carry on the trade in Palm Oil'. Figures for 1857 showed an increase in oil exports over the previous years, though they were to be followed by a decline in the next few years; there was also a striking increase in the export of cotton.

Exports from Lagos, 1856

Palm oil	3,884 tons at £45 a ton	£174,780
Ivory	16,057 lb. at 4s. a lb.	3,211
Cotton	33,491 lb. at 6d. a lb.	837
		£178,828

Exports from Lagos, 1857

Palm oil	4,942 tons	£222,390
Ivory	24,118 lb.	4,220
Cotton	114,848 lb.	3,590
		£230,100
Manufactured cotton fabrics		25,000
		£255,100

Exports of palm oil from other parts of the Bight, all within the consular area, exceeded exports from Lagos by three to four times; Whydah, Badagry and Porto Novo exported between them more than Lagos. But these consular figures cannot be regarded as accurate since there was considerable smuggling from Lagos and elsewhere, especially of ivory; Newbury considers them as 'at best intelligent estimates'.[44]

The dependence of Lagos's new and frail legitimate trade on palm oil was very great, and Campbell cast around for other items of export which might reduce this. In 1856 he hopefully forwarded to London a fragment of local earthenware which had been picked up by Lemagnière and in which some shining particles could be seen. Lemagnière (now established at Palma) and Kosoko, his patron, had suggested that this indicated the presence of gold near Epe, but a few weeks later a reply came back that the glittering substance was only mica.⁴⁵ The next year Campbell succeeded in interesting the authorities in London in a sample of grease produced from shea butter; though the War Office chemist eventually reported that it was unsuitable for greasing cartridges, small quantities of this article seem to have been successfully exported.⁴⁶ But the greatest interest in Britain was shown in the possibility of increasing the West African production and export of cotton and in improving its quality, and throughout 1857 Campbell received a stream of directives on this topic.⁴⁷ By this time the deficiency in the supply of cotton – foreshadowing the cotton famine of 1861–2 caused by the American Civil War – was already alarming, and the consul was told to do all he could to encourage a steady and increasing supply from his part of Africa. His work met with some success, so that by 1860 Lagos could claim to be the biggest cotton port on the West Coast, although by then exports were decreasing from the record figure of 1858. Gins, presses, and various types of seed were sent out for distribution to the chiefs, those at Abeokuta and Ikorodu being the main recipients. Crowther, whom the C.M.S. had now sent to Lagos, took an interest in the matter and advised Campbell that it would be better to direct this aid towards Christian converts rather than the chiefs as in this way model plantations might be formed. He told Venn, the C.M.S. Secretary in London: 'It is very much to be regretted that all the merchants are again [against] the cotton trade, they will not trouble themselves with it'.⁴⁸

With the local European and the more prominent Saro merchants, Campbell's relations during the first years of his consulate were good, and he had their support in his clashes with the missionaries. In March 1854 he negotiated a new agreement between them and Oba Dosunmu, substituting the previous export duties of 2 per cent *ad valorem* paid to the Oba, which had proved impossible to determine satisfactorily, by a fixed duty of two heads of cowries (about 8s.) on every puncheon of 120 gallons of palm oil and three strings (about 2d.) on every pound of ivory exported from Lagos. These payments could be claimed either in cash or cowries. In return the Oba relinquished import duties, previously fixed at 3 per cent, and also the right to trade on his own account. The signatories included Dosunmu, Campbell, and the traders Sandeman, McCoskry, Scala, Hansen and Austin. In reporting this the following June, Campbell estimated the royal revenue at 50,000 heads of cowries (£10,000) annually, of which export dues made up about one-third and market dues and payments on oil brought into Lagos the rest.⁴⁹

Within two years this engagement ceased to be satisfactory to the Oba, partly because of the cowry inflation which followed the breaking of the O'Swald monopoly of the supply from Zanzibar by Régis in 1855–6, partly because of the dishonesty of the Oba's officials, and partly because of evasion of payment of duties by some Sierra Leonean merchants. Eventually, therefore, Dosunmu accepted an offer by Scala to farm the dues. This in turn led to protests by the other merchants, who refused to co-operate in the new arrangements. Characteristically, McCoskry even attempted to ship oil without payment. Already the merchants had fallen out with Campbell over the restrictions placed in the way of their commercial intercourse with Epe, and now they launched the accusation that Dosunmu had been influenced in Scala's favour by Campbell. The consul discussed the matter in an exasperated dispatch of twenty-one pages, identifying the leader of the agitation against Scala as Herman Grote, O'Swald's agent, and concluding that 'Were King Docemo a man of any energy of character, instead of the vacillating, inert creature he is', the trouble would not have arisen.[50] On their side the merchants set about a virtual persecution of Campbell, sending petitions for his removal to Clarendon and to the naval authorities which accused him of exercising 'absolute and irresponsible power in the island of Lagos', reducing the king to a 'mere puppet', and both threatening to reinstate Kosoko and goading him into retaliation.[51] As Campbell pointed out, two of the signatories, McCoskry and Hansen, had personal grievances against him, and he had received the support of the naval officers who investigated the charges. In the event McCoskry and the others were forced to pay their dues, but ill-feeling long persisted.

At home Clarendon minuted laconically 'The English traders at Lagos appear to be a set of turbulent ruffians'. From Downing Street the merchants – not all, nor even perhaps the majority of whom were British – must indeed have seemed hardly different from their predecessors, the slavers, a rough and merry crew, described by Burton as sleeping and smoking their days away, 'with an occasional champagne tiffin on the beach'. But it was necessary to be tough to survive, and it is remarkable how low the mortality apparently was among the merchants compared with that of the missionaries or even the consuls.

The merchants' disenchantment with Campbell stemmed in particular from their resentment of the new export duties and the arrangements for farming them, but more generally from their realisation that the consul was determined not to allow himself, as Frazer had done, to accept direction from any of the factions striving for influence in Lagos, including themselves. There is space to mention here only a few of Campbell's most prominent antagonists. Walter Hansen, the 'man of colour' from Accra, whose deportation by Akitoye Campbell had prevented after the pro-Kosoko rising of 1853, took great offence at being (he thought) accused by the consul of having taken part in slaving, and his complaints to the Foreign Office involved Campbell in lengthy explanations to Lord Clarendon. Then there was Sandeman, known to the Yoruba as *oyinbo onirun*, 'the hairy white man', in whose house Campbell had stayed on more than one occasion but who had now become the consul's inveterate enemy. But Campbell's fiercest opponent seems to have been William McCoskry, his nominee for the vice-consulate of Badagry and destined to act as the last consul and then first governor of Lagos. McCoskry brought a complicated claim against Campbell through the Foreign Office for the recovery of some dollars due to him from the estate of Thomas Hutton, his previous employer, in which he was upheld by the Law Officers. In turn Campbell raked up old scandals in McCoskry's earlier career at Acra and in Lagos.[52]

After the trouble over the farming of the customs, Scala was generally associated with the consul as the object of the merchants' wrath. He, too, now held consular rank, having been appointed as consul (or, as he claimed, consul-general) for Sardinia, a capacity in which he was formally presented by Campbell to Oba Dosunmu in 1856. In January 1857 the committee of Sierra Leone merchants attempted to summon Scala for non-payment of debts, a proceeding for which they were severely rebuked by Campbell, who pointed out that it was beyond their competence. The matter was energetically pursued in London by a Mr Gregory, who complained to Lord Shelburne at the Foreign Office of Campbell's 'aristocratic arrogance and misgovernment'.[53] Early in 1856 (after an exploratory visit in 1855) Scala opened a factory at Abeokuta where he installed machines for cleaning cotton and extracting palm oil, and which, despite vicissitudes and adventures, including incendiary attacks on his property by his enemies in the town, and some initial missionary resentment of the presence of a Roman Catholic, he maintained until he finally left the coast in July 1859.[54]

The 'sort of Court or Tribunal' which sought to try Scala had been set up by the leading 'emigrants' at Campbell's suggestion in mid-1855 in order to hear and determine disputes arising among the 'emigrants' (whether from Sierra Leone, Brazil or Cuba) themselves, or among the 'emigrants' and the Lagosians. A disputed decision in the first type of case was to be referred to the consul and in the second to the Oba. The regulations drawn up by the 'emigrants' committee for the conduct of cases were approved by the Foreign Office with the exception of Article XI, providing for the deportation to Sierra Leone or Fernando Po of any 'emigrant' convicted of disturbing the peace, which Campbell was required to withdraw.[55] In November 1856 the consul reported that the court was working well and sitting regularly every Saturday; many of the European merchants availed themselves of it, with the significant exception of McCoskry, who preferred (the consul wrote) his own 'arbitrary and cruel methods'.[56]

The establishment of the court illustrates the consul's confidence in and respect for the 'emigrants', despite their propensities to slaveholding, and it enabled the latter to develop cohesion as a community. In 1857 Campbell persuaded the Oba to drop the tax which he levied on self-emancipated Africans landing at Lagos from Brazil and Cuba, and in April 1858, before going on leave, he recommended his Sierra Leonean son-in-law Walter Lewis as acting consul, though eventually he appointed the local naval officer to the post.[57] In turn, the 'emigrants' tended to support Campbell when McCoskry, Sandeman and the European party turned against him.[58] On other occasions Campbell drew the attention of the Foreign Office to the tension in Lagos between the indigenes and the Saro, arising mainly, he thought, from jealousy of the former towards the latter who, having often been sold from Lagos not many years before, had now returned with superior skills and had acquired a dominant position in trade. The younger generation of Sierra Leoneans were less tactful in this situation than their parents, and on several occasions Campbell grumbled about their 'arrogance', 'worthlessness', inability to distinguish between *meum* and *tuum*, and the need for them to remember that 'here we are all Foreigners'. He also persuaded Dosunmu to forbid the practice by young 'Creoles' of carrying knives in the street.[59]

With the other important group of 'foreigners', the Christian missionaries, the consul's relations varied, it seems, in inverse ratio to those with the merchants. In the first years of the consulate, Campbell could generally count on the support of Sandeman, McCoskry and their associates in resisting the attacks made on him by Gollmer, Townsend and other members of the C.M.S., and he supported McCoskry's claim to a waterside site near to the Iga which White had obtained in an exchange with Oba Dosunmu.[60]

Charles Gollmer, Campbell's principal adversary among the missionaries, had been born in Württemberg and was presumably brought up as a Lutheran. After four years at the Basle Seminary he spent a further year at the Church Missionary College and in 1841 received Anglican orders, first as deacon and then as priest, from the Bishop of London. He came out to the Sierra Leone mission in the same year, at the age of twenty-nine. In 1845 and 1852 respectively he opened the first Anglican missions in Badagry and Lagos. As we have seen, Campbell was accommodated on his arrival at Lagos in the C.M.S. house with Gollmer and a week afterwards he told the Foreign Secretary that the local prejudice against the missionaries was due entirely to the former slave traders; he was probably yet to learn of the fierce rivalry between the missionaries and the merchants over the much sought-after plots of land along the waterfront. Gollmer, he continued, had been 'a particular object of jealousy and animadversion', but to anyone who knew him and his efforts 'to enlighten the natives' he appeared 'serene and cheerful ... [a] devout, zealous and fearless disciple of his Divine Master'[61] – very different language from that which the consul was to use about him less than a year later when complaining of the missionary's opposition to his pacification of Kosoko.

Another member of the mission with whom Campbell's relations quickly deteriorated was the former naval surgeon Edward Irving, who came out to the Yoruba Mission in 1854 as lay agent. There was something of an alliance between the evangelical C.M.S. and the God-fearing officers of Queen Victoria's Navy,[62] which on at least one occasion caused Campbell to wonder whether his point of view was being properly represented to the Admiralty. In writing to the foreign secretary in 1854 in connection with his restoration of the chiefs at Badagry, he expressed his resentment at the obstruction he had met with from Gollmer, Townsend and Irving, and he hoped that Irving's family and naval background would not lead him to interfere between the consul and the commander-in-chief.[63] In the event Irving's relations with the consul were less stormy than with his colleague Gollmer, but in March 1855 he did go so far as to tell the C.M.S. in London that Campbell should be recalled. Later that year a petition signed by all the European merchants in Lagos, the Wesleyan missionary E. A. Gardiner, and twenty-four African, Saro and Brazilian merchants, asked that Townsend and Irving should not be allowed to return to Lagos after leave, a move of which, Philips considers, Campbell must have been apprised.[64]

After the signature of the Treaty of Epe in September 1854, Campbell had the satisfaction of receiving from the foreign secretary assurance of support in his quarrel with Gollmer, who, Lord Clarendon agreed, had 'interfered in affairs at Lagos with which in his character as a missionary, he had nothing to do'.[65] But very soon the dispute about relations with Kosoko was succeeded by an almost equally bitter dispute over the consular claim to a share of the coveted land along the so-called Lagos River. On the arrival of the famous 'iron house' Campbell applied to Oba Dosunmu for the grant of 'a moderate sized and suitable piece of the vacant land' adjoining the C.M.S. enclosure on the waterfront at Oke Faji. This was granted and measurements were taken. At this point, Crowther, who took over in Lagos in 1855 from the Hildebrandine Gollmer, objected that the land given to the consul was Church property. At his invitation Irving came down from Abeokuta to support him in the matter, and wrote a letter accusing Campbell of 'persecuting' the missionaries. Campbell temporised by putting up a wooden shed, to protect his as yet unassembled consular building, and a flagstaff, and then sent a melancholy report to the Foreign Office about the 'most bitter, systematic, and unrelenting persecution' which he was meeting in his effort to obtain 'a healthy and airy site'. In reply the foreign secretary instructed him to obtain a formal deed of cession from the Oba; he also approved his proposal to invite officers of the Squadron to determine whether C.M.S. rights had been infringed.[66] A remeasurement was carried out by two naval officers in April 1855, and Commander Skene told Campbell that the consular site could not possibly be on C.M.S. land; he advised him to proceed with the erection of the much-needed building. The following day Skene wrote to chide Irving – whose death was to take place later this same month – for the rancorous tone of his letter to the consul.[67] But this by no means ended the dispute, which continued as new quarrels arose between the consul and the missionaries over Campbell's actions at Badagry and his attitude towards the Egba, topics which will be dealt with in a later part of this chapter. Accusations flew to and fro throughout the latter part of 1855 and in 1856, in the course of which Campbell told the Foreign Office that Gollmer's communications had 'more of gunpowder than Gospel in them', while the missionaries, reverting to their grievance over the Treaty of Epe, alleged that the consul had been unduly influenced in Kosoko's favour by the merchants to whom Kosoko and his followers were heavily indebted.[68] The consular site was measured yet again by the Navy in December 1855; Campbell described a report by the C.M.S. legal advisers in London about the matter as 'jesuitical twaddle'; finally a board of naval officers tried to mend matters by deciding that both parties had made errors in identifying the exact sites granted by the Oba but upheld the view that the consulate (now apparently erected) was not on mission property.[69]

It took some two years for this dispute between Church and State to die away, partly overtaken by other matters of discord, partly because the consular building was now an accomplished fact. Much ill-feeling had been generated, though it is pleasant to learn that as Irving lay dying he accepted, at Crowther's prompting, the gift of a bottle of port sent by Campbell. 'That was very kind,' he acknowledged, 'we cannot enjoy a hearty quarrel in this country, being so dependent upon one another'.[70] In July 1857 Crowther was able to tell Henry Venn, the London secretary of the C.M.S., that the consul had 'been regular at Church since the last quarter' and was now displaying friendship towards the missionaries.[71]

The missionaries of the C.M.S. belonged to the extreme evangelical wing of the Church of England, and with at least some of them, especially the German ex-Lutherans, their Anglicanism does not seem to have been deeply rooted. They were uninfluenced by the Oxford Movement with its rediscovery of the historical continuity of the communion of Canterbury, and they recoiled in horror from Roman Catholicism. Townsend, for example, identified affinities between Catholicism and the indigenous religion of the Yoruba with its prayers to the *orisha*, and he asked 'Who can be surprised that white slave-traders at Lagos should consult Ifa before sending their ships to sea? The God of Popery and the God of Heathenism is the same God.'[72] Yet most of the repatriates who came from Brazil and Cuba must already have come into contact with the Church of Rome and many were practising Catholics. One of their number, called Pa Antonio, who had received some education in a seminary at Bahia, opened a chapel in Lagos during the consular period in which non-sacramental services were held. By 1859 there were some 130 'Brazilian' families in Lagos, and when Father Borghero visited the town in 1863 – the first recorded visit by a Roman Catholic priest – he celebrated mass before a congregation of 400.[73]

The only other mission which was established in Lagos during this time was that of the Wesleyan Methodists, though a start was also made by American Baptists. The first Methodist agent to settle in Lagos, following in Freeman's steps, was John Martin, who came from Badagry in 1853. After his early death he was succeeded first by E. A. Gardiner and then in 1857 by Timothy Laing, followed by Alexander Gurney in 1859 and George Sharp in 1860. Mrs Foote, writing about Lagos in 1861, had heard that the Wesleyan Church was 'better attended by the natives than the Episcopal'. Unlike his brethren of the C.M.S. Gardiner was in sympathy with Campbell's policies. In a letter to the consul, he described the C.M.S. accusations against Campbell as 'incomparably strange', since the missionaries in Lagos had benefited greatly from Campbell's services. To his Methodist colleagues at home, he wrote in much stronger language which reflects the animosity bred among these Europeans in the narrow and fevered circumstances of Lagos. Gollmer and Townsend were returning to England on leave, Gardiner warned one of his General Secretaries, and might call at the Methodist headquarters, 'so I beg to say that they are utterly unworthy the confidence either of yourself or your colleagues. The opposition these men have raised against H.M. Consul to thwart his most praiseworthy exertions to bring about a pacific state of things here is incredible. . . . I could name things of which they are guilty, and which I myself have witnessed, at which human nature recoils. . . .' But as to the consul, 'A kinder friend and patron of Christian Missions I never met with. Of him it may be truly said, that he is ready to every good word and work, and to him, under God, Lagos owes its salvation.'[74]

Opening up the consular area

Campbell's interests and activities were not confined to Lagos. The consular area for which he was responsible, described as the Bight of Benin, covered some 300 miles of inhospitable coastline, from the lagoons and remote surf-beaten beaches in the west and centre to the intricate mangrove swamps at the western edge of the vast delta of the Niger. Inland (again moving from west to east) lay first the kingdom of Dahomey, powerful and unfriendly, then the congeries of Yoruba kingdoms, including the Egba federation based on Abeokuta, with the lands of the Nupe and other peoples of the Niger valley and then the Hausa further north, and on the east Benin, capital of a much reduced and now hardly accessible kingdom. The consul's attitude towards these different territories varied, the paternalistic methods practised in the quasi-protectorate of Lagos being reproduced on a diminished scale in Badagry and Abeokuta but entirely discarded in relations with, for example, Dahomey. During the consular period, the European traders were for the most part content to remain in Lagos obtaining their produce and selling their goods through a host of middlemen, and only a few ventured as far as Abeokuta. But the missionaries – Europeans and North Americans – were already advancing deep into the interior, occupying stations at Ibadan, Ijaye, Oyo, Ogbomosho and still further afield,[75] and thus to some extent involving the consular jurisdiction in the affairs of the hinterland.

The first important external problem which Campbell tackled was that of Badagry. Here the Mewu still reigned over the town while the local chiefs, who had opposed Akitoye, remained in exile. So long as this situation continued, Badagry was too unstable for trade to revive there. Moreover, the Mewu was hindering the supply of arms and ammunition from Porto Novo to the Awori town of Ado, under siege by the Egba from 1842 to 1853. This led to retaliation by the King of Porto Novo, the Mewu's suzerain; trade with Lagos was halted and canoe traffic on the western lagoon subjected to interference. The Mewu had agreed to a treaty with the British in March 1852, on lines similar to that with Akitoye, and he enjoyed the support of the missionaries, but during the first half of 1854 Campbell seems to have decided that a change of regime was needed. He paid two visits to Badagry. On the first occasion, in April, he accused the Mewu of violating the treaty by procuring slaves for Domingo Martinez. He then went on to Porto Novo and on his return tried unsuccessfully to persuade the Mewu to retire in favour of the exiled chiefs. He came again to Badagry at the end of June, but found the Mewu still determined to stay: indeed, he made Campbell's visit unendurable by arranging for a concert of drums and horns to be performed through the night outside his bedroom window. In July, however, the two principal exiled chiefs, the Wawu and the Possu, encouraged by Campbell's support for their cause and with reinforcements sent by the King of Porto Novo and the ruler of nearby Ado, drove the Mewu out of the town. Campbell thereupon arranged through Thomas Tickel, an English merchant there, for a safe-conduct for the Mewu to Lagos, where a year later he died.[76]

The consul's intervention at Badagry has been described by E. H. Phillips as 'a classic example of a forward policy undertaken by a local official in direct contravention of the known desires of the [British] Government'.[77] It was vigorously criticised by the missionaries, especially by Gollmer, Townsend and Irving, and put a further strain on relations between them and Campbell. It also met with disapproval at the Foreign Office where Thomas Ward, an official, minuted that Campbell had shown a disposition 'to get into quarrels'. Lord Clarendon informed the consul of his displeasure at the action, which had moreover been taken without consultation with the Navy. Only reluctantly was this disapproval withdrawn at the beginning of 1855, after Campbell had reiterated his charge that by his dealings with Martinez the Mewu had broken his treaty with Britain. The consul was also able to show that with the help of Saro intermediaries he had persuaded the Egba authorities not to attack the restored chiefs at Badagry so long as they were not hostile to Abeokuta. He disassociated himself from the missionary view that the Egba alone were 'worthy of sympathy and countenance of the English, and ought to dominate and rule over all other tribes', and he drove home his argument that if the British Government were to carry out 'its benevolent object' of putting down the slave trade, the missionaries must abstain from involvement in political disputes.[78]

The return of the chiefs did little to arrest the decline of Badagry. In 1855, according to Crowther, it was a base for Dahomean operations against the Egba, and in any case it had now passed into the Aja sphere of influence. Some years later Campbell visited the town and found that the population had shrunk to a mere 600, though there were no fewer than eight chiefs, all claiming equal authority. There was no cultivation, and commercially it amounted to little more than a shipping beach for Porto Novo, whose king exacted a payment of one head of cowries for every puncheon of oil loaded there. Porto Novo, on the other hand, was flourishing, with a population of around 30,000 and the 'neatest' farming that Campbell had seen in Africa.[79]

Campbell's dealings with the important and powerful kingdom of Dahomey, north-west of Badagry, were dominated first by his duty as the agent of a government determined to stamp out the slave trade, which still flourished at the Dahomean port of Whydah, and secondly by the role, imposed on him by missionary enthusiasm, of protector of the Egba and Egbado peoples, who had been the victims of Dahomean aggression from the 1840s onwards. In January 1852 Commander Forbes had obtained an anti-slaving treaty with King Ghezo of Dahomey,[80] but it became almost immediately clear that the Dahomeans had little or no intention of keeping its terms (even if they understood them). When Campbell visited Porto Novo in April 1854 he addressed a letter from there to Ghezo, rebuking him for allowing the shipment of slaves from Whydah.[81] These anxieties continued throughout the consular period, and were increased by repeated reports of large-scale human sacrifices of slave victims carried out in Abomey, the Dahomean capital.

Equally disturbing was the Dahomean threat to Abeokuta. From 1855 on, there were rumours towards the end of each dry season that the Dahomean army was intending to march against the town and repeat its fierce assault of 1851 on the walls. Combined with these were circumstantial reports that Dahomean diplomacy was fostering coalitions against the Egba among neighbouring states.[82] Although in the event the second Dahomean attack on Abeokuta was delayed until 1864, the threat to the state was a constant anxiety to the consul. In February 1855, alerted by a letter from Irving and by other reports that Ghezo was preparing an attack on Abeokuta with the aid of a large Ashanti force and a supply of firearms and ammunition provided by the slave traders of Bahia, Campbell sent up shot and gunpowder for the field pieces which the British Government had earlier presented to the Egba. He followed this with percussion caps and ball cartridges provided by the Royal Navy, while the Sierra Leoneans in Lagos sent 1000 pounds of powder and Dosunmu promised iron bars (for the manufacture of ammunition) and more powder. Campbell also dispatched letters to King Ghezo, to Kosoko, to the King of Porto Novo, and to the chiefs of Badagry, warning them of the consequences of an attack on Abeokuta. At the same time he told the Foreign Office that Dahomean enmity to the Egba was not entirely unprovoked, bearing in mind the long siege of Ado undertaken by the Egba and that 'over twenty towns and villages' in Dahomey had been attacked by them.[83] In June 1856 there were again reports of an impending Dahomean march to the east and also of presents sent by the Dahomeans to win over Ibadan, Ijaye, Ijebu Ode, and Ilorin to their support. The Ilorin, however, realising that Abeokuta was 'the town leading directly to communication with the European traders', sent a friendly warning to the Egba. The next year the Egba authorities appealed to the British for four artillery officers to be sent to instruct them in gunnery, and to bring with them canister shot for their two six-pounders: a request which was not met since Campbell considered that the Egba should have sufficient weapons and ammunition for their defence from what had been supplied two years before. In March and April 1858 the usual reports of Dahomean troop movements against Abeokuta were coupled with a somewhat unlikely rumour that King Ghezo's ambassadors were offering a renewal of the tribute paid in former years to Oyo in return for the support of the Alafin of Oyo against the Egba.[84]

Campbell never visited Abomey. When in September 1855 he heard through J. Dawson, the agent of the Wesleyans in Whydah, that King Ghezo wished to improve relations and was willing to see him, he replied that this would be useless unless the king and his chiefs were prepared to conclude a new agreement.[85] Three years later some disquiet was caused in Lagos when it was reported that Commodore Protet, the commander-in-chief of the French naval forces on the coast, had been attempting to obtain the cession of Whydah to France, but Campbell learnt later that his object had been to arrange for the recruitment and shipping of identured labourers and that he had failed in this (despite his gift to the King of Dahomey of six brass cannon) because of the higher prices paid by the Spanish dealers for true slaves.[86]

The *Columbine* affair illustrates another side of Campbell's relations with Dahomey and of his consular duties. This was one of numerous cases in which a shipwreck off the West African coast was followed by pillaging of the wreck by the local inhabitants. The *Columbine*, a British trader, had gone on shore at Prya Nova, some eight miles west of Whydah, in February 1857. After a fracas with the people of the place, in which, so the Yevogan, or Dahomean viceroy, of Whydah claimed, the ship's carpenter had killed one of the Yevogan's men, the master, supercargo and crew were imprisoned and the ship's cargo and papers plundered. When Campbell went to Whydah to investigate, he found that the prisoners had been released, but he was unable to obtain the return of the salvaged property or the papers, and the Yevogan was treating the matter 'with great nonchalance'. He suggested to the Foreign Office that a fine of 1000 heads of cowries (or about $500) should be demanded from the Dahomean authorities, to be followed by a blockade of the coast if this was not paid. The chiefs of the interior, he added, were shocked at this treatment meted out to white men. Lloyd, an official in Downing Street, minuted on the file that the Dahomeans would not have felt so secure from reprisals had the small steamer requested for use on the lagoon been provided already by the Admiralty. Meanwhile Campbell had urged Commodore Adams to take firm action against Prya Nova, but the commodore, possibly misunderstanding Campbell's intentions, declined, being subsequently supported in this by both the Admiralty and the Foreign Office. Some five months later the property was still unrecovered and rough weather was hampering communications. After this no more is heard of the matter.[87]

Campbell's attitude towards the Egba at Abeokuta was ambivalent. As has been seen above, he gave them such support, military and diplomatic, as was within his power to meet the recurring threat of aggression from Dahomey. At the same time he did not view the Abeokutans through the same rose-coloured spectacles as did Townsend, the resident agent of the C.M.S., and many of the other missionaries, with their pious and enthusiastic supporters abroad. As a federated rather than a unitary state, Abeokuta lacked a stable political authority which could control all the Egba and the other associated people (such as the Owu). The Alake, whose office had been revived only in 1854 at the instance of Townsend, though senior among the chiefs had only a limited authority. 'The civil government at Abeokuta is I fear very weak and unable to contend with the military chiefs and their numerous followers', Campbell told Clarendon in October 1855. During a visit to Abeokuta the following month, he thanked the Alake for protecting the missionaries but at the same time reproved him for allowing a recent human sacrifice. On his side the Alake expressed disappointment at the peace arrived at between the consul and Kosoko, while Campbell countered by blaming the Egba for the failure of Phillips's expedition against Epe.

Campbell now realised that not only were domestic slaves as numerous in Abeokuta as elsewhere but also that the chiefs (especially, he thought, the Muslims) could not be restrained from following their neighbours to the wars and raids which brought in the captives who, either as slaves or as sources of ransom, represented wealth. Thus the treaty signed by them with the English in January 1852 was broken as frequently there as elsewhere. In 1856 the Bashorun of the Egba, despite warnings from the consul and the (perhaps insincere) disapproval of the Alake, followed the Ibadan in raiding 'Esharbey' (probably Shabe) far to the north. In 1857 Campbell learnt of another Egba expedition, undertaken this time against the Aibo, though on this occasion he was encouraged by the news that many of the Egba, having taken to 'honest courses' – trade and farming –, rallied only reluctantly to the call of the war chiefs. But in any event, Campbell's interpretation of these military operations by the Egba as purely slave raids is simplistic and misleading, though understandable in its context: Aibo, for example, an important town some twenty miles to the north-east of Abeokuta, constituted, as K. Folayan shows, the last centre of resistance to the attempt by Abeokuta to absorb the whole of Central Egbadoland into Egba territory.[88]

Commercial relations between Lagos and Abeokuta were of growing importance, but despite the consul's efforts to foster the production and export of palm oil and cotton in the interests of both towns, they generated in this period more ill-will than friendship. In former days, according to Campbell, the Egba traders visited Lagos market to sell their produce twice monthly, but this ceased with Kosoko's raids from Epe across the lagoon. Later, monthly markets were resumed, to which the Egba usually brought about 400 puncheons of oil, but in August 1855 the consul complained that for the last five months all trade with Lagos had been blocked by the Egba chiefs and that in consequence merchants' vessels were being detained in the harbour for lack of oil. He ascribed the action of the Egba to the refusal of the Lagosian and 'emigrant' middlemen to allow them to trade direct with the European exporters and to Egba insistence on being paid in cowries rather than in manufactured goods; McCoskry thought that a revival of slaving was at the bottom of it.[89] The following October a party of Egba traders held a conference with a number of 'emigrant' merchants at 'Eshalli' island – probably Isheri in a bend of the Ogun is meant – where they complained that having adopted the oil trade, previously regarded as an occupation for women, at the insistence of the British, they found themselves poorer than before.[90] After this exchange of views, trade picked up again, but the burning of Scala's premises in Abeokuta in April or May 1858 revealed the existence of dissension in the town between the Parakoyi, or trading chiefs, and those who challenged their monopoly. On a second visit to Abeokuta in May 1858 Campbell persuaded the Alake and other chiefs to sign a commercial agreement under which foreign traders who were provided with a letter of recommendation from the consul were to be allowed to settle in the town and that 'all traders, whether male or female, shall be at liberty to trade with any merchant or trader'. The 'roads' to the embarkation places on the river Ogun were to be improved and it was promised that the transit of goods should not again be interrupted unless required by political circumstances and then only after a month's notice had been given.[91]

The consular decade at Lagos was also the period in which the Ibadan were extending their powerful but short-lived 'empire', which dominated a large part of central Yorubaland from the defeat of Ilorin at Oshogbo in 1838/9 to the beginning of the Sixteen Years' War with a coalition of rival states in 1877. Campbell does not seem to have attempted to establish direct relations with the Ibadan authorities, despite the presence in that town of the influential C.M.S. missionary David Hinderer, and references in his dispatches to the Ibadan mainly concern their wars, described as 'slave raids'. Further afield Campbell heard of the depredations of the 'Felatah' or Fulani, and in July 1856 he suggested to the Foreign Office that he should undertake a mission to explain to the Fulani leaders the advantages of peaceful and legitimate trade, an offer which was received with polite lack of enthusiasm.[92] Nearer home again, there was the problem of the Ijebu, whose country was a major source of palm oil but whose supply to Lagos was threatened by the presence of Kosoko in Epe. Though the Ijebu had signed the treaty of 1852 with the British, Campbell found it difficult to open communications with them, as did also the missionaries. The Awujale put his case in his letter to Forbes (cited in part above on p. 42):

> Hitherto, I have not understood the Treaty, having had nobody to read and explain it to me. And now that it has been read, I do not see how I can agree to allow a white man (missionary) to come and stay in our country: much more to protect him: for our Ancestors never handed it down to us that a white man ever lived among them. Trade is all we want and we are satisfied. We do not want fighting, but if we are attacked in our country, we will defend ourselves.[93]

The consul was occasionally able, however, to pass messages to Ijebu through Saro intermediaries like S. B. Williams, his interpreter. Then in 1855 Hinderer and Irving, shortly before the latter's death, made a tour of the more accessible province of Ijebu Remo, and in 1859 McCoskry succeeded in obtaining an interview at Ijebu Ode with the Awujale, while a short reconnaissance visit in August 1861 by three Methodist ministers, Thomas Champness, George Sharp and Edward Bickersteth, accompanied by the Lagos merchant J. M. Turner, a repatriate relative of the Awujale, was reasonably well received at the capital.[94] However Europeans continued to be generally unwelcome in Ijebu Ode until the British conquest of 1892.

Finally, Campbell was able through the help of the Royal Navy to exercise intermittent supervision over the remote eastern margin of his consular area. He apparently visited the Benin River three times, on each occasion travelling on board H.M.S. *Bloodhound*. The principal object of these visits was to curb the activities of the Ijo, whose piratical attacks on shipping had been the bane of the river from as far back as the seventeenth century[95] and who were now plundering the canoes carrying oil to the British factories on the river and even the boats of those establishments. On the consul's first visit, in March 1856, the *Bloodhound* as usual went aground, so that Campbell was unable to penetrate to the heart of the pirate country, which encouraged the Ijo to step up their raids. The following January he was again in the river, taking the opportunity of holding a court of inquiry on the master of a vessel whom he found had been 'furiously drunk during the passage' and deprived of command. He predicted that when the Niger was developed, the Benin River, as its best entrance, would increase in importance, the estuary being broad and comparatively safe. Later in the year reports of worsening security from the agents of Horsfall & Sons and of Harrison & Co., two Liverpool firms, led Campbell to issue letters warning the merchants against allowing excessive credit to their oil suppliers and to send the *Bloodhound* into the river again. He visited the river himself for the last time in February 1858. On this occasion the gig preceding the *Bloodhound* had to fight off an ambush by Smart, a 'boy' in the service of Chief Jerry (Diare) of Jakpa whom Consul Beecroft had appointed to protect the British traders and whom Campbell now replaced by Abrinomy, chief of Batere.[96]

Benin itself as well as its lower river was considered as being within Campbell's area. This once comparatively well-known city, visited by the Portuguese as early as the fifteenth century, had seen no Europeans since the French trader Landolphe was there in 1787. Little now remained of its past power and glory, and the last attempts of the Oba of Benin to persuade the rulers of Lagos to pay the traditional tribute were rebuffed by Akitoye and Dosunmu (though, as was seen above, there are reports that payments were made by Kosoko at Epe).[97] Campbell, like other observers and writers before and after him, concluded that the decline of Benin was the result of the abolition of the slave trade, an error which, Ryder says, derives from a misconception of Benin's never important share in the Atlantic trade.[98] The consul was chiefly concerned to visit the city because of reports of the human sacrifices which were practised there, and he maintained in a dispatch to the Foreign Office in October 1855 that he had obtained an invitation from the Oba to visit his capital.[99] In the event he was able to get no further than the lower river, and the first visit of a British official was paid by Richard Burton, as consul for the Bight of Biafra, in 1862.

6

The Iron Coffin

Campbell takes leave

Throughout his years at Lagos Benjamin Campbell was subject to those two ailments which so much affected (and still to a lesser degree affect) both visitors to the tropics and the native inhabitants: fever and dysentery. These dangerous and mysterious ailments accounted for the high mortality among Europeans on the West Coast and for the succession of dying consuls in the prefabricated iron house on the waterfront. They were caused not so much by the climate, as many thought, as by physical conditions. Lagos, with its numerous swamps, stagnant inlets from the lagoon, and flooded holes from which building material had been dug, was ideally situated for the breeding of mosquitoes – not yet recognised as the carriers of malaria – while the water table lay so near the surface as to cause serious and constant pollution of the wells.[1] Doubtless the consul's twenty years on the coast and consequent acquirement of some degree of immunity led him usually to treat these ills as unavoidable inconveniences of Lagos life which in his case had happily not proved dangerous. Possibly he used quinine prophylactically against fever, as was now the rule for the sailors of the Preventive Squadron; more probably, like most Europeans on the coast at this time, he kept a bottle in a cupboard at home for use in illness. But though great advances had been made in the empirical treatment of malaria, much less was known about dysentery, 'the fluxes', which was still equated with and treated in the same way as its counterpart in temperate climates.[2]

In 1855 Campbell, who seems to have been unusually disturbed by Irving's death, obtained permission from the Foreign Office to absent himself from his post so as to take a cruise for his health on a naval vessel.[3] It does not appear from the consular papers whether he was able to avail himself of this, and in June 1856 he gave a portentous warning to the Foreign Office that after so long in Lagos and on the coast his health could no longer be relied on and that a vice-consul should be appointed who could take over in the event of his death.[4] Then at last, in the spring of 1858, he was allowed to take home leave, combining this with a business visit to the Cotton Supply Association in Manchester, and carrying presents from the Egba to Queen Victoria.

Campbell embarked for England on 6 June 1858, leaving the consulate in the charge of Lieutenant E. F. Lodder, R.N., commander of H.M.S. *Brune*, the gunboat stationed on the Lagos River. Lodder's appointment, ratified by the foreign secretary the following July, was a success, even though it earned him a rebuke from his senior officer, Commander Wyse, for accepting it without his permission.[5] Lodder was a young officer who spent five years in useful service on the coast, two and a half of them on the lagoon, and who was to act again as consul on a subsequent occasion and to pay several visits to the interior. During Campbell's absence the most notable event was another stoppage of oil supplies by the Egba, which was reportedly the result of an order by the Alake forbidding women – 'the working class in this country' – to trade. Lodder visited Abeokuta and settled the matter with the chiefs, who promised in future to observe the treaty. He was accompanied to the meeting by Townsend, still the resident C.M.S. agent, whose helpfulness on this occasion provides another example of the greater ease of co-operation between the Anglican missionaries and naval officers than between the missionaries and traders or officials like Campbell with a trading background.[6]

Meanwhile Campbell had arrived in Manchester, where his visit aroused interest among members of the cotton trade. He had obtained from the Foreign Office printed copies of his trade report for 1856 (presumably that for 1857 had not been printed) and of his dispatch of 14 March 1857, in which he explained the difference between the conditions of domestic slaves and of those who were exported. Probably, too, he took the opportunity of his conversations in Manchester to stress his views that a primary need was capital to provide for the transport, rather than the growing or cleaning, of African cotton, and that cultivation was more likely to succeed in the savannah country near the Niger than in places like Abeokuta which were near the coast.[7] Early in August he delivered a public lecture at the Manchester Town Hall on the prospects for growing cotton in the Yoruba country and other parts of Africa.[8] He also wrote to the Foreign Office on consular business, reporting the trading agreement he had made at Abeokuta the previous May and other matters. On a draft Order-in-Council conferring magisterial authority on the British consuls in West Africa, with the object of providing more effectively for the government of British subjects and giving added protection to Africans serving on British ships, he commented that it also gave an opportunity to require the numerous Sierra Leoneans who sought the privileges of British citizenship to emancipate their domestic slaves.[9]

From Lancashire Campbell came down to London, where he presumably called on Venn, the C.M.S. Secretary at the headquarters in Salisbury Square, and also on the officials of the consular and slave trade departments at the Foreign Office. They were busily sending him bills for cotton gins supplied to the Yoruba, but more agreeably allowed him £50 for his expenses in Manchester and permitted him to keep the clock which had been presented to him by the Supply Association.[10] Then in December he received from the Foreign Office a copy of the allegations made by the French naval authorities about his earlier connections with a notorious slave trader on the Sierra Leone rivers. A few days later he acknowledged receipt of this in a melancholy, almost pathetic letter from Liverpool where, 'In ill health' – he must have suffered dreadfully from the winter cold of north-west England after so many tropical years – 'and preparing for my departure by the Steam Packet', he asked that he might defer his reply until his arrival at his post.[11]

On 28 January 1859, five days after he landed at Lagos, Campbell addressed himself to the charges made by the French against his character. In a long dispatch he denied that his 'connection' with Mrs Lightburn's daughter had implicated him in the slave trade, which indeed he had tried to persuade her to abandon, confining herself to her lucrative legitimate trade. His liaison with Miss Lightburn (if that is how she was styled) was one which 'so far from shocking the moral sense of the Native Communities, is looked upon as necessary and indispensable, and certainly, so long as it lasts, is attended with many advantages and conveniences'. The connection had ceased soon after he left the Rio Nunez.[12] This explanation seems to have been accepted by the Foreign Office, no more being heard of the matter. An inquiry by Lord Malmesbury about Campbell's character had been answered by W. H. Wylde, an official of the Slave Trade Department, who minuted that 'he is one of our most zealous and intelligent Public Servants on the African coast'. Wylde also drew attention to Campbell's denunciation of the Régis scheme for the recruitment of contract labour; he thought that this was 'the real cause of [the French] attempting to impugn' the consul's character.[13]

Apart from this embarrassing confrontation with a past which he must have preferred forgotten, the consul had other, less personal anxieties. Though Lodder had deputised for him satisfactorily, 'considering the anomalous and arduous duties of this Consulate', the old problems had all revived. These were as usual interrelated: the slave trade had again gained ground; the supply of oil to the market had dropped drastically; there were rumours of renewed hostilities from Kosoko; there had been a great slaughter of human victims for the funeral ceremonies of King Ghezo of Dahomey. Finally, Wyse (now commodore of the Squadron) warned Campbell that he had orders from the Admiralty to remove H.M.S. *Brune*, the mainstay of Lagos security, from the lagoon.[14]

One, perhaps only one, aspect of affairs in Lagos was reassuring. This was the commercial arrangement reached by the European and Saro merchants with Oba Dosunmu at a conference in the palace in February 1859. A new agreement maintained the duty of two heads of cowries for every puncheon of oil exported, with two strings for every pound of ivory and two heads for every ton of shea butter and vegetable tallow. This was signed by twenty-nine merchants, including Vincenzo Paggi on behalf of Scala, McCoskry, Walter Lewis (Campbell's son-in-law), Hansen, Isaac Willoughby, Legresley, Emmanuel Pittaluga, and Giuseppe Carrena. Before this was concluded, four tenders had been opened for farming the export duties, that from William Savage, a Saro, for 1800 bags of cowries, paid quarterly in advance, being accepted, assuring the Oba of an annual income of some £1350. On his side Dosunmu repeated his concessions to the merchants in previous agreements, including the relinquishment of his own right to trade, and also rescinded the law prohibiting the use of certain kinds of roofing tile on any building other than the king's.[15] The last point, which had caused trouble in the past, may have gained importance because of the manufacture of bricks and tiles which Scala began, or planned to begin, in Lagos in 1857. But though tiles gave a much-needed protection against the frequent fires which raged through the thatch, they do not seem to have been much used in the town as yet, probably because of the expense as well as the earlier royal prohibition.[16]

But agreement about the export duties, although it ended the animosity between Scala and the other merchants, did nothing to remedy the growing shortage of palm oil, the main commodity on which the duty was levied. The decline had begun in 1858, as was shown by the consular return of an export of 4612 tons of oil in that year against 4942 tons in 1857, and was under 4000 tons in 1859 (whereas the export of cotton had increased from 114,848 lb. in 1857 to 263,500 lb. in 1858, a record level which was not maintained).[17] The position had considerably worsened since the Ibadan and the Ijebu were now imposing a virtual prohibition on the passage of oil through their territories on the grounds, Campbell reported, that it brought them no revenue. The effect of the Ijebu action was especially damaging as three-quarters of the oil shipped from Lagos (and all the oil from Palma) had to pass through their country. At Ikorodu the Anglican missionary J. A. Maser had seen calabashes of oil brought there for sale to the Lagos traders being smashed by order of the Awujale. 'This king uses every means to suppress legitimate trade, in order to establish the slave trade again,' he wrote. There was now 'not a pot of Palm Oil' to be seen in the markets of Ikorodu and Ejinrin, where normally 7000 to 8000 puncheons were sold every eighth day, and in their place, so Campbell heard, hundreds of slaves were exposed for sale. Campbell blamed this state of affairs on the ever-growing demands of the Cuban plantations and on the French contract scheme, and he alleged that after their failure to obtain labourers at Whydah, the Régis agents had been trying to persuade Kosoko's representatives at Palma to help them.[18]

Campbell applied himself to the problem with his old vigour, setting off up the lagoon on 19 or 20 February on board the *Brune* in order to get in touch with Kosoko. His party included Dr Baikie, leader of the Niger Expedition which had left England in 1857, who travelled in the Niger steamer *Rainbow*.

At Ejinrin the consul was met by Tapa, Kosoko's 'prime minister'. He at once noticed that the latter's canoes had been fitted out for war, 'having stout platforms on which they place their cannon and swivels and benches for the paddlers, all of new wood, rendering them quite unfit to stow puncheons of Palm Oil'. Admitting these warlike preparations, Tapa rather unconvincingly pleaded that Kosoko had been induced to make ready for war by the menacing attitude of the chiefs at Abeokuta. The Epe had not instigated the Awujale to deny oil to the lagoon markets, and he instead placed the blame for the shortage on the Ibadan and the Egba, saying that Epe too was suffering from the halting of the trade. Campbell decided that in the circumstances he could not himself agree to meet Kosoko, but the next day Baikie and his party proceeded in the *Rainbow* to Epe, where the exiled Oba regaled them with a good luncheon.[19]

Before leaving Ejinrin Campbell sent his interpreter Williams, with two other men (probably also Saro), to Ijebu Ode. Here Williams secured an audience with the Awujale, who claimed that in preventing the passage of oil through his kingdom he was acting in concert with the chiefs of Ibadan, Abeokuta, Ijaye and Ilorin, all of whom were opposed to the trade because of its lack of profit.[20] Campbell next dispatched to Ijebu Ode from Lagos a deputation of two European and a number of Saro merchants (none of whose names he gives in his report), accompanied by a messenger from Oba Dosunmu. But they were coldly received and had even less success than Williams in persuading the Awujale and his chiefs to call off their measures against trade. The Ijebu were apparently so horrified by the presence of white men in their town that on their departure they carried out purificatory sacrifices.[21]

The consul seems to have been particularly disturbed at this point by the attitude of the Egba. On his return from Ejinrin he received an excited letter from the Alake and his chiefs claiming that Abeokuta was about to be attacked by the Dahomeans in alliance with the Ashanti, the Portuguese, and the Oyo, and asking for ammunition. The writers added for good measure that Kosoko was preparing again to attack Lagos. Campbell replied by dismissing these fears, but he promised aid against Dahomey 'whenever danger really threatens'. In a second letter he told the chiefs of the charges, by Tapa and by the Awujale, that it was the Egba who were partly responsible for the obstruction of the passage of oil through Ijebu territory and who were encouraging Kosoko to attack Lagos. He warned them that if the interior peoples cut off the oil, the English would retaliate by stopping supplies of rum, tobacco and other articles going inland.[22]

The oil shortage had been affecting the market at Badagry as well as Lagos for the last two months, and at the request of the supercargoes and resident merchants there, Campbell again left Lagos, travelling on board the *Rainbow* with Baikie to Porto Novo, which controlled the bulk of the supply on the western lagoon. Here they were told a new story: that by the king's order the makers of oil in the villages had been required to sell a part of their produce to the royal wives and the chiefs at half-price, and this was causing them to withhold supplies. A more likely explanation is that the Porto Novo merchants were obtaining better prices for their oil at Cotonou, where a narrow channel through the sand-bar connected the port with the open sea. At all events, the king promised in a palaver that for the future the trade should be free from restriction, and accepting this assurance Campbell left for Lagos, which he reached on 30 March. On 5 April he reported these proceedings in one of his characteristically lengthy and leisurely dispatches to the foreign secretary.[23]

This was the last word which reached Whitehall from Benjamin Campbell. On 17 April 1859, after suffering for a few days from an attack of dysentery, his old enemy, he died at Lagos at the age of fifty-seven or fifty-eight. Lodder, the only senior British officer in the town, again assumed the duties of acting consul, taking care this time to obtain the full approval of Wyse.[24]

Consular Lagos

The apparently precarious state of Lagos on Campbell's death is no measure of what had been achieved during the six years of the consulate, in which he had given the lead in so many ways. The regime had now become sufficiently established to weather the ever-threatening storms. It is doubtful whether after 1854 Kosoko again entertained serious thought of returning to his throne, other than as a candidate of the British, or whether the slave traders envisaged restoring their trade there, or whether the officials of Her Majesty's Government in London (*pace* the members of the Parliamentary Select Committee of 1865) contemplated abandoning the 'quasi-protectorate'. Nor could Lagos itself be the same again. In the first place, there had been a dramatic change in its population, the emigrants constituting not just a numerical tenth or more of the total,[25] but an élite, trained in habits of thought and in techniques utterly unknown to their brother Lagosians, and ready to provide leadership in many spheres. Moreover, building on the foundation laid for them by the Sierra Leoneans, the Christian missionaries continued to labour in the interests of change, and the fruits of this labour were now becoming apparent: 'the whole face of this furnace of Satanic Cruelty is changed', Gollmer wrote ecstatically; more prosaically, Hinderer observed that 'every corner in the town has assumed the appearance of respectability'. Many fell away from the missionaries' teaching, for 'love of money and debauchery' were as prevalent in Lagos as elsewhere, and the 'emigrants' showed a strong tendency to relapse into the polygynous ways of their forbears and relatives, and Islam was already a serious rival. Nevertheless, the work went on. Oba Dosunmu forebade manual labour on Sundays, especially house building and the making of casks, and the beating of drums near to places of worship, and even the palm-oil merchants were thought to observe a Sabbath rest. (The Oba's measures were mentioned with approval in a memorial to Parliament in 1856 from an English provincial town campaigning for a 'godly Sunday'.) Primary schools had been started alongside

Sunday schools almost as soon as services began, and in June 1859 the Reverend T. B. Macaulay opened with six pupils what was to become Nigeria's first secondary school, the Lagos C.M.S. Grammar School.²⁶ Nor were the Anglicans alone in the educational field since, apart from the Wesleyans, a black American pastor, J. M. Harden, had opened a Baptist primary school in 1855, though it was soon to close when the American Civil War cut off its funds.

The physical aspect of Lagos too was changing much during these years. As Burton steamed down the river in McCoskry's *Advance* in 1861, he saw a 'thin line of European buildings' strung along the waterfront from the entrance to Five Cowrie Creek (or 'Forbes Point', a short-lived name) to the north-western end of the island at Olowogbowo:

> first, the French comptoir, prettily surrounded with gardens; then a large pretentious building, white and light yellow, lately raised by M. Carrena, a Sardinian merchant – it is said to be already decaying; then the Wesleyan Mission-house; the Hamburgher's factory; the Wesleyan chapel, with about five times its fair amount of ground; the British Consulate, like that at Fernando Po, a corrugated iron coffin or plank-lined morgue, containing a dead consul once a year; the Church Mission-house, whose overgrown compound caused such petty squabbles in days gone by, and which, between whiles, served as a church; another Sardinian factory; a tall white-washed and slated house, built by Mr. McCoskry; and at the furthest end, another establishment of Hamburghers, who at present have more than their share of the local commerce; these are the only salient points of the scene.²⁷

This thin line was backed at its eastern end by the new Brazilian quarter, called Popo Aguda or Popo 'Maro, where the first 'Brazilian' style houses with their exuberant plasterwork were already built,²⁸ and at the west by the 'native town'. Much of the area now thickly built over was then swamp, as is shown by a plan prepared in 1885,²⁹ and on the north-eastern side of the island there was a large inlet from the lagoon known as Idumagbo. The original Lagosians of Isale Eko still lived clustered around their Oba's palace, the Iga Idunganran, 'a red-tiled and partially whitewashed barn, backed by trees of noblest stature'. So far nothing had been done to lay out proper roadways, with the exception of the 'broad, well kept road slightly raised from the beach' which, according to Mrs Foote, the wife of one of Campbell's successors, was 'the one promenade in Lagos' in 1861. As for the muddy, sandy lanes which ran between the buildings, they wanted, as Burton said, 'only straightening, widening, draining and cleaning'.³⁰

The population had risen by 1861 to some 30,000. Of these, 800 were said to be Muslims, and Burton was delighted to find a Moroccan sheikh who had wandered there from Tripoli.³¹ Trading remained the Lagosian's favourite work, though there was also much fishing and the shallow waters of the lagoon were everywhere obstructed by bamboo shrimp baskets attached to poles, while the wealthier had also acquired farms on the mainland. The land on the island itself continued to be alienated from its traditional owners as Oba Dosunmu made numerous grants to both European traders and 'emigrants'; these grants doubtless increased the Oba's influence over the indigenous and mercantile population and at the same time aroused resentment as he became ever more dependent upon British protection.[32] Meanwhile, life centred round the yearly cycle of festivals associated with the land and the ancestors, characteristic of Yoruba towns; especially important in Lagos was the fishing festival dedicated to the goddess of the lagoon.[33] Doubtless there was much sharing among the different elements of the town in such public amusement as was going; the Europeans, for example, inaugurated their annual regatta and race-meeting in 1859, the latter on a ground laid out behind the eastern end of the waterfront.[34]

Regular communication with the wider world beyond the shores of Africa was now maintained by means of the mail steamers of the African Steam Ship Company. A timetable of 1859 shows that the steamer called at Madeira, Teneriffe, Bathurst, Freetown, Cape Palmas, Cape Coast and Accra before reaching Lagos after a trip of some four weeks from Liverpool. It went on to call off the Benin River and at Nun, Brass and Bonny, before returning to Lagos and thence to Liverpool.[35] The service provided means for the European residents to keep in touch with their distant homes and facilitated the import of European goods by the lesser African merchants. It also enabled the Africans to move up and down the coast, seeking work or education or new outlets for commercial enterprise. The humbler of these embarked as deck passengers, and from early days the consulate was concerned by intermittent allegations of rough treatment meted out to them by the company. Another frequent complaint, which came usually from the mercantile community, was that the steamer all too often was unwilling to wait long enough off the bar, particularly if the seas were high, for delivery of the mail and packets.[36]

The bar remained as hazardous and unrelenting as ever. On a still, rainy day when the waters of the harbour were 'as smooth as the river Exe', Townsend described how from the town one and a half miles away the line of breakers could be seen, with the hulls of the waiting ships beyond, and how the roar of the surf sounded all day and night.[37] Burton wrote of the bar as it appeared from a ship in the 'French' or eastern roads: 'Against the purple-black surface of the eastern sky the bar was smoking forth a white vapour, as if afraid to break, and we could hear from afar the muffled roar of the sullen surf'.[38] Its dangers were much increased by its instability, which made charts of little use. A typical mishap occurred on New Year's Day 1856 when the steam sloop H.M.S. *Hecate* went aground on the western bar and had to jettison two of her ten-inch guns. Later in January Campbell asked the master of the *Puffin*, Messrs Harrison's small iron steamer, to help recover the guns, but as the *Puffin* was doing so 'a heavy swell with breakers' set in and she was lost.³⁹ In September 1856 two merchants, Thomas Hutton and a Mr Swanzy, after being seen off from the beach by Campbell and other European residents, were drowned when their boat upset while crossing the bar to join the steamer *Candace*. Burton estimated the average number of lives lost on the bar at fourteen a year, excluding Europeans, and in 1858 there had been forty-five deaths. Sharks were said to swarm in the water so that even a good swimmer had small chance of surviving.⁴⁰

Thus the harbour at Lagos was little used by seagoing shipping. Scala writes that all goods brought into and exported from the town were taken over the bar in open canoes or on lighters from the beach, while transport between the beach and the river bank was by porterage, and between the river bank and the town by canoe. He estimated that this system led to a loss of 30 per cent on imports, because of thefts, breakages, the deterioration caused by salt water, and the wages of the porters.⁴¹ As at the turn of the century when Adàms had visited Lagos, Fanti canoemen were still employed for the passage through the breakers over the bar, but as they were unable to carry more than two puncheons of oil at a time in their canoes, the loading of a cargo was a lengthy and costly business.⁴² Mails also had to be sent aboard the packet steamer via the beach, causing considerable delay and loss.⁴³ It was little wonder that, as Burton wrote, 'No one seems to visit Lagos for the first time without planning a breakwater'. He mentions a project by an American firm in or about 1858 for building a floating breakwater on condition that the firm received a grant of the harbour dues for twenty years⁴⁴ – an offer of which there seems no trace in the consular records. In the event harbour works were not begun until 1907.

Campbell's successors and the Ijaye War

The two years following Campbell's death in April 1859 saw the 'iron coffin' occupied by two acting consuls, both naval officers who survived their ordeal on shore, and by two substantive consuls who both died of fever and dysentery after only six months in their post. Campbell's immediate successor, Lieutenant Lodder, still also commander of the *Bruñe*, acted in the post until the much-deferred arrival in November of George Brand, a Scot and former naval officer who had recently served as vice-consul in Luanda, where he had encountered some of the slave traders known in Lagos. Then on Brand's death in June 1860, Lieutenant-Commander Henry Hand, who had taken over the *Brune* on Lodder's much regretted departure for England in May, became acting consul until the arrival six months later of Henry Grant Foote.

The political and economic problems which had beset Campbell in his consulate continued after his death: the threat to the Egba and Egbado from Dahomey and to Lagos from Kosoko, the slave shipments from Whydah, and the shortage of palm oil for the export trade. The last was causing particular concern because of the steady decline in the prices paid for palm oil by the consumers from a peak of about £48 a ton in 1854 to about £38 a ton in the early 1860s. As Newbury points out,[45] the exporters' rate of profit was narrowing, despite cheaper freight rates, and interruptions to the flow of oil from the interior were viewed with increasing alarm by traders like William McCoskry. The situation worsened as the intermittent wars between the states in the hinterland concentrated into the major conflict known as the Ijaye War, the first actions of which were fought in April 1860 and which made movement on the roads ever more difficult and dangerous. Although this war had its origins in the long-standing rivalry between the main successor states to Oyo for the domination of Central Yorubaland and particularly in the fear felt by the Egba and the Ijebu Ode of the growing power of Ibadan, it was interpreted at Lagos in economic terms as arising from the selfish denial of free trade along the roads from the interior by Egba and Ijebu middlemen. In London, meantime, the return of Palmerston to office in June 1859 presaged a more forceful British policy in West Africa, especially directed against the slave trade. It also enabled the Anglo-French negotiations for a convention allowing the French to recruit contract labour in India, broken off the previous year, to be resumed and tackled with some urgency.

The first event of interest in Lodder's second consulate was the visit which McCoskry succeeded in paying to Ijebu Ode in May 1859, hardly two months after the failure of the deputations arranged by Campbell. McCoskry, who gives the first account by a European of a visit to the Awujale's capital, spoke frankly to the courtier who, in the presence of the Awujale, acted as the royal interpreter, threatening a stoppage of deliveries of gunpowder and rum if trade continued to be hindered. In reply the intermediary ('a plump old man, of rather waggish appearance') was even more forthright. Speaking without apparent consultation with the king, he described the Oba of Lagos as the descendant of a runaway slave of the Oba of Benin and asked why his messenger was accompanied by two white men. The Ijebu wanted no missionaries: the Ibadan, Ijaye and Egba had received missionaries and were never at peace. Next morning, after a chilly exchange of presents, the deputation left for home. As they were denied guides to take them back to their boats at Ejinrin, they followed the people who were making their way on foot to the market there, a walk of just under six hours through forest and farmland. On their way they noted loads of 'native', presumably sea, salt being taken up to Ijebu Ode.[46]

Two months later, Lodder reported that oil was now reaching Lagos again from Ibadan, Ijaye and Ilorin, coming via Abeokuta, and he hoped that the Awujale would take note of this. He could suggest no course but the use of force against Ijebu Ode, but he pointed out the difficulty of this as the town lay twenty-two miles inland (this underestimated the distance by a few miles). In Lagos, meanwhile, he had called on Oba Dosunmu to apply the 'country law' by executing four thieves, one of them a chief's son, who had been caught stealing puncheons of oil; this sentence seemed too severe to the Foreign Office.[47] A year later, the Ijebu were still refusing to allow oil to be sold at Ikorodu and Ejinrin, and in June 1860 Dosunmu wrote to Lord John Russell, who had now become foreign secretary, that this was the result of presents made to the Awujale by Kosoko, an allegation which, so Consul Brand thought, exaggerated Kosoko's influence.[48] The next month, Commander Hand, now acting consul on Brand's death, received a letter from the Awujale saying that the Ijebu wanted trade with the British which would not be in 'rum or common cloth but such things as are best', and advising that guns and powder should not be supplied to Ibadan – an indication of Ijebu sympathies in the Ijaye War.[49] In October Hand reported that the Ijebu had relaxed their restrictions, implying that the markets on the north shore of the lagoon were again selling oil, and that for the first nine months of 1860 exports of oil had risen to 3413 tons, compared with 2476 in the same period of 1859.[50] But now the alternative route through Abeokuta was being obstructed. Through Townsend, the Alake told Hand that this was because the local merchants had been refusing the payment of duty to him. The merchants privately told Lieutenant John Richards, R.N., whom Hand sent up to Abeokuta to discuss these difficulties, that the main reason for the closing of the Egba roads was to prevent desertions from the war camp by conscripts more anxious to trade than to fight. Nevertheless, after forming themselves into an association, they eventually agreed to pay a duty of 1 per cent on all exports of oil, shea butter, ivory and cotton.[51]

The closing of the roads and the river routes by the people of the interior was the major hindrance to the trade of Lagos, but not the only one. As Scala pointed out, the transit of goods by canoe and porterage via the beach resulted in delays, theft and damage. Trading operations were also cumbersome. The traditional system was described by Brand:

> It is usual to sell the whole cargo to a single individual on shore, the vessel being at the disposal of the purchaser of the cargo during the six, eight or twelve months within which the homeward cargo in payment is supposed to be in the course of collection. The original cargo is landed as suits the convenience of the purchaser and the vessel moves from place to place for that purpose as he directs.

This was rendered the more unsatisfactory by the dishonesty of the middlemen, to whom the European and Saro merchants perforce allowed long credit, and by the absence of any authority to compel the recovery of debts.[52]

Another problem seems to have been oversupply of cowries, the major currency in use at Lagos. About 1845 A. J. Hertz, a Hamburg merchant, had begun to ship cowries direct from Zanzibar to West Africa. Eventually these East African cowries drove the higher-priced Indian shells out of circulation, so that the Hamburg firm of O'Swald, who had taken over imports from Zanzibar, were able to establish a virtual monopoly of the supply of cowries in Lagos. As has been noted above, this monopoly was broken in 1855–6 by the French firm of Régis, with the result that cowrie imports into Lagos (and also Whydah) quadrupled during the period 1855–60, causing rising prices and a constantly falling value of the cowrie.[53]

The internal affairs of Lagos and of the consulate during this period were relatively placid, despite the frequent changes of consul. There continued to be a trickle of slaves who registered their redemption at the consulate, and the Foreign Office gave formal approval to the device of issuing consular certificates (called 'passports' by Campbell and Brand) to ex-slaves going inland.[54] In December 1859 Oba Dosunmu assented to the treaty with Great Britain whereby magisterial authority over British residents was conferred on the consul.[55] In May 1860 Brand reported that he had refused an application from Madame Tinubu, now trading at Abeokuta where she was said to have acquired many debts, for permission to return to Lagos.[56] Threats of invasion from Kosoko, though growing less serious, still merited the occasional attention of the consul and the Royal Navy. As a result of increased apprehension of this in November 1859, Lodder, as acting consul, paid a two-day visit to Epe. Kosoko told him that 'it was only the late Consul [Campbell] that kept him away' from Lagos, and he asked Lodder's support for his return, apparently in his rank as a prince and not as Oba. Lodder did not take seriously this new, modest proposal, having noted that the war canoes again seemed to be in readiness, and told him that he should stay quiet where he was.[57] A year later Kosoko persuaded the Oba of Benin to send messages to Dosunmu pressing him to allow the ex-Oba's return. Commander Hand, as acting consul, reported to the foreign secretary that Dosunmu had replied, doubtless at his prompting, that 'he only recognized the British Government now, not as in former times when Lagos was under the King of Benin to whom annually a tribute was paid'. Hand was at the same time advising the Oba to fortify the island against possible invasion and begging him to show 'more energy'; he also applied to the commander of H.M.S. *Alecto* (presumably then in the roads) for rocket tubes, signal rockets, a gun and a European gunner. But once again the threat from Epe, which Hand seems to have exaggerated, did not materialise.[58]

There is little information about conditions at Epe during this time. It is evident that Palma continued to prosper as an outlet for a part of the important oil supplies from Ijebu, and from 1855 Régis Aîné had found it worthwhile to keep an agency there which extended credits to Kosoko.[59] But Kosoko was growing tired of his exile, and probably too of the cares of his tiny, barren coastal state and of his dependence at Epe on the goodwill or at least tolerance of the Awujale of Ijebu Ode. After the flurry of anxiety in November 1860 and Hand's attempts to stir up the lethargic Dosunmu, little more is heard of

Kosoko in the consular records, and soon after the annexation of Lagos he was allowed to return there.

The affairs of Abeokuta constituted another recurrent preoccupation for the consuls. Every dry season brought reports of an imminent repetition of the Dahomean invasion of Egba territory and attack on the capital, and appeals to Lagos for help were strongly backed by the missionaries, who could bring powerful influence to bear in England in support of their cause, and by the European merchants in the town. Anxiety came to a head in February 1860, and Consul Brand found himself beset by requests for various kinds of aid. Though reproving the Egba through Townsend for having left the requests so late, he responded energetically enough. Apart from trying to stimulate the Egba in Lagos to join the armed forces of their homeland, he obtained sufficient supplies from the Royal Navy to send four canoes up the Ogun loaded with twenty barrels of gunpowder, two hundredweight of lead, and 224 pounds of iron shot. But his request to Lodder for the loan of crew members of the *Brune* as artillery instructors was refused, and Commander Bowden of the *Medusa* supported this in language characteristic of the Navy's determination not to become involved in the interior: 'I am unaware', Bowden wrote pompously to Brand, 'of any treaties or obligations which would authorize us taking any offensive measures against the Dahomey people even in supplying their adversaries with ammunition'. But his unhelpful attitude and perhaps wilful misunderstanding of the issues were not supported by his senior officer, Commander W. N. W. Hewett, V.C. (a hero of the Crimea), of H.M.S. *Viper*, who assured Brand that he fully appreciated the importance of Abeokuta.[60]

Hardly had all these preparations been made when reports came that the Dahomean army, after a battle with the Ketu, had turned homeward, and with the approach of the rains tension slackened. By the end of March 1860 the Egba felt confident enough to take a decision to intervene in the war between Ibadan and Ijaye, and in May their army took up position in its war camp outside Ijaye, just in time (so thought a missionary observer) to save the beleaguered town from falling to the Ibadan.[61] Meantime, two members of a 'National Emigration Convention of Coloured Men', organised in Cleveland, U.S.A., Dr Martin Delany and Robert Campbell, passed through Lagos. These harbingers of the sentimental obsession of the blacks in the New World with an indifferent Africa were returning from a visit, despite the unsafe condition of the roads, to the Yoruba interior, including Abeokuta, where they had concluded (or thought they had concluded) an agreement for the settlement of a North American colony, which the Egba authorities soon repudiated.[62]

In Abeokuta the Alake continued to press for help in the defence of his town, and in October 1860, as the dry season approached, Hand paid a visit of several days there during which he advised the Egba to strengthen their fortifications. He received a letter from a group of seven European residents of Abeokuta, reinforcing the Alake's request for instructors in gunnery and contending that the Egba deserved support in their war with Ibadan as they were 'politically right' and the war had been 'unavoidable' for them. On his return Hand wrote to the foreign secretary about references in recent debates in the House of Commons to the human sacrifices made by the King of Dahomey and he put forward the suggestion that detachments of West Indian troops should be brought to Abeokuta (presumably from the Gold Coast) so that with their help the Egba would be able to take the offensive against Abomey, despite the swamps and marshes which were believed to surround that town.[63] But once again the dry season passed without an attack. Not until March 1864 did the Dahomeans make their long expected, and again unsuccessful, second assault on the walls of Abeokuta.

The Ijaye War, in which the Egba of Abeokuta were now taking a principal part, had become a matter of great concern for the people of Lagos and the condominium there of Oba and consul. Many contemporary observers, especially the Europeans (though not Townsend), saw the war, as they saw other 'native wars', merely as a large-scale slave hunt undertaken with the aim of taking as many captives as possible for the trade in slaves. Later historians have stressed the clash of economic interest between the Ibadan, who wanted a route to the sea, and the Egba, who stood in their way. These were important motives, but behind and overshadowing them were the struggle for political power and the territorial rivalry between the new states which had emerged from the collapse of the major Yoruba kingdom and empire of Oyo and the earlier wars of the century.[64] Beginning as a duel between Ibadan and Ijaye, the war soon drew the Egba to the weaker side of the Ijaye, and after the fall of Ijaye in March 1862 it openly assumed the character of a contest between Ibadan and Abeokuta for the political control of western and central Yorubaland. Material, both primary and secondary, is comparatively abundant for the history of the war,[65] which continued well after the period studied in this book. From the point of view of the Lagos consulate, its interest lies in its effect on the hinterland of Lagos and thus on Lagos trade and internal politics; the 'emigrants', for example, had divided but strong sympathies. Consular policy, even before the arrival of instructions to this effect from the Foreign Office,[66] was directed at reconciliation of the warring parties, a role in which the officials concerned – Brand and his successors – were seconded by the merchants, both European and emigrant, and by the missionaries.

At the outbreak of the war, Brand was exposed to the strong pro-Egba sympathies of his frequent correspondent at Abeokuta, Henry Townsend. In March 1860 Townsend warned him that there was a danger of the whole Yoruba country becoming involved in the war. 'Ibadan is already too strong. . . . In fact a balance of power is useful now. The advance of Civilization and Christianity would be retarded, I think, by the uprising of a strong native Government in the country,' he wrote, and he urged the consul to make an effort to bring about peace. Meanwhile, a threatened invasion of

Egbaland by Dahomey had been overtaken by the onset of the rains and Brand, having failed to persuade Lodder to go up to Abeokuta in order to help with the artillery there, now dispatched him into the interior (by permission of the senior naval officer) on a peace mission, accompanied by two merchants of Sierra Leonean origin, Messrs J. M. Turner (who was related to the Bashorun at Abeokuta as well as to the Awujale of Ijebu Ode) and J. R. Thomas. The deputation left Lagos in mid-April 1860, succeeded in reaching Abeokuta and Ibadan, where they were coolly received, but were prevented from continuing either to Ijaye or Oyo. Passing again through Abeokuta on their return two weeks later, they found the Alake and his chiefs greatly alarmed by reports of a possible alliance between the Ibadan and the Dahomeans.[67] The Egba renewed their requests for arms, complaining that the Ibadan were obtaining guns and powder from the Benin River, from Epe, from Ijebu and even from Saro sympathisers in Lagos. Many of these arms transactions took place in the market at Ikorodu, where the Ibadan were selling slaves to finance their purchases. Accordingly Hand, as acting consul, arranged in July for canoes leaving Lagos to be searched by his staff, together with representatives of the Oba, for arms, the export of which Dosunmu had presumably been constrained to forbid.[68]

Consular anxiety about the war and its effects was reinforced by the fear of Dahomean intervention. Hand believed that the Ibadan were keeping hostilities going in the hope of this. But he was also concerned about the attitude of the Ijebu who, he foresaw, would soon take an active part on the side of the Egba.[69] In July Richards, the second master of the *Brune*, in the course of his expedition to Abeokuta on trading matters, heard that the Ijebu were about to abandon their neutrality in favour of an alliance with the Egba.[70] In September Hand sent a messenger, disguised as a trader, to Ibadan with a letter asking Hinderer, the C.M.S. representative there, for his views. Hinderer's reply put the other side of the case in forceful terms. The consul, he wrote, had been misled by prejudiced statements from Abeokuta about the origin of the war, which in fact had been provoked by the Are (ruler) of Ijaye. Egba intervention was extending a war which until then had been confined to the 'Yoruba' (in the original sense of the inhabitants of the former large kingdom of Oyo, and thus including both the Ibadan and the Ijaye). It was a 'vile insinuation' that the Ibadan were planning to join the Dahomeans in the destruction of Abeokuta; on the contrary, they realised that Abeokuta constituted their only barrier against Dahomean ambition. Meanwhile, Ibadan's trade was suffering because of the closing of the roads against them by the Egba and the Ijebu Ode, who wanted to monopolise trade. Thus the best course for the consul and for Lagos would be to encourage the friends of Ibadan in Ijebu Remo to take a stand against both Ijebu Ode and Abeokuta so that the Ibadan could obtain a safe and direct route to the market at Ikorodu. Even more emphatic was Hinderer's assessment in a letter to the C.M.S. Secretary in London: 'As long as Ilorin stands a Mohamedan power in this country, it is by no means to be wished that Ibadan's war power should diminish.[71]

But the fact remained that the consul at Lagos, whether he was a British civil servant or a naval officer, did not dispose of resources which would enable him to take any decisive action in the interior away from the lagoon. Even the purely local influence which was based on the presence within the bar of a naval gunboat was now threatened. In November 1859 Lodder complained to Lord John Russell that the *Brune* had been deprived of her white crew and was left with but nine Kroomen, while a warship called in the roads off Lagos only about once every ten days. Bowden, the senior officer on the Bights, responded tartly to Lodder's appeal for greater protection, writing that 'I do not intend to expose my men, after three years in this station, in the Lagoon until I have received further instructions'.[72] In April 1860 Commodore W. Edmondstone told Brand that he had orders to remove the *Brune* from the river. Brand protested in a long letter: Lagos was surrounded by hostile, warring states, and Kosoko, 'our old enemy', had many supporters in Lagos and was merely biding his time. He enclosed letters supporting his plea for the retention of the *Brune* from Oba Dosunmu and the merchants. In response the commodore agreed to refer the question to the Admiralty, and the *Brune* remained, though her effectiveness was doubtless reduced by the changes in her crew.[73]

Throughout all these preoccupations the consulate maintained its watch on the slave trade, while the Royal Navy continued their patrols and made their occasional captures of slaving vessels. Just as constantly the prices paid for slaves continued to rise with the insatiable demands of the sugar plantations of Cuba and the cotton plantations of the southern United States, where breeding among the slaves was unable to keep pace with the demand. There was a hint of the co-operation soon to be achieved with the American navy in the permission given to Brand to pass on to their commanders routine information about slaving vessels in the area, but the American flag (like the French and Mexican) was still used to cover slavers.[74] In September 1860, when there were only two English warships on the Bight (H.M.S.s *Alecto* and *Triton*), Hand told the foreign secretary that the only way to deal with the suspect American vessels, which camouflaged their activities by continually receiving and transferring small quantities of palm oil as though they were traders, was to persuade the United States Government to place a few warships in the Bight.[75]

On the last day of 1859, Brand sent an analysis of the current state of the trade to London.[76] A feature of the past year, he wrote, was the sale and embarkation of persons previously held as domestic slaves, reflecting either a scarcity in the supply of slaves for export or an increase in demand or (as was surely the case) a combination of the two. By far the greatest number of shipments was from the coast between Porto Novo and Whydah, from which there was also a considerable trade in palm oil, traders like Domingo Martinez being still able to carry on slaving and legitimate trade together. The area was under the suzerainty of the King of Dahomey, with whom Portuguese, Brazilian and other slave dealers had much influence, and Brand concluded that 'it seems absolutely necessary that energetic measures should be adopted towards the king' – against which someone in the Foreign Office commented: 'This would be a very difficult and costly enterprise'.

An irritation to the consul in this period was the allegation made by Dr William Balfour Baikie and Lieutenant J. H. Glover, R.N., the leaders of the 1857 Niger Expedition, that British subjects in Lagos, and in particular three consular employees, were not merely owners of slaves but also dealers in them. After the wreck of their vessel, the *Dayspring*, at Jebba in October 1858, the expedition had continued by exploring the overland route from the coast at Lagos to the Nupe capital at Rabba and thence to the confluence of the Niger and the Benue.[77] Both Baikie and Glover spent some time in Lagos in the early months of 1859, Baikie (as we have seen) accompanying Campbell in visits on the lagoon while Glover charted the Lagos River and parts of the lagoon. Eventually, in May 1859, Baikie, followed some days later by Glover, both accompanied by numerous carriers, left for Abeokuta on the first stage of the journey to the interior. Shortly after leaving Lagos Baikie's party was attacked by a group of enraged Lagosians who claimed that their domestic slaves had been recruited as carriers by Baikie's interpreter without their knowledge. At Abeokuta similar allegations led to the seizure of the 'loads' carried by Glover's party, which included a number of Hausa (or Hausa-speaking) former slaves recruited in Lagos as well as a group of ex-slaves whom Glover had attached to himself in Sierra Leone. These events formed the background to the complaints addressed to Lord Malmesbury, the foreign secretary, by Glover and Baikie about slave-dealing, associated with complaints about the robbery – or impounding – of their loads.[78]

Brand contended that the whole trouble had arisen because of the interference by the members of the Niger Expedition with the property in domestic slaves of the inhabitants of Lagos and Abeokuta. The institution of domestic slavery was a recognised evil which admitted only of a long-term solution. As the British Government knew, all Sierra Leoneans of sufficient wealth were slave-holders as much as were the indigenous inhabitants; though they probably also engaged in the occasional sale or purchase of a slave, it had never been possible to bring home such a charge. Moreover, in Lagos society as Brand understood it, slavery was 'extremely mild but universal'; the king's chiefs were his slaves, and so on down the line, so that everyone had a master, and beside the Europeans only the Sierra Leonean, Brazilian and Cuban emigrants could be considered as free men (this echoed in part what Campbell had written in 1857). From the three consular employees, S. B. Williams, J. P. Boyle, and J. B. Pearce, Brand produced letters denying the holding of slaves. The foreign secretary accepted the consul's explanation and agreed that Baikie and Glover had 'acted injudiciously in encouraging slaves to desert their masters and return with them into the interior of Africa'. Nevertheless, this did not excuse the robbing of the loads, and Hand, as Brand's successor, was left with the task of trying to recover the value of the property from the Alake.

It was probably their experiences at Lagos and Abeokuta, combined perhaps with an understandable and characteristic desire to emphasise their own achievements as travellers, which led Baikie and Glover to report discouragingly on the prospects for opening up the land routes through the Yoruba country to European trade and travel. Brand commented sharply on this issue in his memorandum of May 1860.[79] The 'Yoruba road' had been 'a road from time immemorial', he pointed out; travellers passed daily between Lagos and Abeokuta and between Abeokuta and Ilorin, and onward from Ilorin to Rabba in five days, and these towns had all been reached by the missionaries long before Baikie came on the scene. In this, Brand, who might appositely have also cited the experiences of Clapperton and the Landers, was entirely correct. Yet even as he wrote, the Ijaye War was making movement along these roads much more hazardous than in previous years.

Consul Brand and the problem of Lagos

The predominance of British political influence in Lagos grew clearer and more strongly established as the years of the consulate wore on. British commercial predominance, on the other hand, was not unchallenged. The Hanseatic, or more prosaically the Hamburg, merchants had won a considerable place in the economy of Lagos and the coast. When the Hansa minister in London complained of hindrance to his countrymen's trade in Lagos, referring to the burning of their stores on the beach on one occasion and to Dosunmu's imposition of a fine on Peter Diederichsen, O'Swald's agent, for breaking the interdiction of trade with Epe, Campbell complied with the request for his good offices by informing the Oba that he was directed by Her Majesty's Government to protect Hanseatic citizens. At the same time he told the merchants that he could give them no help if they endangered the security of Lagos. To the foreign secretary he complained that the firm of O'Swald, 'through their large capital and the fleet of vessels employed by them between this place [?] and Zanzibar in importing cowries to Lagos, enjoy the lion's share of the large and increasing trade of this country'. Nevertheless, he had helped them to obtain a new site for their factory on the waterside.[80]

The Sardinians, represented by Scala, had insufficient resources to provide serious competition, though Giambattista Scala in his *Memoirs*, published in 1862, hoped to interest his country's ministers in the development of the trade of Lagos,[81] and after his return home in 1861 the Italian connection was maintained by his partner or assistant, Vincenzo Paggi, and also by Carrena and Emmanuel Pittaluga.

The French Government took a more aggressive interest in the affairs of Lagos and of the Bight. The Marseilles firm of Régis Ainé was evidently able to count on a good measure of official support in Paris, and their factory at Lagos had been opened against local opposition under the guns of a French man-of-war.[82] There was an important branch of the firm at Whydah and they also maintained a factory at Palma in Kosoko's territory. It seems reasonable to assume (as did Wylde at the Foreign Office) that the accusations made against Campbell's private conduct by the imperial government during the last months of the consul's life were actuated by a desire to damage the man who had uncovered the real nature of the contract labour scheme operated for them by Régis. In November 1859 Lodder reported the visit to Lagos of the French cruiser *Renaudin*. The commander, Captain Barbotin, when calling on Oba Dosunmu, apparently using very threatening language, protested against the expulsion from the town of the trader Louis Lemagnière for non-payment of the fine imposed on him in 1856 for trading with Kosoko; he then went on to visit Kosoko at Epe, rejoining his ship at Palma. These proceedings led to rumours that the French intended to station a gunboat in the Lagos River, and Lodder forwarded a protest to London against this signed by thirty-eight 'native traders'. The French Government repeated the protest about Lemagnière to the Foreign Office in February 1860. Consul Brand later confirmed Lemagnière's slaving antecedents from personal knowledge of him in Luanda, and he also alleged that in March 1859, when Campbell was absent on his visit to Epe with Baikie, Lemagnière had urged Kosoko to attack Lagos.[83]

The actions of the French and Hanseatic governments recorded above show that internationally the British consular regime had won tacit though provisional recognition as the *de facto* authority in Lagos. Suggestions that this 'informal' system should be converted into a form of government known to international law were first made in Lagos not in order to increase the standing of the regime or to legalise its position, but with the aim of strengthening the effectiveness of British efforts to suppress the slave trade and such practices as human sacrifice, to which the kingdom of Dahomey now represented the greatest obstacle. As with the restoration of Akitoye, the idea may have originated with the missionaries. At any rate, Earl Phillips has drawn attention to a letter of January 1855 in which the medical missionary Edward Irving told Campbell that in his opinion unrest would continue at Lagos until the place was occupied on a permanent basis by Britain. The suggestion first occurred to Palmerston when reading the indictment of domestic slavery at Lagos made by Lieutenant Glover, one of the Niger Expedition leaders, though, as Phillips points out, he seems not to have understood the distinction between the Atlantic and the domestic trades. It was next raised officially by Consul Brand in a dispatch to Lord John Russell of April 1860. Every year, he wrote, the threat of Dahomean aggression unsettled the country, and the King of Dahomey's influence on the coast from Badagry to Great Popo allowed the slave trade to flourish and hindered legitimate trade. 'The cause of humanity, peaceful commerce and Christian civilization loudly demand that some restraint be put on the power and influence of this Barbarian Chief who annually causes confusion and bloodshed in the Interior. . . .' To this end, Brand suggested the occupation of both Whydah, where there was some reason to think that the King of Dahomey was little loved, and Lagos, 'either as a possession or by way of a Protectorate'. He pointed out that exports from Lagos in the last year had increased to the value of nearly a quarter of a million pounds; the island was 'the natural entrepot of an immense country abounding in unlimited resources' and also the natural base for operations to expand industry, commerce and Christian civilisation to this part of central Africa. But it could not serve these high purposes fully under a native government. The Oba and his chiefs were averse to progress; the payment of debts due to Europeans could not be enforced and there was no effective protection of property. 'To do justice to this place, therefore, and to put it in a position to become what it seems by nature intended to be', it was necessary to take steps to remedy all this, and these, Brand thought, would be welcomed by the inhabitants.[84]

There is no direct evidence that attention was given to this dispatch on its receipt in London, but it was probably in recollection of Brand's advice that four months later, after his death, Wylde, now head of the Slave Trade Department in the Foreign Office, minuted on Commander Hand's warning of possible Dahomean intervention in the Ijaye War that the fall of Abeokuta would 'put an end almost entirely to legitimate trade in the Bight of Benin and all the good we have succeeded in effecting during the last ten years will be effaced. It is in a great extent the demand for slaves that is at the bottom of these desolating wars' fought by the King of Dahomey, 'and the only measure that would counterbalance and thwart his proceedings would be the taking possession of Lagos'. The logic and accuracy of these statements were not impeccable: the British colony at Lagos could not shield the Abeokutans from a second Dahomean attack on their walls in 1864 nor was the slave trade the only or the most important cause of Dahomean aggression.[85] Yet the argument was forceful and convincing enough for Lord Wodehouse, the strongly Palmerstonian under-secretary at the Foreign Office, to suggest (in what was doubtless a polite command) that 'We might ask the Colonial Office their opinion as to taking possession of Lagos'.[86]

7

The Last Consuls

Consul Foote's forward policy

At the beginning of June 1860 Consul Brand wrote to the Foreign Office that he was delayed in setting up the cotton-pressing machine sent out to him for use in Lagos by an obstinate attack of dysentery. A week later, evidently much weakened by his illness, he embarked on a Hamburg sailing vessel in the desperate hope of effecting a cure by a change from the fetid air of Lagos. But he had left his retreat too late. He was transferred on 15 June to the captain's cabin on board H.M.S. *Alecto* of the Preventive Squadron, and he died the following day. His body was taken to Badagry where it was placed in a brick vault built, ironically, by Señor Jambo, the Brazilian ex-slaver, who would take no payment.[1] Two months later the Foreign Office received an application from Her Majesty's consul at Salvador for transfer to a post in West Africa. The applicant, Henry Grant Foote, wrote that his previous service in India, China, and on the Mosquito Coast of Central America, had inured him to the dangers of a bad climate. An official minuted that the application came opportunely for Lagos; the foreign secretary, Lord John Russell, concurred, and the appointment was made. Like his predecessor, Foote paid a visit to Venn at the C.M.S. offices in London before leaving to take up his post.[2]

On 21 December 1860 Foote landed at Lagos from the African Mail Steamer *Ethiope*; on Christmas Eve he and Commander Hand, who had now completed almost six months as acting consul, were received and feasted by Oba Dosunmu, and on New Year's Day 1861 he took over the consular archives. The new consul was a man of thirty-nine years, energetic, confident and optimistic. As a boy of sixteen he had seen service with the loyalists in Canada, carrying dispatches to Port Erie during the disturbances of 1837; he later worked as a clerk in the secretariat at Bombay and fought with the East India's Company's navy against the Chinese in the first Opium War, before entering the consular service in Latin America. Now he threw himself with zest into the affairs of his new post, losing no time in putting before the foreign secretary his recommendations for solving the problems of Lagos, and where he could take action himself within the limits of his means and authority, he did not hesitate to do so. The contrast between Foote and his predecessors, especially Campbell, is instructive, indicating not only differences in background, generation and way of life, but also a new outlook among British officials, readier now to take initiatives and assume responsibilities in a way which presaged the confident, full-blooded imperialism which was to appear towards the close of the century.

Two months after his arrival Foote was joined at Lagos by his wife and young daughter. Mrs Foote, who was later to publish a slight but interesting account of her life in Central America and in Lagos, was pleased with her new home, freshly painted, set in a garden of oleander and acacia, and commanding 'a view of a noble sheet of water, with low green shores nearly surrounding it'. After her passage on the 'burning hot' mail steamer from Madeira, even the iron consulate with its wide verandah seemed cool. The number of servants made up for their apparent lethargy and she abandoned housekeeping, defeated by the cumbersome and inflated local currency; asking one day for a sovereign to be changed, she was brought three heavy sacks of cowries. Food was abundant (except that beef was almost unknown) and good, and the cooks were 'generally first rate'. She had one glimpse of Oba Dosunmu when he called to congratulate her husband after the successful expedition against Porto Novo in April 1861. 'The native king of Lagos', she wrote, 'was a good tempered easy going sort of man, much given to pomp and show, but quite under English rule.'[3]

Foote had hardly been a month at Lagos before he sent to the Foreign Office an ambitious plan for an expansion of the consular establishment. In this he suggested that non-trading consular agents should be appointed at Badagry, Abeokuta and Benin, and a European vice-consul, who could trade and so would be unsalaried, to assist him at Lagos. To the surprise of the Foreign Office he submitted the names of the 'emigrant' C.M.S. agent Samuel Pearce for the post at Badagry and of his clerk J P. Boyle, another 'emigrant', for that at Abeokuta, which caused an official in Whitehall to minute, 'I don't think we ought on any account to send a man of colour to Abeokuta' (though a similar suggestion for posts on the coast had been made by Commodore Bruce in 1852). Foote supported his scheme by an account of the onerous nature of his work. From Mondays to Saturdays, he wrote, he and his clerk were busy from 6 a.m. to 6 p.m. On the day of his dispatch he had written letters for the mail from 6 to 10 a.m., then the consulate opened for general business: and thirty-seven separate visitors had been interviewed, some from Abeokuta and Badagry. On Mondays and Thursdays he attended his court (presumably that set up under the magisterial authority conferred on the consul at the end of 1859), but the settlement of petty disputes was a daily occupation.[4]

One of Foote's first actions was to despatch H.M.S. *Brune* under Lieutenant Stokes to Badagry, where the merchants thought themselves and their property to be endangered by quarrels in the town over a disputed chieftancy succession — that perennial source of trouble in West Africa. Stokes, who was something of a diplomatist in the naval tradition, managed to settle the matter, and in reporting this Foote asked for his retention in command of the gunboat, which he took the opportunity of criticising as 'not only too long' but also drawing too much water in proportion to her armament.[5]

Badagry, with its community of European and emigrant merchants in a town of mixed Egun and Yoruba origins, had continued to be an anxiety to the consuls at Lagos. There had again been serious trouble there in January 1860 when part of the premises of Novelli & Co. of Manchester had been deliberately fired as a result of a quarrel between Novelli's acting agent and the local people. Consul Brand had been confronted by the usual dilemma of adjudicating between a high-handed Committee of Merchants and an incensed local populace which, from the European point of view, had taken the law into its own hands, and Commander Bowden of the *Medusa* had been shocked by the lack of co-operation shown by the merchants in his inquiry.[6] There had also been reports from Samuel Pearce, the C.M.S. agent there, of executions for witchcraft carried out in the town.[7] The suggested appointment of a vice-consul to superintend affairs in the town and also at Porto Novo, and especially to promote British trade, offered a solution to these troubles, and Foote forwarded a letter from Pearce, his nominee for the post, in which the missionary wrote that 'if the Lord' (by whom he presumably did not mean Palmerston, the prime minister) 'is pleased to make me useful', he thought that his employers, the C.M.S., would raise no obstacle. In the event the foreign secretary's reluctance, like that of his official, to appoint coloured consular agents was conveyed to Foote, who thereupon found that 'your Lordship's doubts are well-founded' as the local rulers and merchants were likely to object (an argument which he should have thought of before). He then appointed Thomas Tickel, described as 'one of the few reputable British merchants in Badagry', to the post.[8] At the same time he also appointed Tickel's former business associate, William McCoskry, who had briefly acted as vice-consul in Badagry in 1855–6, as vice-consul at Lagos. Both were to be unpaid, and so continued trading. Overlooking, or perhaps ignorant of, Campbell's troubles with McCoskry, Foote wrote in enthusiastic though patronising terms that he was 'an excellent fellow, clean [clear?], shrewd and well-informed and what is of vast importance here, he is sober and steady'.[9] For the time being no action was taken on Foote's recommendation for a third consular appointment to be made at Abeokuta.

The new consul equally rapidly assessed the problem of the slave trade. After a month he thought that he had 'arrived at a pretty clear estimate not only of what has already been done but of the means most likely to put an end to the Traffic in slaves'. This traffic, he wrote, was carried on through the inland waters parallel with the beaches and was based on numerous trading establishments where small groups of captives meant for export could be passed off as domestic slaves. His remedy would be to place detachments of negro soldiers – a 'Sergeant's guard' – at Badagry, Porto Novo, 'Agoue' (Agoueye), and Benin, with a consular guard of a hundred men at Lagos, whence with a steamer of shallow draught he could send reinforcements wherever needed. Such a measure 'would be of more service in putting down the Slave Trade than a dozen additional Cruizers on the Coast' and half the gunboats could be dispensed with.[10]

In London, Foote's despatch was noted by Palmerston as 'deserving of serious attention', while a minute in another hand adds, rather naively, that if liberated Africans made slaves of their countrymen, 'the prospect is not a bright one'. But at this very time the export trade in slaves was drawing to its end. In March 1861, a month after Foote wrote his dispatch, Lincoln assumed the presidency of the United States, and by the Treaty of Washington in April Anglo-American naval co-operation against the trade began in earnest, while in Cuba General Francisco Serrano, the new captain-general, was taking steps to enforce the long-ignored anti-slaving laws. This at once brought the question of domestic slavery to the fore, and again Consul Foote was beforehand with his measures. Realising that many 'emigrants' in Lagos were slave-holders and yet at the same time claimed British citizenship, and possibly aware of Campbell's similar suggestions in 1858, he issued a notice during his first month in the post which required all British subjects to register as such at the consulate. As no 'emigrants' came forward, he posted a second notice fixing a time-limit for enrolment and warning that his protection would be withheld from anyone who held or in any way dealt in slaves.[11] Though this probably accounted for a pronounced increase in the number of liberated slaves registered at the consulate during the next few months,[12] the move seems not to have had long-term success. There are no further references to it in the consular records and the holding of domestic slaves continued at Lagos down to the end of the century, while the issue of British citizenship was settled within a few months by the annexation of Lagos as a colony.

The prevalence of domestic slavery at Lagos was a relatively unimportant part of a wider problem. As has already been observed, the growth of legitimate trade had increased the domestic demand for slaves as labourers on the farms and as porters to carry the oil to the markets, while the intensification of the wars (in which the Ijebu now joined in attacking Ibadan) increased the supply of captives whose fate was often enslavement.[13] The raids which the Dahomeans carried out every dry season into Egba and Egbado country and their long-standing threat to Abeokuta had now merged into the general conflagration of the Ijaye War, and the Alake and his chiefs were still haunted by the spectre of a possible coalition between Dahomey and Ibadan.[14] The roads were again closing all around, partly to prevent the movement of arms and enemies and partly to check desertion from the war camps. Thus the effects of the war were quickly felt in Lagos, where the export of palm oil began to drop.[15]

In the Foreign Office opinion was coming more and more to favour a limited intervention by Britain in the affairs of the interior in order to impose a solution of the problems of Lagos and its hinterland. At the beginning of 1861 a plan drawn up by Commodore Edmondstone for an attack on Dahomey was under consideration and in March the commodore was on the point of leaving Sierra Leone with a detachment of 250 West Indian troops and four mountain howitzers intended for the defence of Abeokuta.[16] Meantime Foote was encouraged in his project of visiting Abeokuta; he also received permission from the Foreign Office to visit the King of Dahomey, though he was warned not to commit the British Government so far as to involve them in hostilities in the interior. Because of Foote's report that the Dahomeans were quarrelling among themselves and unlikely to launch an invasion that year, the project of sending troops was called off.[17] Foote continued, however, to urge the dispatch of the West Indians. He thought, rather ambitiously, that 1000 of them would be more than enough – it was in fact unlikely that such a large number was ever in contemplation – and asked that 200 be sent at once (March 1861) in order to begin drilling the Abeokutans, and the remainder in November after the rains. His first expedition against Porto Novo, carried out in February, had made him more sanguine than ever and he described the Dahomean army, about which he could have had little reliable information, as 'the most contemptible soldiers in the world', adding that in nine out of ten cases their flintlocks exploded on firing.[18]

Before Foote set out on his visit to Abeokuta in April 1861, news had reached Lagos of Egba reverses in their battles with the Ibadan at Ijaye,[19] and on his journey by the road through Otta he passed many towns destroyed in war. He was accompanied by the Reverend S. A. Crowther, whose services proved 'of great importance', and on arrival at Abeokuta he was cordially received by the Alake. He was also greeted by Campbell's old enemy, Madame Tinubu herself, and by a deputation of thirty market women. He spent nearly two weeks in the Egba capital, from his arrival on 4 April to his departure on 17 April. He found it very unlike the glowing accounts he had heard and read from the missionaries: the houses were scattered, the streets crooked and filthy, the wall surrounding the town – on which the Dahomean assault had been broken – was low and its outer ditch shallow. Like other visitors, he remarked on the constitutional restraints imposed on the Alake, who could do nothing without the consent of his elders and chiefs in council. Nevertheless, the discussions went well, the Alake saying that he would gladly receive British troops in his town, would sign no treaty with any nation or individual without the consent of the English, and would open the roads and the river to trade – the last being a promise which remained unkept. He professed to believe that the war at Ijaye would soon be successfully concluded and that Abeokuta would then be able, with British help, to take the offensive against the Dahomeans.[20]

The consul returned to Lagos down the Ogun, travelling in a small canoe which accomplished the journey in twenty-six hours, including a stop of nine hours; he was impressed by the high degree of cultivation and by the wealth of timber which he noticed as he was poled along the river. In the reports which he then made to the Foreign Office, he seems to have been won over, to a greater extent than his predecessors, to the policy of support for the Egba advocated by the missionary party led by the Reverend Henry Townsend. He told Wylde that the only course for the British was to launch a vigorous attack on Dahomey in the next dry season, and in his official dispatch to Russell he wrote that:

> If the Egba could make themselves masters of the country, the whole of the petty chiefs on the coast would rejoice at their occupation; and certainly the great object we have in view, viz the abolition of slavery, would be finally secured if our friends the Egbas did extend their possessions to the coast, including Whydah and the other Dahomian slave trading ports.[21]

Foote's policy of vigorous support for the Egba now received a heavy setback in the cancellation by Commodore Edmondstone of the despatch to Abeokuta of the company of West Indian Troops already assembled in Sierra Leone, on the grounds that the Dahomeans were unlikely to attack at this end of the dry season. In their place there arrived at Lagos in May a small detachment of ten West Indian soldiers under Captain A. T. Jones, sent for service in Abeokuta, where they were to teach gunnery to the Egba.[22] On Edmondstone's advice the detachment remained at Lagos as a temporary consular guard while Captain Jones paid a visit to Abeokuta, whence he continued to the Egba camp at Olokemeji on the Ogun and then to the main war camp of the Egba outside Ijaye. On his return to Abeokuta at the end of May Jones wrote a detailed and on the whole discouraging report addressed to his commanding officer on his visit and describing the 'Constitution and Military Capability of the Abbeokutan Army for carrying on an offensive war'.[23] He then returned to Lagos, where he found that William McCoskry had taken over the consulate on Foote's death. Though he accepted the plan of stationing a small British force in Abeokuta, McCoskry was opposed to proposals for helping the Egba to achieve victory over their enemies, and it was probably because of his advice that the dispatch of the main body of the West Indian company was countermanded. He saw little prospect of ending the war by such intervention and he advocated instead the denial of supplies of war material to both sides. Meanwhile he wrote to the Alake counselling him to give up the war at Ijaye and return to trade, and he also asked Jones to undertake a mission to Ibadan and Oyo in order to try to bring about a truce. Jones started for Ibadan by way of the Ogun river on 3 July apparently in good health, but he was taken ill with fever and died four days later.[24]

The last major acts of the consular regime were the two expeditions undertaken by Foote in February and April 1861 against Porto Novo where King Sodji, under pressure from Dahomey, was diverting trade away from Lagos to Whydah. Foote took as his *casus belli* the seizure of a cargo of palm oil belonging to a British subject, but his object was undoubtedly to open the western lagoon to the free passage of oil to the Lagos market.[25] The undertaking was not an alternative to action against Dahomey or in support of the Egba, but rather the complement. As Campbell's experiences had shown, Porto Novo, unlike Ijebu Ode twenty miles or more inland (or, more appositely in this case, unlike Abomey), was accessible by water to steamers of shallow draught; an expedition there could be mounted rapidly from local resources and without recourse to the Foreign Office, War Office or Admiralty for permission or reinforcements; finally, the news of any success against Porto Novo, Dahomey's coastal satellite, would be likely to impress the authorities at Abomey and to encourage the Egba.

The first expedition left Lagos on 23 February on board HM.S. *Brune*, on which seventeen British seamen and marines and a gunner were added to the Kroomen who now comprised the normal ship's company. Porto Novo was reached on 24 February and on 25 February a messenger arrived from King Sodji, promising that the king would soon visit the consul on board. But the king failed to appear and in the meantime preparations could be seen going on ashore for the defence of the town. Eventually the *Brune* fired a warning shot at a high elevation. This precipitated a heavy fire from the town on the *Brune*, which was returned. At 150 yards from the shore, the small vessel proved to be almost beyond the range of the Porto Novan flintlock muskets and nearly all the shots fell short, whereas the Enfields used by the expedition 'soon stretched several of the natives on the beach'. But matters were not entirely to the advantage of the expedition as the *Brune* was proving difficult to handle – her commander, Lieutenant Stokes, having to con her and to give orders from the bridge at the same time – and in the course of the three-quarter-hour engagement it was possible to fire no more than three shell and five shot from the broadside gun. After some 500 rounds of rifle cartridge had been expended, it was suggested to the consul (presumably by Lieutenant Stokes) that rockets should be used to burn the town, the wind being favourable. Foote rejected this as he believed that at least half the population were friendly, and at the end of the day the *Brune* returned down the lagoon, convoying a number of Lagos trading canoes which had inopportunely appeared at the hottest moment of the battle. The next day at Badagry, where the *Brune* had anchored, overtures were received from Porto Novo, and on 27 February it was reported that the lagoon had been reopened to trade. Foote thereupon returned to Lagos and prepared for his visit to Abeokuta.[26]

Foote's account of the February expedition to Porto Novo was greeted in the Foreign Office with an enthusiasm disproportionate to what had been achieved;

the protests of a number of English and other merchants against the consul's proceedings were brushed aside and the foreign secretary's approval of 'the prompt decision and energy' of the consul's action was conveyed to him.[27] An unsigned and undated minute, almost certainly by Palmerston, pointed out how much might be accomplished 'by a little local vigour' and endorsed the policy of making a 'lodgement' at Abeokuta. The minute castigated the attitude of the Royal Navy to their wearisome task on the West Coast:

> All naval lords of the Admiralty hate everything connected with service on the coast of Africa for suppression of [the] Slave Trade and if left to themselves would take no adequate means to accomplish the object. They look upon the West Coast with the same vague apprehension with which our Fleet in the Bosphorus looked upon the *Black* Sea before they entered it.

If Dahomey refused to come to terms, the British should 'bombard Whydah and drive all the Slave Trading vermin out of that haunt'. Foote himself was jubilant. In an excess of self-congratulation he told Wylde: 'You will see by my despatches . . . that I have already commenced in earnest with the slave trading chiefs and that I have accomplished in ¾ of an hour of *sharp firing* what all the sheets of foolscap written by Campbell and Brand could not effect.' He hoped now to make an ally of the King of Porto Novo and had sent Thomas Tickel to him in his capacity of vice-consul. He admitted to having suffered a slight bout of fever on returning from the expedition, but he had recovered and now considered that 'The climate will not kill any man who is constitutionally strong if he is sober and steady. . . . Lagos cannot be so unhealthy as people have represented it.'[28]

Less than a month later news came that both the King of Dahomey and Kosoko were urging Sodji at Porto Novo to stand up to the English, and Foote's confidence somewhat abated.[29] Next he learnt that Sodji, so far from keeping the western lagoon open to trade, had now constructed a barrier across it behind which he had stationed his war canoes. The consul made ready to meet this challenge. Preparations were at once put in hand for a second expedition, and on 24 April, six days after Foote's return from Abeokuta, the hired steamer *Fidelity*, with Foote and Commodore Edmondstone on board, followed by H.M.S.s *Brune* and *Bloodhound*, steamed up the Badagry creek – though the *Bloodhound* soon went aground, a familiar experience for her, and had to be left behind.[30]

The following day, 25 April, the expedition reached the barrier thrown across the lagoon (or river Ossa, as it is generally called in the reports) between Badagry and Porto Novo. This consisted of stakes 'well tied under water with ropes', the interstices being stuffed with coarse grass. As the ships approached, they were fired on from war canoes in the rear of the barrier, which then made off. The seamen pulled up a few of the stakes and the *Fidelity* pushed her way through, followed by the *Brune*. Early the next morning, 26 April, the two steamers, with the *Fidelity* towing a number of armed boats, came under heavy fire from positions in the grass and scrub at the edge of the water as they approached the town, where an army, estimated by Foote at some 10,000, 'all well-armed', awaited them. But again many of the Porto Novan shots fell short, and the ships moved without difficulty into position before the king's palace where they anchored. They then opened fire with their rockets and with grape, canister and shell. 'Each rocket set a line of houses on fire', and in less than an hour the whole town was ablaze. Yet the Porto Novans held to their positions in the long grass, and were not dislodged until a sally from the ships' boats drove into their midst. 'The Enemy were now mowed down in dozens and a general retreat commenced.' When the seamen and marines landed, only dead were to be seen, numbering, Foote thought, about 500, while the expedition had lost only one man killed with five or six lightly wounded.

The steamers weighed anchor that same morning and two days later reached Lagos. Foote was delighted with his success. He told Russell that the affair had been much better managed than the attack on Lagos ten years before, and he praised the commodore for holding back his men and 'well thinning the ranks of the enemy' before landing. Hastily readjusting their sympathies, or at least their policies, the Awujale and Kosoko sent messages of congratulation to the consul, while King Sodji sent to tell him that he would 'sign any treaty but not fight against us any more'. Foote wrote to Wylde that 'We can do anything we like now with the Chiefs. They are terrified beyond belief. The rockets are called fearful war fetiches.' In London Russell minuted that 'Whydah unless given up should be treated like Porto Novo', to which Palmerston added his agreement, saying that 'great praise is due to Mr. Foote and Commodore Edmondstone'.[31] Just over two weeks later King Sodji and his chiefs signed a treaty with three officers of the Royal Navy on the lines of that signed at Lagos in January 1851, abolishing the export of slaves, permitting European traders to exercise their calling, forbidding human sacrifice, and promising protection to Christian missionaries. Almost at once supplies of palm oil began to flow to Lagos down the western lagoon.[32]

When the news of the expedition reached England, the consul's proceedings, according to Burton, were 'grossly abused by a portion of the Manchester press, from which officers and gentlemen have nought to fear save praise'.[33] But in the meantime, on 17 May, Henry Foote had died, 'after suffering some days from a combined attack of fever and dysentery'.[34] Only a little more than a month before, when writing to Wylde from Abeokuta, he had felt 'uncommonly well'. His last official letter seems to have been that written on 10 May, when he admitted to being 'fairly down with African fever', adding that 'Mrs. Foote and nearly all the servants' were also ill. Now this buoyant and ambitious man lay dead in the consulate, at the very time when in London the matter of Lagos was moving rapidly towards a decision.

Lagos annexed

The case for taking direct control of Lagos and Whydah put forward by Brand in April 1860 seems not to have aroused the sympathy or attention of the foreign secretary, Lord John Russell, or of the Colonial Office under the Duke of Newcastle. But, as we have seen, Hand's account of the ever-recurring Dahomean threat to Abeokuta and of the worsening conditions in the Yoruba hinterland led to a decision in the Foreign Office to consult the Colonial Office about the possibility of 'counterbalancing' and 'thwarting' the King of Dahomey by taking possession of Lagos where, unlike Whydah, British interests and influence were already installed. This had the enthusiastic support of the prime minister, Lord Palmerston, who continued to study the papers from Lagos, but it was not until some point in the latter months of 1860 or the first months of 1861 that Russell's caution (or his 'stubborn but brittle resistance', as R. J. Gavin rather oddly calls it) changed to acquiescence in the project, at least so far as Lagos was concerned.[35] The arguments for annexation were well known: to further the suppression of the slave trade by preventing its recrudescence at Lagos – and as Cell points out, this was not yet an anachronism[36] – to encourage legitimate trade, to check Dahomey and protect the Egba, and – considerations more apparent to the consuls on the spot than to politicians and officials in London – to protect property, especially that of Europeans and 'emigrants', provide stability of government, and regulate if not suppress the widespread use of domestic slaves.[37] At the beginning of 1861 a marked increase in French interest in the Bight of Benin added yet another argument in favour of British annexation, and one which seems to have been decisive in the sense that it precipitated action.

In January 1861 Foote announced the arrival off Lagos of the French naval steam frigate *Danae*. He noted the visit paid to the vessel by the agent of Régis Ainé and learnt from a Hamburger clerk in that firm that the captain, Commander Bosse, was intending to visit Kosoko, as Captain Barbotin had done in 1859.[38] The consul considered, however, that the Awujale of Ijebu Ode, on whose territory at Epe Kosoko was 'a mere squatter' and who was now allied with the Egba, would not tolerate any agreement between Kosoko and the French: an argument which seems to reflect Foote's failure as yet to master the complexities of the situation. Bosse did in fact make a hurried trip to Epe by canoe, but on his return behaved in so conciliatory a manner to Foote as to imply full recognition of the special British position at Lagos. He accompanied the consul to the Iga, where Foote presented him to Oba Dosunmu, and three days later, on 18 January 1861, Dosunmu returned the visit at the British consulate, arriving by water with a fleet of fifty canoes, each flying an English flag and discharging its cannon in salutes. After a banquet in the consulate, the canoes performed 'a series of manoeuvres' for the edification of the French visitor, and the Oba then withdrew to his palace.[39]

As J. W. Cell has recently shown,⁴⁰ French interest in Lagos and its neighbourhood – both coastal and in the interior – was associated with the shortage of labour in their colonies and their consequent schemes for labour recruitment in West Africa. The *Regina Coeli* affair and Commander Protet's visit to Abomey, both in 1858, had increased Campbell's suspicions of their activities at Whydah and elsewhere. Foote's reports of Commander Bosse's visits gave urgency to the probably somewhat desultory sounding of Colonial Office opinion in London. On 7 February 1861 Russell had written to the Duke of Newcastle, the colonial secretary, setting out the position of Lagos. After stressing the value of its exports, he pointed out that the Government could not allow the town to fall again into the hands of the slavers nor could they 'view with indifference the establishment there by French Agents of a Depot for Negroes to be exported as Labourers to the French Colonies, a measure which might still be carried into effect if the French should fail in procuring a supply of labor for their Colonies from other than African sources'. Its occupation would facilitate its defence and increase its trade, and he therefore asked the duke to consider whether it should not be taken into possession. There was 'no cause to doubt that the inhabitants would gladly become British Subjects', and the expense would not be great.⁴¹ On 3 March 1861 Palmerston asked: 'As it is supposed that the French want to form a military establishment at Lagos might it not be useful that we should get this Lagos Chief [Dosunmu] to enter into Treaty with us to place himself and his territory under British Protection with engagement not to alienate any part of his Territory without our consent,' to which Wylde added a note the following day that the question of taking possession of Lagos was 'still under the consideration of the Colonial Office', and that if their advice was opposed to this, then a proposal in the sense of Lord Palmerston's minute might be made to Oba Dosunmu.⁴² Two weeks later Wylde minuted on Foote's dispatches of 9 February about the position at Abeokuta that 'a small detachment of black troops' and an efficient artillery, in place of the inefficient *Brune*, 'would do more to check the Slave Trade than several cruizers'. To this Palmerston added that 'the expense (which would not be great) would be justified. If we do not take this step, the French will be beforehand with us, and to our great detriment.' Accordingly letters were drawn up asking for the consent of the War and Colonial Offices to the military measures (the provision of detachments of black troops) suggested by Foote.⁴³

On 20 March Palmerston made an even stronger annotation on Foote's account of his conversations with Commander Bosse, by whose politenesses he was not reassured: 'This strongly confirms the expediency of losing no time in assuming the formal Protectorate of Lagos ... we may find ourselves in difficulties if we don't take time by the forelock.' As to Foote's complaints about the *Brune*, 'The naval lords of the Admiralty for the time being have always done as little and that little as grudgingly as possible in the way of furnishing Cruizers for suppression of Slave Trade [sic]. If there was an old Tub fit for nothing else she was sent to the Coast of Africa. Of late things have been better done but this Lagos steamer was evidently a mistake.'[44]

A policy had thus been decided upon both in the Foreign Office and in the mind of the prime minister, but the consent and agreement of the other interested government department, the Colonial Office, was awaited before it could be implemented. Towards the end of March Foote was told that the question of taking possession of Lagos was still under consideration. Meanwhile Wodehouse was complaining of Colonial Office dilatoriness; 'At all events they might send us an answer to our letters,' he wrote.[45] In June McCoskry, now acting consul, repeated Foote's recommendation for the establishment of a consular guard at Lagos in order to counter the tendency of the local chiefs to revert to their old slaving practices. Wylde commented on 11 July that this showed the anomalous position of the Oba and 'is an additional reason for our taking possession of Lagos. The Consul has in fact for some years been the *de facto* ruler of the place. . . .'[46]

At last the agreement of the reluctant Colonial Office and its minister to the annexation was received. In reply to Russell's inquiry of the previous February and subsequent Foreign Office letters in March and June, Sir Frederic Rogers, the permanent under-secretary at the Colonial Office, wrote on 19 June that though the Duke of Newcastle was 'very much averse' to any extension of British dependencies, yet he 'could only concur . . . in the present case'. As no troops could be spared from other parts of the West Coast and no money was available from 'the small Parliamentary Grant for the Gold Coast', it would be necessary to ask the War Office 'to find some Black Troops' and Parliament to vote funds.[47] On 22 June the foreign secretary thereupon wrote to the consul that the matter had now 'been decided in the affirmative'. After stressing the reluctance of the Government to add their dependencies, he continued that they were convinced that the occupation of 'this important point in the Bight of Benin is indispensable to the complete suppression of the Slave Trade in the Bights', as well as to the support of legitimate commerce and to check the aggressions of the King of Dahomey. The consul was to take no step without first consulting with either the commodore in command of the African Station or the senior officer of the Bights Division, but if he thought it 'advisable at once to take temporary possession of Lagos pending final arrangements' – that is, before the transfer of responsibility to the Colonial Office – he was then authorised to do so. He was to explain the proceeding to Oba Dosunmu, for whom a pension or a position of remuneration would be provided, and was advised first to secure a treaty of cession from the Oba. Finally, he was to report on the material requirements of the new colony as regards means of administration, revenue and armed forces. He was particularly asked whether the troops which would be needed could be supported out of the local revenue and he was to bear in mind that the policy of Her Majesty's Government was to avoid 'all aggression upon the surrounding Chiefs' and to keep down expenditure 'within the narrowest limits compatible with the safety of the place'. A minute by 'W' – probably Wodehouse rather than Wylde – on the draft of this dispatch commented 'I don't see how we can go to Parliament for a prospective vote as to a territory which is not yet ours' and that much would have to be left to 'the discretion and judgement of Mr. Foote'. A postscript to Foote of 24 June advised that if he foresaw that force would be needed in the operation, he was to await further instructions.[48]

Foote had been dead over a month before this dispatch was written, and the foreign secretary's instructions came to the hands of the Acting Consul, William McCoskry. Though the language of the instructions was permissive, their intention was clearly mandatory, and they coincided with the views and advice of the man in Lagos who – with the probably less ardent support of the Royal Navy – was to carry them out. McCoskry wasted no time. He got in touch with Commander Bedingfeld, now the senior officer, who promptly brought his cruiser, H.M.S. *Prometheus*, at some hazard across the bar into the river. A conference was held on board on 30 July at which the British intentions were explained to Oba Dosunmu, who agreed to lay the matter before his chiefs and to give his answer on 1 August. Meanwhile, McCoskry sounded European (though not missionary) opinion in the town, which he found to be favourable to the project, and also the Sierra Leoneans, who were, he thought, mainly favourable.[49]

The acting consul addressed himself at the same time to the administrative questions asked by the Foreign Office.[50] He dealt first with the finances of Lagos, with which he was already intimately concerned since he had won the contract to farm the dues from the beginning of 1861. Revenue, derived from a duty of nearly 2 per cent on all exports except cotton (which had been exempted in order to encourage production), had risen from 11,500 heads of cowries (£1035) in 1856 to 20,000 heads (£1800) in 1860/1. Out of this the Oba had to meet the cost of his government, so McCoskry concluded that a pension of £1000 a year would suffice to maintain Dosunmu in his dignity. As to future revenue, increased stability and security at Lagos would make it possible to levy heavier taxes, but these should not be so high as to drive away trade to the neighbouring ports of Badagry and Palma. He thought that the present methods of taxing exports was bad in principle, adding that the trade from Brazil, mostly in rum and tobacco, was escaping duty, and he recommended instead a tax of 4 per cent on imports, which might raise about £5000 a year. He felt incompetent to estimate expenditure on government, but he rightly forecast that 'It will at first probably be beyond income'. Much was needed: there were no police, no gaols, and (in his sense) no laws; in the town there were no streets, no sanitary regulation. Nor was there accommodation for the necessary military garrison which, in view of the troubled state of the interior, should consist, he thought, of 200 men. Finally McCoskry had consulted Bedingfeld, who had recommended the stationing of a paddle steamer in the Lagos River off the Badagry creek, with two small steam tenders.[51] 'A few white men' were needed for this at first, but they could later be relieved from the dangers of living on the river. The *Brune* (and in particular her boilers) was now worn out, though her engines were still good. McCoskry added that the provision of light draught steamers, burning wood as well as coal, would make possible the penetration of the interior, and with a vision of the future importance of Lagos harbour, he concluded: 'As it has been shown that vessels can be safely towed over the bar into the river at Lagos when not drawing more than 10 feet we may expect in a short time a revolution in the old mode of carrying on the commerce of the place'.

Among the Oba and chiefs, opposition to the cession was now rallying, and they began to ask whether the acting consul and the commander had authority for their proceedings. Eventually McCoskry and Bedingfeld, growing impatient for the Oba's answer, told him that they intended in any event to take possession of Lagos on 6 August. According to the letters of protest afterwards addressed by the Oba, his chiefs, and 'certain natives' to Queen Victoria, this ultimatum was presented by the acting consul and the commander in person, who arrived at the Iga on 5 August in 'two brass-gun boats' with 'lots of well-armed marines', and it was accompanied by a threat to open fire on Lagos.[52] According to Bedingfeld, the marines were drawn up outside the palace, 'so that they could not in any way interfere with the palaver, but were near enough, if wanted'. In any event, this pressure, Dosunmu told the Queen, combined with a general panic in the town as the inhabitants prepared to flee, induced him to give way, and he agreed to sign a treaty ceding 'the port and island and territories of Lagos', a definition whose vagueness was later to bring trouble. Two articles were added as minor concessions to the Oba: the first, Article II, allowed him to continue to use his title and to settle disputes between the natives of Lagos, and the second, Article III, established his authority in the transfer of lands. At 1 p.m. on 6 August 1861 the Oba, accompanied by four chiefs, landed at the consulate and appended his signature to the treaty of cession.[53] Let the sardonic Burton, a visitor after the event, describe the final scene, rather than the prosaic McCoskry or the staid Bedingfeld:

> Our Union Jack was hoisted in the town, another on the beach, *Prometheus Vinctus* saluted with twenty-one guns. The marines presented arms; three hundred fetish, or sanctified boys, as the convert people call them, sang a hymn, headed by their missionaries. And as we Englishmen celebrate any event with a dinner ... forty-four Oyibos, Europeans, and Afro-Europeans, officials and merchants, sat down to meat upon the quarter-deck of the *Prometheus*, and by their brilliant speeches and loyal toasts added, as the phrase is, *éclat* to the great event. Thus Lagos — rose.[54]

The new colony

The news of the annexation of Lagos was received by the British prime minister with satisfaction, and no account was taken of the protests by Dosunmu and his chiefs and subjects which reached the Foreign Office through Townsend, the local agent of the C.M.S., and Venn, its London Secretary. 'The possession of Lagos will give great additional means for putting an end to [the] Slave Trade in [sic] that part of the African coast, and will afford a valuable and increasing development to legitimate trade. The Results will amply compensate for any expense which may be incurred,' Palmerston wrote.[55] He did not mention the French threat to the British position in Lagos, which six months before had seemed to him so alarming; only a month before the annexation, the Anglo-French negotiations for a coolie convention had at last been successfully concluded, and French contracts for the supply of labour from West Africa now came to an end.[56]

The reaction in the Colonial Office, which was to become responsible for the new colony, was less enthusiastic, glum but resigned. For the present, however, the channel of communication between the British Government and the authorities in Lagos continued to be through the Foreign Office, Russell conveying approval of the annexation itself[57] and then, two months later, of McCoskry's suggestion that the Egba of Abeokuta might be brought to acquiesce in a settlement of the Ijaye War by the cutting off, so far as was practicable, of supplies to them of arms and ammunition.[58] The policy of encouragement and support for the Egba, so strongly urged by some leading members of the Anglican mission and recently taken up with such enthusiasm by Consul Foote,[59] was now buried, and as Russell explained, the Alake and his chiefs were to be made to understand that the British had 'no predilections' among the peoples of the interior, but would support any or all who pursued peace and legitimate trade – statements which McCoskry must have read with pleasure.[60] This, combined with the avoidance of further involvement on the mainland and the practice of a strict economy, amounted to the policy which the new governor, H. S. Freeman, was required to implement.

To the missionaries, who had played so large a part in the events of 1851, the cession came as a surprise. If at first they welcomed it, they soon changed their opinion. As E. H. Phillips points out,[61] the policy of the C.M.S. was to encourage a self-supporting church among the Africans and to this end they preferred to work through independent though converted African governments. Apart from passing on the petitions received from the Lagos chiefs, Venn interviewed Layard, the parliamentary under-secretary at the Foreign Office, on their behalf in November 1861. From their point of view, the annexation represented a victory for the open-trade policy of the merchants and a defeat for the hopes and plans which they had built around the Egba of Abeokuta.

Freeman's appointment had originally been made to the post of consul at Lagos, and when the Duke of Newcastle at the Colonial Office accepted Russell's recommendation that he should become the governor he was also given a commission as consul for the Bight of Benin.[62] He left his post as vice-consul at Janina on 21 August and, after spending nearly three months in London, did not reach Lagos until late in January 1862. Meanwhile, the acting and last British consul of Lagos became the acting and first British governor. This was in a sense the consummation of William McCoskry's career on the coast. As will be recalled, in his first years at Lagos he had enjoyed the confidence of Consul Campbell, who had appointed him to the position of vice-consul at Badagry. The two men had fallen out when McCoskry, with the other leading European merchants, opposed the consul's policies, especially his measures against Kosoko, and McCoskry's appointment to Badagry – where in any case he usually deputed his duties to Thomas Tickel – was rescinded. It is impossible on the present evidence to determine how far Campbell's subsequent allegations against McCoskry's conduct (both at Lagos and earlier on the Gold Coast) were justified, but a picture emerges of the first acting governor as a man who was ruthless, energetic and resourceful. To the Lagosians he was Oba Apongbon, 'Chief Redbeard'; he seems to have impressed the sceptical Richard Burton, and in the Foreign Office Wylde had heard of him as a man 'of considerable energy and experience in the trade and politics of the Bight of Benin'. Towards the end of the consular period, he had succeeded in taking over the farming of the Lagos customs, outbidding his Saro rivals[63]: a significant victory for the European interest. He had evidently accumulated some wealth since when visiting Britain early in 1861 he bought a small iron steamer, built as a tug for the Clyde. He brought this out to Lagos where the *Advance* (or, as the Yoruba described it, *oko elefi Apongbon*, 'Redbeard's steamer') did yeoman service across the bar, carrying goods, mail and passengers and towing other vessels of light draught, though according to Burton, 'She is nearly lost about once a year and the engineers cannot be kept alive even by drink'.[64] All subsequent generations of Lagosians have had reason to remember McCoskry with gratitude since it was he who, despite the opposition of a number of Saro, cleared and laid out a roadway, the first in the town, along the waterfront, Mrs Foote's 'promenade', which has been famous since then as the Marina of Lagos.[65]

The consular age at Lagos, this ten years of 'informal rule', was ended. There began the long, slow, often hesitant expansion of the small colony into the hinterland which at the beginning of the last decade of the nineteenth century was to culminate in a Protectorate covering the major part of Yorubaland and eventually to form the Western State of Federal Nigeria, which existed until 1967. Oba Dosunmu retained his crown and stayed in his palace, but neither he nor his descendants were again to reign over the island kingdom. In 1862 he was prevailed upon to give up his revenue from the customs in return for a pension of 1200 bags of cowries, or about £1030 – a poor bargain.[66] One wound was healed, or at least bound up, early in the colonial administration, for by the end of 1862 Kosko had at last been allowed to return to Lagos, where he resumed the title of Oloja of Ereko and was given a pension of £400 a year[67] – as against the £1030 paid to Dosunmu. Tapa and others of his followers settled in the north-eastern part of Lagos, which came to be called Epetedo, 'the settlement of the Epe', while the majority, led by the irreconcilable Possu and Ajenia, remained in Epe, where their descendants still form a large, and largely Muslim, element in the town. In February 1863 Kosoko signed an agreement with the British authorities under which Palma and Leke were to 'revert' to the Lagos Government – to whom, despite Kosoko's claims, they had probably never previously belonged.[68] Possu, however, who had taken Kosoko's place at Epe, refused to acquiesce in the cession, apparently encouraged in this by Régis Ainé, who had maintained their establishment at Palma. He repelled an attack made on him by a force from Lagos in the same month as Kosoko's cession, and only after the destruction of his town by gunfire during a second attack in March did he admit defeat and sign a treaty recognising the new regime at Lagos. When the boundaries of the colony and protectorate were defined in 1864 by Colonel Ord, sent out from England as commissioner for the purpose, Epe was excluded,[69] though the coast from the river Addo in the west to Leke in the east was confirmed as coming under British rule.

8

A Deadly Gift?

One theme dominates any consideration, historical or contemporary, of Lagos: its physical situation at a point where highways from the interior, by river, lagoon and through the forest, meet the highways of the ocean. The first settlers sought probably only security from the troubles of the mainland, and for a long time — perhaps for about two centuries — they and their descendants remained as fishermen and farmers, at first under their own chiefs and then under a dynasty imposed by the imperialists of Benin. But the converging routes, especially the waterways, made this the natural site for a market, and with the shift in the Atlantic trade in slaves eastwards along the coast of West Africa, Lagos attained an importance, commercial and political, which from the eighteenth century onwards has not ceased to grow. It was this importance which drew the British, for motives which were inextricably mixed, into the assault which inaugurated the consular regime, a regime which was unintended and (unless perhaps by Captain Bruce) unforeseen at the time of the reduction and which after only ten years became formalised into a colony. Now began the rise of Lagos harbour, as gradually the difficulties of the bar were overcome, and it was the harbour, or its potentialities, which dictated that here should be the southern terminus of a railway, suggested in the very first year of the new colony and finally begun by the colonial government in the last decade of the nineteenth century.[1] In the making of Nigeria, and even more in the holding together of Nigeria through many dangers and threats, this combination of harbour and railway has been decisive, overshadowing the Niger itself, which to the men of the mid-nineteenth century had seemed the natural 'highway to the interior'. Thus Lagos became, for all its inconveniences, the capital of Federal Nigeria.

Such reflections are induced by a study of the consular period, short as it was. But two specific questions, of more limited range, were posed in the first chapter of this book: how was it that the establishment of a British consulate led, and led almost at once, to what was early realised in London to be a 'quasi-protectorate', and then why was this quasi-protectorate after only ten years found inadequate to the aims and needs of British policy, and so transformed into a colony – a far from popular step in mid-nineteenth century England and one requiring financial support on an unforeseeable scale? The causes of these developments seem less difficult to identify than to assess in terms of their relative importance and their place in the hierarchy or (to use Professor G. R. Elton's word) 'morphology' of causes.[2] But an analysis which did not attempt such an assessment would seem superficial indeed. Again, there are two elements which must be added to any historical assessment before it can carry conviction: an awareness of time and a demonstration of the interconnectedness of events. These can be supplied only by a narrative. Thus the preceding chapters of this book have tried to show how from month to month, sometimes from day to day, the problems of political and economic life in Lagos were tackled by those whose responsibilities they were, and how, to put it most simply, one event or one act led not just to another event or act but to a whole range of consequences, consequences which might perhaps have been forecast but not foretold.

The answer as to why the British consulate at Lagos took the form almost from its inception of a second government of the island, senior partner in a condominium with the Oba, lies partly in what the British Government set out to do in its West African policy: to abolish the slave trade, to prevent its revival at Lagos or elsewhere in the Bight of Benin either in its old form of slave exports for the plantations or in the new form of contract labour, and to promote 'legitimate' trade in order to fill the economic gap – objectives which by their nature involved the continuous assertion of British authority in the area. It lies partly too in the local situation: in the circumstances of the reduction of Lagos, the restoration of Oba Akitoye and the deposition of the reigning Oba Kosoko, in the subsequent weakness of the monarchy and the threat from the dethroned but still formidable Kosoko, in the rivalry with the French, and in the commitment, brought about mainly by the Anglican missionaries, to the cause of the Egba of Abeokuta against their rivals, especially the fierce Dahomeans and the Ibadan. This local situation was the challenge taken up by the succession of dutiful, in some cases remarkable, men who represented British authority on the ground: the consuls and those naval officers who found themselves directly concerned on numerous occasions in the affairs of Lagos. It was the consuls who bore the brunt of the daily routine and the daily dangers – above all to health and life – of carrying out British policy within the fairly wide limits set by a meagre flow of instructions from London, many of which had on arrival been overtaken by events. Despite Foote's rather unworthy suggestion that his predecessors preferred writing lengthy dispatches to engaging in military expeditions, Campbell's achievement in establishing a firm base of authority in his consulate was considerable, and his successors – Lodder, Brand, Hand, and Foote – built on his foundations. Finally, all these consuls, substantive or acting, knew that despite the opposition at home to any increase in British commitments abroad, there was still powerful and organised support there for measures which could be seen to be directed against the lingering slave trade, and from 1855 to 1858 and again from 1859 the government in London was headed by the doughtiest of all opponents of the trade, Lord Palmerston. 'While Palmerston and Russell lived', writes Hargreaves, 'it was usually the Foreign Office that was most active in supporting the use of British power in West Africa. These robust elder statesmen retained enough Whig idealism to regard the final extinction of the slave trade as a solemn duty.' Realising that commerce was (in Palmerston's words) 'the best pioneer for civilization' and the most effective means of supplanting rather than merely suppressing the slave trade, they also 'understood that commercial development in the tropics might occasionally require unfashionable demonstrations of British power'.[3]

As the reduction of Lagos in 1851 took place soon after the virtual ending of the Brazilian slave trade, so did the annexation of 1861 come at a time when political changes in the United States and in Cuba were bringing to an end the whole of the Atlantic trade.[4] This may induce scepticism as to the British Government's declared purpose in the annexation, defined in Russell's dispatch of 22 January 1861 as the complete suppression of the slave trade in the Bight of Benin. Ajayi and Austen, in particular, unable to accept that altruism played any part in the calculations of the British Government, have written that 'as the example of Lagos shows, abolition was a mere pretext for seeking economic and political domination'.[5] This is to substitute one over-simplification for another. Such scepticism, so far as Lagos is concerned, cannot be reconciled with the evidence adduced throughout this book as to both the motives and the actions of the British officials. It is, moreover, a perversion of the historian's advantage of hindsight, for there could be no foretelling the results of the political changes in the New World. At the same time as Bedingfeld reported the annexation of Lagos to his naval superior, he was lamenting yet another revival of slave shipments from elsewhere in the Bight, incidents impossible to check 'as long as there is no American man-of-war here'.[6] Moreover, the shortage of labour in the tropical colonies of France had brought about from the early 1850s a steady drive by French agents to recruit contract or indentured labourers on the West African coast, whose conditions of service and method of recruitment were only little removed from those of the slaves sold outright for the Atlantic trade. Again, the internal trade in slaves was on the increase, paradoxically encouraged by the success of the legitimate trade in palm oil, and though this was not explicitly urged as a reason for annexation by Russell or the consuls, it was implicit in their references to the political conditions of the interior. The internal wars among the Yoruba greatly increased the numbers of captives available for the market in slaves. They also threatened the legitimate commerce of Lagos port (at a time when the exporters of palm oil were feeling the pinch of lower prices) and the security of the town itself. This issue of security provided another argument, for although the capacity of Kosoko to overthrow the regime of Oba and consul at Lagos and to regain his throne had diminished, the threat of Dahomean attack on Egba territory almost immediately to the north of Lagos seemed to be growing from year to year.

These were real arguments, urged in Lagos and accepted in London, for the annexation. But the precipitating cause, though one in itself no more important than the others, seems to have been the increased activity of the French navy and French commercial firms in the neighbourhood of Lagos from 1858 onwards, mainly but not wholly actuated by the pressing need for the recruitment of contract labour. Hence the decision was taken in London to strengthen the British position at Lagos and in the Bight of Benin by making the informal formal and the provisional permanent, and to regularise the sending of British troops who could protect and extend British interests, commercial, humanitarian and political. In the event the French Government abandoned its recruitment of West African labourers when they concluded the convention with the British allowing them to recruit coolies from British India. This was in July 1861, a month after the crucial instructions had been sent to Lagos from Downing Street and less than a month before they were put into effect. Yet this did not cause Palmerston to regret or draw back from the consequences of his foreign secretary's instructions. Nor did it end French ambitions, especially commercial ambitions, in the Bight of Benin since it was followed in July 1862 by the declaration, at the instance of the ubiquitous Messrs Régis, of the first and short-lived French protectorate over Porto Novo.

The authorities of the Colonial Office received their new territory with a marked lack of enthusiasm. Confronted by the news of the annexation, an official there asked sourly whether the Foreign Office 'sufficiently represses over-zeal' among its consuls[7] – an interesting recognition of the degree to which the annexation had originated in local conditions and the views of local officials – while some years later another wrote: 'Lagos is a deadly gift from the Foreign Office.'[8] 'The price of Lagos was high', C. W. Newbury points out.[9] Its trade depended upon the maintenance of peaceful conditions in an interior which, until the British intervention of the early 1890s, was beset by war, and the Colonial Office's ideal of a self-sufficient colony never came near to realisation. Apart from this, the British were embarrassed to find that their new possession, the child of the crusade against the slave trade, was itself riddled with domestic slavery, an institution impossible to reconcile with British law or practice and yet so deeply entrenched in the Lagosian way of life that it persisted for the rest of the century.

It may next be asked why the consular system in the Niger and Cross river deltas, the eastern half of the original consular area assigned to Beecroft in 1849, was to continue unchanged down to 1885, when Great Britain declared a Protectorate over the Niger Districts. The answer is partly that the maintenance of the degree of order needed for profitable and uninterrupted trade was easier among the tiny city states of the delta and the politically fragmented peoples of the interior than at Lagos. Nor was there the same rivalry with the French. Thus, as K. O. Dike writes, 'The informal control which Britain exercised in the Niger Delta flourished as long as she remained the undisputed master in the Bight of Biafra'.[10] Moreover, when it was decided in 1861 to follow a forward policy in the Niger valley as at Lagos, serious difficulties prevented the fulfilment of this. The Liverpool traders who monopolised the coastal trade of the area, in co-operation with the African middlemen, objected so strongly to the proposal to offer a government subsidy to a private company prepared to develop direct trade up the rivers that it had to be withdrawn, and by the time that these firms realised the importance of inland trade, the Parliamentary Select Committee of 1865 had recommended a policy of retreat rather than expansion in West Africa, thereby discouraging further official support for ventures into the interior.[11]

The consular period in Lagos stands at the beginning of Britain's long presence and long-exercised influence in Nigeria, formally brought to an end a century later. In 1853, a Yoruba emigrant, the catechist James White, wrote: 'By the taking of Lagos, England has performed an act which the grateful children of Africa shall long remember.... One of the principal roots of the slave trade is torn out of the soil'. Another, the Reverend Samuel Ajayi Crowther, contrasted the sad condition of the Lagos from which he was shipped as a slave for the Brazils thirty years before with Lagos as it was in 1852, when 'The resources of the country [were] being called forth'.[12] This contemporary evidence provides a real and important criterion for an assessment of the consulate, though not for subsequent developments. From another point of view and looking back over a longer period, the historians Robinson and Gallagher write that: 'The colony [of Lagos] remained a failure, a skeleton in the imperial cupboard. Only determined British intervention in the politics of the hinterland could have turned it into a success; but no British Government was willing to contemplate such a step.... On the eve of the Scramble, Lagos was still regarded as a liability.'[13] But the concepts of 'failure' and 'success' can have meaning in history only when measured against that most elusive element, human motive, and though it was certainly Colonial Office doctrine that the expenditure of a colony should be balanced against its revenue, success in this would be too narrow a criterion. Moreover, the very use of such terms diminishes the historian's integrity by involving his sympathies with one party or another. An evaluation of the consular regime at Lagos, as also an evaluation of the whole colonial period there, must take account of the changes which it wrought or which it fostered in the politics and economy of the island and in the lives of the people there. The slave trade was abolished; the Christian religion was introduced, and with it Western education; a flourishing export trade was brought into being. There must then be considered the loss of national independence and, much more gradually, of national identity — losses never regained, since Lagos and all the Yoruba kingdoms were merged into Nigeria. But it is not the historian's duty to issue a verdict on 'gains' and 'losses' such as these, which defy measurement and serious comparison; he sees and assesses them as change, and it is with change and the explanation of change that he is concerned.

APPENDIX A

Treaty between Great Britain and Lagos, 1 January 1852

Commodore Henry William Bruce, Commander-in-chief of Her Majesty's ships and vessels on the West Coast of Africa, and John Beecroft, Esquire, Her Majesty's Consul in the Bights of Benin and Biafra, on the part of Her Majesty the Queen of England, and the King and Chiefs of Lagos and of the neighbourhood, on the part of themselves and of their country, have agreed upon the following Articles and Conditions:—

Article I

The export of slaves to foreign countries is for ever abolished in the territories of the King and Chiefs of Lagos; and the King and Chiefs of Lagos engage to make and to proclaim a law prohibiting any of their subjects, or any person within their jurisdiction, from selling or assisting in the sale of any slave for transportation to a foreign country; and the King and Chiefs of Lagos promise to inflict a severe punishment on any person who shall break this law.

Article II

No European or other person whatever shall be permitted to reside within the territory of the King and Chiefs of Lagos for the purpose of carrying on in any way the Traffic in Slaves; and no houses, or stores, or buildings of any kind whatever shall be erected for the purpose of Slave Trade within the territory of the King and Chiefs of Lagos; and if any such houses, stores, or buildings shall at any future time be erected, and the King and Chiefs of Lagos shall fail or be unable to destroy them, they may be destroyed by any British officers employed for the suppression of Slave Trade.

Article III

If at any time it shall appear that Slave Trade has been carried on through or from the territory of the King and Chiefs of Lagos, the Slave Trade may be put down by Great Britain by force upon that territory, and British officers may seize the boats of Lagos found anywhere carrying on the Slave Trade; and the King and Chiefs of Lagos will be subject to a severe act of displeasure on the part of the Queen of England.

Article IV

The slaves now held for exportation shall be delivered to any British officer duly authorized to receive them, for the purpose of being carried to a British Colony, and there liberated; and all the implements of Slave Trade, and the barracoons or buildings exclusively used in the Slave Trade, shall be forthwith destroyed.

Article V

Europeans or other persons now engaged in the Slave Trade are to be expelled the country; the houses, stores, or buildings hitherto employed as slave-factories, if not converted to lawful purposes within three months of the conclusion of this Engagement, are to be destroyed.

Article VI

The subjects of the Queen of England may always trade freely with the people of Lagos in every article they wish to buy and sell in all the places, and ports, and rivers within the territories of the King and Chiefs of Lagos, and throughout the whole of their dominions; and the King and Chiefs of Lagos pledge themselves to show no favour and give no privilege to the ships and traders of other countries which they do not show to those of England.

Article VII

The King and Chiefs of Lagos declare that no human being shall at any time be sacrificed within their territories on account of religious or other ceremonies; and that they will prevent the barbarous practice of murdering prisoners captured in war.

Article VIII

Complete protection shall be afforded to Missionaries or Ministers of the Gospel, of whatever nation or country, following the vocation of spreading the knowledge and doctrines of Christianity, and extending the benefits of civilization within the territory of the King and Chiefs of Lagos.

Encouragement shall be given to such Missionaries or Ministers in the pursuits of industry, in building houses for their residence, and schools and chapels. They shall not be hindered or molested in their endeavours to teach the doctrines of Christianity to all persons willing and desirous to be taught; nor shall any subject of the King and Chiefs of Lagos who may embrace the Christian faith be on that account, or on account of the teaching or exercise thereof, molested or troubled in any manner whatsoever.

The King and Chiefs of Lagos further agree to set apart a piece of land, within a convenient distance of the principal towns, to be used as a burial-ground for Christian persons. And the funerals and sepulchres of the dead shall not be disturbed in any way or upon any account.

Article IX

Power is hereby expressly reserved to the Government of France to become a party to this Treaty, if it shall think fit, agreeably with the provisions contained in Article v of the Convention between Her Majesty and the King of the French for the suppression of the Traffic in Slaves, signed at London, May 22, 1845.

In faith of which we have hereunto set our hands and seals, at Lagos, on board Her Britannic Majesty's ship *Penelope*, 1st January, 1852.

           (L.S.) H. W. BRUCE
           (L.S.) JOHN BEECROFT
           (L.S.) KING AKITOYE
           (L.S.) ATCHOBOO
           (L.S.) KOSAE

APPENDIX B

The Treaty of Epe, 28 September 1854

Agreement entered into this 28th Day of September 1854 between Kosoko his Caboceers and Chiefs, and Benjamin Campbell Esquire Her Britannic Majesty's Consul for the Bight of Benin, and Thomas Miller Esquire Commander H.M. Sloop "Crane" Senior Officer in the Bights of Benin and Biafra.

1st. Kosoko his Caboceers and Chiefs solemnly pledge themselves to make no attempt to regain possession of Lagos either by threats, hostilities or stratagem.

2nd. Kosoko his Caboceers and Chiefs claim Palma, as their port of trade, and Benjamin Campbell Esquire Her Britannic Majesty's Consul, and Thomas Miller Esquire Commander and Senior Naval Officer in the Bights, engage to recognize Palma, as the port of Kosoko and his Caboceers and Chiefs, for all purposes of legitimate trade.

3rd. Kosoko his Caboceers and Chiefs do most solemnly pledge themselves to abandon the slave trade, that is the export of slaves from Africa, also not to allow any slave trader to reside at their port or any other place within their jurisdiction and influence.

4th. Kosoko and his Caboceers and Chiefs solemnly bind themselves to give every protection and assistance to such merchants and traders as may wish to reside among them for the purpose of carrying on legitimate trade – also to assist Her Britannic Majesty's Consul to reopen the markets on the Jaboo shore viz Agienu, Ecorodu, and Aboyee, and in maintaining order and security at those markets.

5th. There shall be levied at the Port of Palma, an export duty of one head of cowries for every Puncheon of Palm Oil of the average size of one hundred and

Appendix B

twenty gallons and two strings of cowries per lb. on all Ivory exported from the above Port for the benefit of Kosoko.

6th. Benjamin Campbell Esquire Her Britannic Majesty's Consul engages on behalf of Her Magesty's Government that for the due and faithful performance of this engagement on the part of Kosoko his Caboceers and Chiefs there shall be paid to Kosoko by Her Majesty's Government an annual allowance for his life of Two thousand heads of cowries or one thousand dollars at his option.

7th. This engagement to have full force and effect from this day and until annulled by Her Britannic Majesty's Government.

Signed up the Lagoon at Appe this 28th day of September 1854

    Kosoko X
    Oloosema X   Bagaloo X
    Oloto X   Apsee X
    Pelleu X   Oleesau X
    Tapa X   Ettee X
    Agenia X   Lomosa X
    Bosoopo X   Otcheodee X
    Agagoo X
    Obatchi X
    Whydobah X

  B. Campbell (Her Britannic Majesty's Consul for the Bight of Benin)
  Thos. Miller (Commander H.M.S. 'Crane' and Senior Officer of the Bights of Benin and Biafra)

in the presence of

  Herbert L. Ryves, Lieut. Commander of 'Minx'
  W. P. Braund, Master H.M.S. 'Crane'
  Francis Wm. Davis, Assistant Surgeon, 'Minx'
  Geo. Batt. Scala, merchant of Lagos
  W. R. Hansen, merchant of Lagos
  Jose Pedro da Cousta Roy, merchant of Lagos
  S. B. Williams, merchant of Lagos and interpreter.

APPENDIX C

The Treaty of Cession, 6 August 1861

Treaty between Norman B. Bedingfeld, Commander of Her Majesty's ship *Prometheus*, and Senior Officer of the Bights Division, and William McCoskry, Esquire, Her Britannic Majesty's Acting Consul, on the part of Her Majesty the Queen of Great Britain, and Docemo, King of Lagos, on the part of himself and Chiefs.

Article I

In order that the Queen of England may be the better enabled to assist, defend, and protect the inhabitants of Lagos, and to put an end to the Slave Trade in this and the neighbouring countries, and to prevent the destructive wars so frequently undertaken by Dahomey and others for the capture of the slaves, I, Docemo, do, with the consent and advice of my Council, give, transfer, and by these presents grant and confirm unto the Queen of Great Britain, her heirs and successors for ever, the port and Island of Lagos, with all the rights, profits, territories, and appurtenances whatsoever thereunto belonging, and as well the profits and revenue as the direct, full, and absolute dominion and sovereignty of the said port, island, and premises, with all the royalties thereof, freely, fully, entirely, and absolutely. I do also convenant and grant that the quiet and peaceable possession thereof shall with all possible speed, be freely and effectually delivered to the Queen of Great Britain, or such person as Her Majesty shall thereunto appoint for her use in the performance of this grant; the inhabitants of the said island and territories, as the Queen's subjects, and under her sovereignty, Crown, jurisdiction, and government, being still suffered to live there.

Article II

Docemo will be allowed the use of the title of King in its usual African signification, and will be permitted to decide disputes between natives of Lagos with their consent, subject to appeal to British laws.

Article III

In the transfer of lands, the stamp of Docemo affixed to the document will be proof that there are no other native claims upon it, and for this purpose he will be permitted to use it as hitherto.

In consideration of the cession as before-mentioned of the port and island and territories of Lagos, the Representatives of the Queen of Great Britain do promise, subject to the approval of Her Majesty, that Docemo shall receive an annual pension from the Queen of Great Britain equal to the net revenue hitherto annually received by him; such pension to be paid at such periods and in such mode as may hereafter be determined.

LAGOS, August 6, 1861.

(Signed) DOCEMO his X mark.
TELAKE "
ROCAMENA "
OBALEKOW "
ACHEBONG "
NORMAN B. BEDINGFELD,
    Her Majesty's ship
    Prometheus, Senior Officer,
    Bights Division.

W. McCOSKRY,
    Acting Consul.

Notes and References

Chapter 1

1. See Ajayi and Smith (1971) passim, and Smith (1969a) chaps x–xii.
2. See Smith (1969a) pp. 151–2, and Law (1970) passim, for suggested chronologies of the opening stages of the wars. Law dates the beginning of the second Owu–Ife war and the siege of Owu (in the south) and the alliance of Afonja with the Fulani and the revolt of the Hausa slaves (in the north) all at c. 1817.
3. p. 34.
4. p. 34.
5. Robinson and Gallagher (1961) use both these terms, e.g. on pp. 33–4. 'Informal empire' is used by Dike (1956a), passim, to describe the consular system in the Niger Delta.
6. This account of Lagos history is based on Smith (1969a) pp. 89–94, 168–9. See also Forde (1951; 1969 reprint) pp. 65–70. References to traditional history are from Losi (1967), Davidson and (less often) Buckley Wood, passim.
7. The name Curamo or Kuramo seems to be applied by Dapper, *Description*, p. 307, to a different place, to the east of Lagos, but Osifekunde, in Curtin (1967) p. 239, says that 'Korume' is the Bini (Edo) name for Lagos, and Robin Law in a private communication suggests that it derives from the Edo for 'the war camp by the sea'. There are traces of other names for Lagos: Onim and Aunis, and also Awani, Awane (which must be Awori). See Osifekunde again, Robertson (1819) p. 287, Burton (1863b) p. 231, and Verger (1959).
8. Pacheco (trans. Kimble) (1937) pp. 123–4.
9. Mabogunje (1962) pp. 26–7.
10. Mabogunje (1962) p. 15, points out that the nearest natural harbour to the west is the Rokell River, 1300 miles away, and to the east the Benin River, 130 miles away.
11. There are two other villages called Isheri near Lagos: Isheri Olofin, some ten miles to the north-west, and Isheri Osun, some eight miles west-north-west. Isheri Olofin claims to be the original home of the people of the three villages, but only the village on the Ogun is ruled by an Olofin.
12. Davidson (1954) p. 52. This measurement excludes the eastern end of the island, called Ikoyi, a suburb which developed only in the present century. The swamps

separating Ikoyi from Lagos were drained into the former MacGregor Canal which until recently divided the island.

13. Ryder (1969) pp. 14, 72–3, dates the establishment of a tributary relationship by Benin over Lagos to the 1540s. Bini influence was being felt at this time as far west as Ardra and Labedde, well to the west of Lagos.
14. Egharevba, pp. 30–1.
15. Wood (1878) pp. 18–19.
16. Lander (1832) 1, pp. 47–8, also Law (1968), p. 51.
17. FO84/920, Frazer to Malmesbury, 14 Jan 1853; Adams (1823) p. 100; Herstlet (1909) p. 95. An Idejo chief of Lagos, the Onibeju Agbe, claims overlordship of the waterside up to Leke. But Osifekunde, in Curtin (1967) pp. 239–42, describes the coastal strip on the east as belonging to the kingdom of Ijebu. The present, sparse population there is mixed, containing both Ijebu and Awori. On the west, according to Frazer, Lagos territory extended to the boundaries of Iwori, some twenty-six miles distant.
18. M. Heyman, cited by Ryder (1969) pp. 157–8. The bar was especially dangerous at ebb tide when the waters poured through the narrow gap with the weight of the lagoon behind them.
19. For the role of the canoe in Lagos, see Smith (1970) pp. 521, 522–5, 531–2.
20. Lloyd (1971) passim, especially pp. 1, 47.
21. Ward-Price Commission (1933), evidence of the Eletu Odibo, the Ashogbon, the Oluwa, and the head of the Ibiga (palace slaves). The Obanikoro claimed that an Oba could be succeeded by a brother, though this was exceptional. Most Yoruba kingships rotated between a number of ruling houses.
22. Ward-Price, pp. 34, 41. Enu Owa is an open space at the intersection of Upper King and Great Bridge Streets in Isale Eko. The Idejo are significantly absent from these ceremonies marking the relationship with Benin, and perform their own ceremonies.
23. Egharevba, pp. 47–8. The delegation from Benin consisted of the Osodin, a senior palace chief, and two other officials. Egharevba places the event in 1840, but the civil war took place in 1845. The payment made, or resumed, by Kosoko is alluded to in a letter, CO147/15, from Glover to Kennedy of 17 February 1869, enclosed in Kennedy to Granville, 28 February 1869, which states that for the beach east of Lagos 'with the territory of Lagos, King Kosoko paid tribute to the King of Benin until his return to Lagos in 1862 when he ceded his rights to the British Crown; and the ambassadors of the King of Benin who up to this date had always resided with the King of Lagos returned to Benin, and called upon me to take leave, informing me that they had been recalled and that no ambassadors would in future be accredited to the King of Lagos.' On 4 March 1879, CO147/37, Governor Moloney reported to the Colonial Secretary another visit to Lagos by messengers from the Oba of Benin, who arrived in February and interviewed Oba Dosunmu and his chiefs as well as himself. (I am indebted for these references to Dr E. R. Turton.)
24. Attempts to interpret the word 'Idejo' as meaning in Yoruba 'land-owning' should be discounted, according to Dr E. R. Turton.
25. In early times, according to Davidson, p. 54, the Oba and the Oloto were thought of as equals, but with increasing wealth derived from the slave trade the Oba

eventually become dominant.
26. Johnson, p. 123, describes the Aromire as 'an admiral in the olden days of sea fighting', but the present holder of the title in an interview in April 1969 stated that his predecessors had never been among the war chiefs, nor did the Lagosian war canoes operate at sea.
27. Ward-Price, p. 100: Macaulay's evidence; also Davidson, p. 53.
28. Ward-Price, passim.
29. *Report* (1967) pp. 10 (evidence of the Oba), 27–8 (evidence of Prince W. Akinshemoyin).
30. *Report* (1967) pp. 48–51 (evidence of the Ashogbon). The first Erelu was apparently mother of the Oba. The chieftaincy is now classed for convenience among the Abagbon but previously does not seem to have belonged to any of the four grades.
31. Ward-Price, p. 12; information from the Oloto and the Asajon Oloja.
32. *Report* (1967) p. 45 (evidence of Mr K. Akinshemoyin).
33. Robertson (1819) p. 287; Adams (1823) p. 100; Scala, p. 22; Bowen, p. 218. Freeman, cited by Newbury, p. 56, n. 1, thought that in 1844 there were some 25,000 to 30,000 inhabitants.
34. FO84/950, Campbell to Clarendon, 1 May 1854; Robertson, p. 287; Payne, p. 1; Lander, I, pp. 48–9 (I am grateful to Dr Robin Law for these references).
35. Burton (1863b) pp. 222–3, and H. B. Brown (1964) chaps I and II.
36. See p. 74.
37. Adams (1823) pp. 96–9.
38. Verger (1964) pp. 24–6.
39. Ryder (1969) p. 180 n. 2.
40. Verger (1964) pp. 42–6.
41. Curtin (1969) p. 227. There was, however, a revival of the slave trade at Whydah after the Anglo-Portuguese treaty of 1810 which permitted its continuation there. Akinjogbin, pp. 194–5. See also Verger (1964) pp. 19, 23–6.
42. Adams (1823) p. 219. Verger (1959) p. 346, cites a Portuguese report of 1807 ascribing the growth of the slave trade at Lagos to a war between Dahomey and Porto Novo which interrupted supply to the western ports of the Slave Coast.
43. Ryder (1969) p. 229.
44. Adams (1823) p. 96.
45. Cock (1816) p. xxxvi.
46. Bowdich, pp. 223–6. Bowdich's informant was 'An officer in this service [the African Committee?], who resided at Lagos three years, and is the only European merchant who has survived of those who have made the attempt'. The Mahi live north of Dahomey. Robertson (1819) p. 295, writes that many of the palace servants at Lagos were Mahi.
47. Law (1977) p. 13, citing James Fawckner, *Narrative of Captain Fawckner's Travels* (London, 1837) pp. 100–1, and Gollmer's list of rulers in FO84/920 (see note 63).
48. Curtin (1969) p. 235 and table 68 on p. 237; Robertson (1819) p. 292.
49. Curtin (1969) table 71 on p. 245. The trade in Hausa slaves at Lagos, mentioned by Adams (1823) p. 222, seems to have ceased by this time.
50. Wright in Curtin (1967) p. 330.
51. Crowther, ed. Ajayi, in ibid., pp. 292, 307, 309–10. Crowther was born in

Oshogun, in the Ibarapa district of the kingdom of Oyo, to which his family apparently migrated from Ketu, further west. He refers to Oyo as his 'own dialect' in his narrative. In a discussion at Abeokuta with Richard Burton in November 1861, one of the Egba chiefs claimed that Crowther was 'a subject of the Alake' of Abeokuta, but apart from Ibarapa being subject to Egba raids at this time there seems no ground for this: Burton (1863a) p. 285.

52. CA2/067, journal of W. Marsh.
53. Ross (1965) pp. 79–80. Marsh, in a letter of 13 April 1848 to Venn (CA2/067), wrote that Martinez controlled two factories, one 120 miles west of Badagry and one eight miles to the east.
54. Law (1968) p. 51.
55. Losi (1967) pp. 15–16.
56. Ajayi (1963a) pp. 169–71. No references are attached to this seminar paper.
57. C. Lloyd (1949) p. 61. He establishes on p. 67 that the Preventive Squadron was probably created in 1819, but from 1808 there was a small but continuous anti-slavery patrol off the coast of West Africa. By 1851 the number of vessels employed had risen to twenty-seven (twelve sloops and brigs, fifteen steam). Subsequently it fell to fifteen in 1855, twenty-one in 1858, and eleven in 1860 (Lloyd, pp. 282–3).
58. The motives are discussed in Kopytoff (1965) pp. 38–43. See also Newbury (1965) pp. 196–200.
59. Townsend, pp. 15–19; Freeman, pp. 229–30. The latter writes of 265 emigrants landing at Lagos from three vessels, all of whom were robbed. He mentions, incidentally, that the Oba, who participated in the robbery, had lately died, which goes some way to confirm Gollmer's date of 1841 for the accession of Oluwole.
60. Ajayi (1965) p. 29.
61. Kopytoff, p. 70. Some legitimate trade may have been done much earlier. For the reported establishment of the English merchant Houston at Lagos in 1825, see CO2/16, Bathurst to Clapperton, 30 July 1825, in Newbury (1965) p. 63. When the C.M.S. missionaries reached Badagry in 1845 they found that an English factor, Captain Parsons, representing Thomas Hutton's firm, had been living there for several years (Phillips (1966) p. 97).
62. Austen (1970) pp. 257–9, 274.
63. See Law (1968) passim, for the dating of the reigns of the Lagos Oba. A list of rulers, with dates, was compiled by the Rev. C. A. Gollmer and is enclosed in FO84/920, Campbell to Clarendon, 11 September 1853.
64. Ajayi (1963a) p. 169; Losi (1967) p. 19; Law (1977) p. 13, citing Clapperton, *Journal of an African Mission,* entry for 4 Dec. 1825.
65. Lander (1832) I, pp. 37, 48–50, describes how the young Oba fled to Badagry accompanied by his infirm mother, whom he had placed in a 'cage or box' on the shoulders of four slaves, and carrying his father's skull – the headless corpse having been buried at Benin. According to the Landers, the Hausa slaves, whom they describe as mallams, or learned Muslim, were 'very respectable, and are never called on by their master except when required for war, supporting themselves by trading for slaves which they sell to the Europeans'.
66. Lander (1832) on his second visit does not allude to the presence of Europeans in Badagry and at one point (I, p. 16) almost implies that none were then resident there. But in his account of his visit in 1827 (returning from Sokoto after Clapperton's

death), he describes how three Portuguese living there denounced him to Adele as an English spy (Clapperton (1829) p. 325).
67. Lander (1832) I, pp. 51–2.
68. Ibid. I, p. 14.
69. Law (1977) p. 20.
70. Quoted in Yoruba by Losi (1967) p. 26. The English translation is: 'If it ends in war, let it end in war. If it ends in revolt, let it end in revolt.'
71. p. 29.
72. Ajayi (1961) p. 99.
73. This event is precisely dated by Gollmer, writing in September 1853 (see note 63 above). The detail of the narrative derives from Losi, pp. 29–34. The Eletu's return is also mentioned in Townsend's journal entry for 21 July 1845 (CA2/085(b)). Euler Ajayi ('A Yoruba Historian', 1905–6) p. 12, attributes Kosoko's enmity to the Eletu, and also the civil war during Adele's second reign, to the Eletu's having brought about the conviction and drowning of Opolu, Kosoko's sister, as a witch.
74. Phillips (1966) p. 110.

Chapter 2

1. For the 'colonial' thesis, see for example Geary, p. 2, and Burns, chap. x. It is embryonically present in Burton (1863b), for example, on p. 189, despite his detached and sardonic tone (and his criticisms of British rule in his Indian books). The 'abominable traffic' was a common phrase, used for example by Beecroft in his despatch to Palmerston, FO84/858, 21 February 1851.
2. For the 'anti-colonial' thesis, see Ajayi (1961) p. 97, and Gavin (1958) chaps IV and V. Gavin (1961) summarises his views.
3. Robertson (1819) pp. 290–1.
4. C. Lloyd (1949) p. 156; Phillips (1966) pp. 105–6, citing CA2/O5 and CA2/M1. On 25 March 1847 Townsend wrote to the C.M.S. in London (CA2/085(b)) that the efforts of the British cruisers had no visible effect on the trade. 'How then is this monster evil to be put down? The natives say, drive away the Portuguese etc. If there be a moral right to capture the slaves at sea I cannot see why it is bounded by the limits of the ocean.' The American missionaries of the Southern Baptist Convention were also stressing the importance of Lagos. See, for example, Baptist papers, Bowen to Taylor, 21 November 1851, describing the harbour and the 'rich . . . almost vacant' hinterland.
5. FO84/816, Palmerston to Beecroft, 25 February 1850.
6. FO84/816, Beecroft (on board H.M.S. *Bonnetto*) to Palmerston, 22 July 1850.
7. FO84/858, Sagbua and Chiefs of Abeokuta to Palmerston, 15 August 1851, under cover of Beecroft to Palmerston, 15 August 1851.
8. C. Lloyd (1949) pp. 92–7.
9. PP, LIV (1852), Addington (FO) to Admiralty, 11 October 1850. Beecroft figures in most works dealing with the making of Nigeria in the nineteenth century and is the subject of a short study by Dike (1956b).
10. *CMI* (1851) p. 162. See Ayandele, pp. 5–6, for the general positions taken by the pro- and anti-mission factions in the area.

11. Akitoye's letters of 1845 to the British commodore and to the governor of Cape Coast Castle, professing his intention to abjure the slave trade, to which he refers in his petition to Beecroft of February 1851, must have been written after his deposition.
12. Phillips (1966) pp. 113, 122, based on references in CA2/082. Ajayi (1965) p. 38, writes that this connection with Martinez 'destroys the simple picture that the Lagos dispute was between slave traders and anti-slave traders'. But this need not affect an interpretation of the motives of the British missionaries and officials who, doubtless without trusting Akitoye far, nevertheless saw in him a useful instrument in their war against the slave trade.
13. PP, LIV (1852) missionaries at Abeokuta to Fanshawe, 3 November, 1850. See also Adams to Fanshawe, 24 March 1851, Gollmer to Fanshawe, 26 March 1851, and Fanshawe to Admiralty, 29 April 1851. Verger (1964) p. 37.
14. FO84/858, Beecroft to Stanley, 4 January 1851.
15. FO84/858, Beecroft to Palmerston, 21 February 1851; Losi (1967) p. 35. For the help given Akitoye by Gollmer in preparing the petition, see Ajayi (1965) p. 69, n. 3.
16. FO84/858, Beecroft to Palmerston, 24 February 1851.
17. Phillips (1966) p. 161, citing FO84/858, Beecroft to Palmerston, 19 April 1851.
18. FO84/858, Palmerston to Beecroft, 20 February 1851, 21 February 1851. Ajayi (1965) p. 71, describes the instructions as 'a veritable cocktail of imperialistic gin and philanthropic tonic'.
19. Gavin (1961) p. 25.
20. The delay was not unusual. Dispatches dated in October 1850, for example, reached Lagos only in July 1851, according to FO84/858, Beecroft to Palmerston, 27 July 1851. Beecroft suspected that delays occurred in the Secretary's office at Freetown.
21. Gollmer in his letter of 5 July 1851 in *CMI*, II, p. 252 estimates the force at 600, while Beecroft in FO84/858, Beecroft to Palmerston 4 October 1851, passing on a report from Frazer, then vice-consul at Whydah, says 1000. See also PP, LIV (1852) 221, Heath to Bruce, 11 July 1851, estimating the temporary Egba occupation force at Badagry under Bashorun Shomoye at 200 to 300 men.
22. *CMI*, II (1851) p. 253, Gollmer to C.M.S., 5 July 1851.
23. CA2/044c, Gollmer's journal, 7 July 1851, 22 July 1851; FO84/886, Gollmer to Frazer, 4 August 1851.
24. Bowen, p. 121.
25. 'Obba Shorun' to Jones, 3 July 1851. PP, LIV (1852) 221, pp. 130–1. The Bashorun since March 1852 had been Shomoye: Biobaku (1857) p. 42.
26. PP, LIV (1852) 221, Palmerston to Admiralty, 27 September 1851; Phillips (1966) pp. 179–81. According to Stock, II, pp. 111–13, Crowther was also received by Queen Victoria at Windsor and was told by the Prince Consort that Lagos 'ought to be knocked down by all means'.
27. FO84/858, Palmerston to Beecroft, 28 October 1851. A reference to Kosoko as 'the usurper who has unfortunately obtained possession of the chief power at Lagos' was deleted from the draft of this despatch.
28. PP, LIV (1852) 221, Admiralty to Bruce, 14 October 1851; Bruce to Admiralty, 6 December 1851.

29. Cell, p. 216.
30. FO84/892, Bruce to Admiralty, 1 November 1851. Bruce also expressed doubts about Akitoye's personal qualities as a ruler.
31. PP, LIV (1852) 221, Admiralty to Bruce, 14 October 1851.
32. FO84/858, Beecroft to Palmerston, 5 September 1851.
33. FO84/858, Beecroft to Palmerston, 26 November 1851; Losi (1967) p. 35.
34. Losi (1967) p. 35.
35. FO84/858, Beecroft to Palmerston, 26 November 1851, enclosing a note of the conference held 'at the Chief's house at the Town of Lagos' on 20 November 1851, signed by the British representatives on 24 November 1851.
36. FO84/858, Beecroft (on board H.M.S. *Bloodhound*) to Commander Forbes, 22 November 1851.
37. FO84/858, Beecroft to Palmerston, 26 November 1851.
38. Gavin (1961) p. 25.
39. See note 17 above.
40. Phillips (1966) points out that the specific instructions for the attack on Lagos were issued by Sir Francis Baring, First Lord of the Admiralty and a close associate and parliamentary supporter of the C.M.S. (PP, LIV (1851) 138, Baring and Dundas to Bruce, 14 October, 1851).
41. FO84/886, Granville to Beecroft, 24 January 1852.
42. Burns, chap. X; C. Lloyd (1949) chap. XI; Ward, pp. 205–15. The consular accounts are in FO84/858, Beecroft to Palmerston, 26 November 1851 (the first attack), and FO84/886, Beecroft to Palmerston/Granville, 3 January 1852 (the second attack). See also PP, LIV (1852) 221.
43. The fortification of the western as well as the eastern bank of the river has been overlooked by the authorities cited in note 42 above.
44. Burton (1863*b*) p. 212.
45. Bowen, pp. 122–3.
46. FO84/886, Beecroft to Palmerston/Granville, 2 March, 1852, enclosing Beecroft to Oba of Benin, 4 December 1851.
47. FO84/886, Beecroft to Palmerston/Granville, 3 January 1852; *Destruction of Lagos*, p. 19; Losi (1967) p. 36. The site of the Exhibition Centre on the Marina of Lagos – opposite to the site of the former consulate – is remembered as having been one of the focal points of the battle: Davidson, p. 65 (remarks added by the Rev. J. A. J. Ogunbiyi). Loopholes in the walls of a house surviving until recently near the Yacht Club at the east end of the Marina were said to have been made for the defence of Lagos in 1851: letter from C. R. Niven, *Nigerian Field*, XXVI (1961) 2, p. 93.
48. Burton (1863*a*) vol. I, p. 17. 'Takpa' is probably the same word as Tarkwa, now applied to the beach near the lighthouse and between the main and subsidiary moles.
49. PP, LIV (1852) 221, Forbes to Bruce, 9 December 1851. For Yoruba fortifications, see Ajayi and Smith (1971) part I, chapter 3.
50. See Map. p. 29. This chart, dated November 1851, seems to be the first detailed map of Lagos and its harbour, though Captain Horsley of Liverpool had published a map of 'Lagos and its channels' in Laurie's *African Pilot*, 1789.
51. This is probably the village now called Ogogoro (which could mean 'the tall one' or is otherwise the word for locally distilled spirits).

52. 'Agidingbi' seems to be an onomatopoeic word to convey the sound of the guns.
53. According to the young Samuel Davis (or Davies), formerly a pupil of the Sierra Leone Grammar School, who had been on board the *Bloodhound* during the second engagement, Kosoko's men 'armed and manned their canoes' for the battle (*CMI*, III, 1852, pp. 62–1), but none of the accounts, including Davis's, mention any part played by these canoes. For an account of the training of James and Samuel Davis by the Royal Navy, see FO84/950, Campbell to Clarendon, 14 August 1854.
54. PP, LIV (1852) 221, Gardner to Jones, 29 December 1851, and Coote to Jones, also 29 December 1851, list forty-six guns which were disposed of by these means. They were described as guns or 'carronades', of iron or brass. One eighteen-pounder, placed near the palace, was mounted on 'a well-executed carriage'.
55. Ajayi (1961) pp. 96–7.
56. Idem, p. 98.
57. Gavin (1961) p. 26.
58. Phillips (1966) pp. 1, 6, 194.

Chapter 3

1. See Crowder (1971) for examples of West African resistance, mostly in the last quarter of the nineteenth century.
2. FO84/886, Malmesbury to Beecroft, 23 February 1852.
3. *Destruction of Lagos*, pp. 19–21.
4. This lack of interest extends to later historians. Robinson and Gallagher, for example, p. 35, dismiss the event in one sentence: 'In 1852 Palmerston imposed an anti-slave treaty on Lagos'.
5. *BFSP*, XLII, Bruce to Admiralty, 11 February 1852; Bruce to Senior Naval Officer, 15 June 1852; FO84/894, Bruce to Baudin, 6 April 1852.
6. FO84/893, Wilmot to Bruce, 11 February 1852; FO84/894 Wilmot to Bruce, 28 February 1852; FO84/920, Wodehouse to Campbell, 28 February 1853. For the Ijebu treaty, see also *CMI*, III (1852) p. 131. Gollmer took pains to entertain the Ijebu chiefs in the hope of being allowed to visit their king and capital.
7. Dike (1956a) p. 100.
8. Dike (1956a) p. 145, comments that 'There was some unity between the events.'
9. The reception of the two chiefs at Lagos is described in White's journal, 13 and 14 January 1852 (CA2/087(a)). Gollmer, *CMI*, IV (1853) p. 273, identifies Akinpelu Possu with a chief at Badagry who was expelled from there in 1851 and came to Ado. Crowther, journal, 21 June 1851 (CA2 031), corrects this: 'This Possu of Badagry has often been confounded with Possu of Lagos ... both were adherents of Kosoko and their characters assimilated.'
10. FO84/894, Wilmot to Bruce, 28 February 1852; FO84/920, Frazer to Malmesbury, 11 March 1853; Newbury (1961) pp. 57–60. Sandeman came to Lagos to start trading in August 1852 while McCoskry did not remove from Badagry to Lagos until July 1853, according to FO84/1002, Thomas Hutton to Campbell, 25 June 1856, cited by Folayan (1969) pp. 28–9. Had these merchants been resident in Lagos, as Newbury implies, they would in all probability have signed the

commercial agreement of 28 February 1851. For the price of palm oil see Newbury (1961) pp. 43, 60.
11. Newbury (1961) p. 58. See also Newbury (1972) passim.
12. See Marion Johnson, parts I and II, and A. G. Hopkins (1966) both passim.
13. PP, LXI (1862) no. 2, pp. 2–4. The merchant signatories were two Britons (Duggan and Sillis), an Austrian subject (the Hungarian Amadie), a Portuguese (Furra), and a Hamburg supercargo (Oitzmann). Akitoye signed with four chiefs, who included Ajenia and Possu. Lieutenant-Commander Bedingfeld, R.N., of H.M.S. *Jackal* witnessed the document.
14. Scala (1862) pp. 21–47, section headed 'Lagos' (the *Memorie* are not divided into numbered chapters).
15. See FO84/920, Campbell to Clarendon, 29 July 1853, in which Campbell recounts how on meeting Scala at Freetown in 1853 he recognised him as 'one of those clever shrewd Genoese captains sailing under the Sardinian flag' who had often baffled the English captains. Scala affirmed to Campbell his intention of confining himself to legitimate trade. See also Smith (1973b).
16. Scala, p. 39, adds that these chiefs were afterward found to be supporters of Kosoko, and it seems probable that they were Ajenia and Possu.
17. Bowen (1857) p. 218, estimates the population of Ibadan and Ilorin as 70,000, Abeokuta as 60,000, and Ijaye as 35,000, compared with 20,000 at Lagos.
18. *CMG*, 1853, p. 57.
19. Miss Tucker's *Abeokuta, or Sunrise within the Tropics*, was published in 1853.
20. *CMI*, III (1852) p. 59; C.M.S., CA2/043, Gollmer to Venn, 7 January 1852, cited by Ayandele (1966) p. 8.
21. Enclosed in CA2/043, Gollmer to Venn, 12 March 1852. A copy was also enclosed in FO84/976, Campbell to Clarendon, 28 May 1855. The Idejo landowner in the Marina area was apparently Chief Onitolo whereas the chiefs who witnessed the grant were Ojinnia, Pellu, the Olumegbon, Koka and the Olisa.
22. The services are described in White's journal, reproduced in *CMI*, III (1852) pp. 125–6. The first sermon was based on I Kings, iii, 5–14 (Solomon's Dream). The first eucharist was presumably celebrated soon after Gollmer's arrival.
23. *CMR*, XXIV (1853) pp. 126–30, extracts from White's journal. See Kopytoff, p. 300, for a biographical sketch of White, who was ordained priest in 1857.
24. *CMP* (1852/3) p. 37; *CMR*, XXIV (1853) extracts from Gollmer's journal, pp. 132–3; *CMR*, XXV (1854) p. 121f., extracts from Gollmer's journal, and p. 130, extracts from White's journal. The Ile Alapako is seen in the background to a group photograph in Gollmer (1889) p. 144.
25. MP, Gold Coast, 1853: Report of the Badagry, Lagos and Abeokutan stations for the year ending December 1852; Thompson to Freeman, 10 June 1853; Moses to Freeman, also 10 June 1853. Martin was buried in the new premises allotted to the mission.
26. C.M.S., CA2/043, Gollmer to Venn, 6 April 1853, cited by Kopytoff, p. 86.
27. Kopytoff, p. 96.
28. Kopytoff, p. 87, writes that 'Amaro' 'meant commonly "those who had been away from home"', but this seems rather unlikely.
29. *CMR*, XXV (1854) p. 122.
30. See Laotan, passim.

31. Gbadamosi, pp. 44, 49, 50, 57–9.
32. According to H. Macaulay in his evidence to the Ward-Price *Commission of Inquiry re the Head of the House of Decemo*, p. 93, Kosoko went first to Badore on the south shore. The anonymous *Historical Background of Epe* (a manuscript in the possession of the Oluepe, or chief of the Lagosian element in Epe) mentions that he stayed at 'Igbodu near Ejinrin', which is probably Iboju on the south shore to the south of Ejinrin. The Oloja Epe (ruler of Ijebu Epe) believes that Kosoko went first to Badore and thence to Epe, where he was forced by the inhabitants to withdraw; he then went to Iboju and from there negotiated with the Awujale for permission to stay at Epe. A similar account is given by T. Ola Avoseh (1960) pp. 16, 20.
33. See 'Osifekunde of Ijebu,' ed. P. C. Lloyd, in Curtin (1967). Osifekunde's account refers to a period just before 1820.
34. FO84/886, Beecroft to Granville, 3 January 1852. Macaulay in Ward-Price, p. 93, estimated Kosoko's original followers at about 2000, adding that they travelled in fifty to sixty canoes. This seems too large a number, though it may have swelled to this at Epe.
35. For Tapa (whose name is Yoruba for 'Nupe'), see Losi (1967) pp. 80–2. Losi lists Kosoko's war chiefs on p. 10. Commander Wilmot had given Tapa permission to return to Lagos, telling Bruce that he enjoyed great credit there and 'will take the cargo off a vessel off hand at once' (FO84/894, 28 February 1852). Tapa did not avail himself of this permission and remained at Kosoko's right hand. Lima may have been a member of the Cerqueira Lima family prominent at Bahia, mentioned by Verger (1964) p. 35. The Muslims in Kosoko's emigration were in such force, or of such influence, that according to Gbadamosi, p. 44, they 'virtually turned Epe into a Muslim settlement'.
36. Palma was the name given, presumably by the Portuguese, to Orimedu.
37. According to the Oluepe, Kosoko sent representatives, to whom he gave the Oyo title of Bale for a village head, to govern the outlying parts of his state. They were placed at, for example, Leke, Orimedu and Oriba.
38. According to the *Historical Background*, Leke was unoccupied when Kosoko's men arrived, although local Ijebu used to gather salt from the beach there. Osifekunde, in Curtin (1967) pp. 239–43, refers to the land between the lagoon and the sea as 'Ikebekou', an old chart name mentioned by Burton (1863b) p. 231, but now unknown, and says that it was Ijebu territory from Lagos in the west to Makun in the east. The present names given to the area are Ehin Osa, 'the other side of the lagoon', that is, the south shore, and Etikun, 'by the ocean', or the seashore.
39. A copy of the Awujale's letter of 2 November 1852 is among the C.M.S. papers (CA2/08).
40. The relationship was through Olufaderin who was either (according to tradition at Epe) daughter of an Awujale and mother of Kosoko or (as related at Ereko) granddaughter of an Awujale and grandmother of Kosoko. Avoseh (1960) p. 16, gives the woman's name as Erelu and says that she was Kosoko's great grandmother.
41. Ayantuga, pp. 70–3. The dating of the death of Awujale Fagbajoye Anikilaya and the accession of Ademiyewo Fidipote derives from Payne (1893).
42. Dalzel, p. 83.
43. Ayandele (1966) p. 36. The Ilaje canoemen carried on a considerable trade across the lagoon, eastwards with Benin and westwards with the coastal Ijebu and Lagos. A

tradition recorded in the nineteenth century claimed for the Ilaje the privilege of conveying the remains of a dead Oba of Lagos to Benin.
44. FO84/895, Townsend to Bruce, 20 May 1852, covering the chiefs' letter to Bruce of 'this day's date' (the copy is dated 28 May, apparently in error for 20 May).
45. FO84/893, Bruce to Admiralty, 11 February 1852. See also Bruce to Forbes, 13 February 1852, severely discouraging Forbes's suggestion that the British Government should purchase a part of Abeokuta.
46. FO84/895, Bruce to Abeokuta chiefs, undated (but probably June 1852); Admiralty to Stanley, 26 August 1852, enclosing Bruce to Admiralty, 13 July, 1852, minuted by Stanley on 28 August 1852; Admiralty to Foreign Office, 26 August 1852, enclosing correspondence with Townsend and Abeokuta chiefs, minuted by Malmesbury on 29 August 1852. FO84/891, Stanley to Hamilton (Admiralty) 30 August 1852, FO84/886, Malmesbury to Beecroft, 14 September 1852. See also Baptist papers, Bowen to Taylor, 7 September 1853: 'Lagos is in fact a British possession and I suppose will soon be formally reckoned a colony.'
47. PP, LIV (1852) 221, Bruce to Admiralty, 7 January 1852. Bruce also suggested the appointment of ten consular agents at various places on the coast. The latter might be West Indians or Sierra Leoneans.
48. Until 1825 British consuls were usually merchants. After the reform in that year nearly all became members of the civil service, drawing a fixed salary instead of fees and answerable to a separate department in the Foreign Office. After 1832 non-salaried consuls and some salaried ones (as in the case of Campbell) were again allowed to trade.
49. FO84/886, Beecroft to Malmesbury, 28 June 1852; Malmesbury to Beecroft, 13 September 1852.
50. PP, LXXIII (1854), Beecroft to Malmesbury, 4 February 1853. In FO2/9, writing to Malmesbury on 13 January 1853, Frazer gives 10 December 1852 as the date of his return to Lagos to take up his post.
51. FO84/816, Palmerston to Beecroft, 11 December 1850; Palmerston to Frazer, 12 December 1850; Frazer (from Knowsley) to Beecroft, 29 January 1850. FO84/920, Clarendon to Campbell, 15 September 1853; Campbell to Clarendon, 19 September 1853. See also FO84/886, Beecroft to Malmesbury, 19 February 1852, transmitting Frazer's journal of his mission to Abomey. Frazer also annoyed Palmerston by asking the Foreign Office to provide him with books on navigation, a watch and a compass. See FO2/5, Palmerston's minutes on Frazer's letters of 20 December 1850 (on FO2/4) and 10 January 1851.
52. FO84/886, Russell to Frazer, 20 December 1852; Russell to Beecroft, 22 December 1852. FO84/920, Frazer to Russell, 13 January 1853; Clarendon to Frazer, 28 February 1853. FO2/9, Frazer to Gollmer, 27 January 1853; Gollmer to Frazer, 1 February 1853. Rev. J. White thought that McCoskry and Sandeman, angered by their failure to stake claims for waterside plots on their own first visits to Lagos, had caused the trouble over the C.M.S. land: CA2/087(a), White to Straith, 18 April 1854. See also Phillips (1966) pp. 190–1.
53. *CMR*, XXI (1850) p. 50. 'The Chief Mewu is disposed to listen: he attends Service on the Lord's Day with much regularity, and is friendly to the missionaries; yet he serves his own gods.' C.M.S. sources at this time refer constantly to the 'spiritual indifference' at Badagry.

54. PP, LXXIII (1854), Bruce to Admiralty, 3 March 1853 and enclosures; Phillips (1966) p. 217.
55. *CMR*, xxv, p. 124, extracts from Gollmer's journal, 16 April 1853. Gollmer was invited to this meeting but did not attend as it was 'of a political nature'.
56. FO84/920, Frazer to Clarendon, 8 April 1853.
57. FO84/920, Frazer to Clarendon, 30 May 1853; Clarendon to Campbell, 18 July 1853, enclosing Akitoye's complaint to Bruce.
58. *CMR*, xxv (1854) pp. 124–7, Gollmer's journal; Losi (1967) p. 38. Losi adds that the Egba force numbered 800 and was commanded by Bashorun Shomoye.
59. PP, LXXIII (1854), Phillips to Bruce, 23 June 1853, and numerous enclosures.
60. Scala, pp. 61–4, gives another version of the affair which, though probably less accurate than that in the Admiralty and consular papers, supplements the official account. According to Scala, Oba Akitoye was under the influence of Madame Tinubu and implicated in her clandestine slaving activities. The consignment in question had been sent by Tinubu to Martinez and had reached Porto Novo in such poor condition that Martinez demanded a reduction in the agreed price. Tinubu refused, saying that she would rather drown her slaves, whereat Martinez seized her agent and the slaves and sent them in revenge to the British consul in Lagos. The embarrassed Oba tried to put the blame on Ajenia and Possu, who were also associated in the enterprise, ordering their arrest. To avoid this the two chiefs prepared to offer resistance. Scala says nothing of the parts played by Amadie or Ojo Martins. His version is probably that preferred by the European merchants at Lagos. Ross (1965) does not mention the affair in his study of Martinez.
61. FO84/920, Frazer to Russell, 13 January 1853.
62. FO2/9, Frazer to Clarendon, 27 June 1853.
63. FO2/9, Wodehouse to Beecroft and to Frazer, both 19 February 1853; Wodehouse, to Campbell, nos 1 and 2, 28 February 1853, FO2/10, Admiralty to Wodehouse, 20 January 1853; FO to Treasury, 19 February 1853; Foreign Office to Bruce, 28 February 1853.
64. FO84/920, Frazer to Clarendon, 30 May 1853. There is more correspondence from Frazer on FO2/12, mostly about his financial claims against the Foreign Office. In his last letter in this volume (Frazer to Wodehouse, 21 February 1854) he writes that he is leaving next day for Lagos, presumably to trade, but he has not been traced further in the papers.
65. FO2/9, Campbell to Clarendon, 21 July 1853.

Chapter 4

1. FO2/5, Governor of Sierra Leone to Grey, 28 November 1850; Fyfe (1962) pp. 203, 226–7, 232; Brooks (1970) pp. 202, 204, 210; Kopytoff, p. 320, n. 67; private communications from Mr Christopher Fyfe.
2. FO84/976, Campbell to Clarendon, 4 October 1855, in which Campbell mentions that he had attained his fifty-fifth year on 27 July 1855. In FO2/17, Campbell to Clarendon, 28 June 1856, the consul writes of his twenty years on the coast, but in his application for the post, FO2/10, Campbell to Bruce, 27 December 1852, he

3. FO2/11, Foreign Office to Campbell, 29 August 1854 and subsequent correspondence about the French Foreign Ministry's allegation that Campbell had improperly withheld certain monies belonging to the French consulate in Freetown (see p. 67).
4. Fyfe (1962) p. 318; Kopytoff, p. 292. Mrs Lewis was born Mary Anne Campbell (or Potts?).
5. FO84/1002, Campbell to Clarendon, 26 June 1856.
6. Photography does not seem to have reached Lagos in Campbell's time, though there survives a purported photograph of Oba Akitoye (Nigeria Museum, Lagos, envelopes 118/2 and 206/1).
7. FO84/950, minute on Campbell to Clarendon, 1 May 1854. It is interesting that the Foreign Secretary should have regarded it as his duty to read dispatches from the consul at Lagos. The volume of correspondence in the Foreign Office was rising throughout the nineteenth century, and dispatches received from and sent to posts abroad increased between 1841 and 1853 from 20,047 to 35,104 (Jones (1971) pp. 32, 80).
8. Frazer in correspondence with Malmesbury, FO2/9, 12 January 1853 and 11 March 1853, had complained of having no 'proper place to reside in'. Presumably he hired lodgings with a local European merchant, though Akitoye had agreed in November 1852 to put him up in the Iga until he could erect a house for himself: PP, LXXIII (1854), Beecroft to Malmesbury, 4 February 1853. Also, Phillips (1966) pp. 228–9, citing CA2/043.
9. FO2/11, Campbell to Clarendon, 13 June 1854; FO84/976, Campbell to Clarendon, 25 October 1855.
10. All lagoons are called *osa* in Yoruba, as opposed to *okun* for sea and *odo* for river. The eastern or Lagos lagoon is known by the various names of the places on the shore, for example, Osa Eko (Lagos lagoon), Osa Ikorodu, Osa Epe. Nineteenth-century European observers mistook the word *osa* for the proper name of the lagoon itself and its extension towards Badagry.
11. The following maps cover the area: Nigeria 1:50,000, Sheet 279, Lagos SE; Sheet 280, Ijebu–Ode SE: Sheet 281, Ijebu Ife SW; Sheet 281 A, Abigi NW, NE. For some remarks on the lagoon system and its possible changes over the last few centuries, see the introduction to Newbury (1961).
12. Smith (1970) pp. 522–5.
13. Ibid., pp. 525–32; Ajayi and Smith (1971) appendix II.
14. The Iso, living near Whydah and speaking a dialect of Egun, were well known as mercenaries in the canoe warfare of the lagoon, and continued to use spears as well as muskets. Burton (1863b) p. 195, writing about the British attack on Porto Novo in 1861, describes Iso tactics as being to hurl a club, causing an adversary to duck his head, and then to transfix him with a spear.
15. For West African diplomacy, see Smith (1973a) and Smith (1976) chapter II.
16. Argyle, p. 25, citing Dalzel, pp. 175, 205, 213. But Argyle's contention that an Oyo embassy was established, that is, resident, in Abomey, is not substantiated by Dalzel in these passages or elsewhere.

17. Most cases of the use of the word *ajele* by the Yoruba refer to representatives living in subject towns, so there is not an exact equivalence. But the British consul in Lagos did occupy a position of greater authority and influence than was normally the case, and in this resembled the ajele of, for example, the Ibadan empire of the mid-nineteenth century.
18. FO84/920, Campbell to Clarendon, 30 July 1853.
19. PP, LXXIII (1854), Price to Stuart & Douglas, 2 August 1853.
20. The following account of the events of August 1853 is based on: FO84/920, Campbell to Clarendon, 1 September 1853; FO84/976, Campbell to Clarendon, 30 July 1855, replying to charges made against him by the missionaries; *CMR*, XXV (1854) p. 128, extracts from Gollmer's journal, and pp. 131–3, extracts from White's journal.
21. The account in *CMI*, IV (1853) pp. 267–9, claims that Akitoye's men spent 5 August in distributing guns and powder, and did not begin hostilities until 9 a.m. on 6 August, when they interpreted the arrival of the boats from the *Waterwitch* as a signal to take action against Ajenia and Possu. The consul's detailed and explicit account seems likely to provide the more accurate version of events, and also agrees with the account in the missionary journals.
22. Scala's allegation (*Memorie*, pp. 66–8) that Madame Tinubu collaborated with Ajenia and Possu to bring about a pro-Kosoko rising is uncomfirmed by the contemporary reports of Campbell and the missionaries. It is, moreover, inherently unlikely, even though she must have grasped the implications of the new regime for her slave trade.
23. This was widely believed by the merchantile community, who were in general hostile to the missionaries and sympathetic towards Kosoko. Scala, p. 68, says that Gollmer, after consulting Commander Phillips, sent a white hankerchief to Akitoye as a signal to open fire, which bears out subsequent recollections by the consul and Commander Gardner in FO84/1002 (Phillips (1966) pp. 231–3).
24. Gollmer, letter of 8 September 1853, *CMI* (1853) p. 268, estimated the number there at 4000. They had built sheds against the rain and the compound looked and sounded like a busy market.
25. Canoes even of this size must have been constructed in the traditional manner, from felled trees, trimmed by axes and then dug and burnt out. See R. Smith (1970) pp. 519–21.
26. Newbury (1961) p. 55.
27. Akitoye, pp. 34, 54, explains how the hostility engendered among the Ijebu by the southward move of the Egba in the late 1820s was abating in the 1850s. Egba use of the Ogun, their highway to the lagoon and Lagos, depended in part on Ijebu goodwill, and Akitoye says that they obtained this in 1852.
28. FO84/920, Campbell to Clarendon, 10 September 1853, with enclosures of 23 August 1853.
29. FO84/920, Campbell to Clarendon, 11 September 1853, no. 11. The letter to Kosoko is dated 1 September 1853 and the reply from Epe 7 September 1853.
30. It was usual for an Oba's death to be kept secret in the palace for at least some days, but on this occasion, probably because of the dangerous situation, the news seems to have been promptly given to Gollmer.
31. FO84/920, Campbell to Clarendon, 3 September 1853; Losi (1967) p. 39. Scala,

p. 69, ever dramatic and ever hostile to Akitoye, the protégé of the 'Protestant' (actually Anglican) mission, writes that the Oba's death was caused by his 'sensual excesses'.

32. Campbell to Clarendon, 3 September 1853. For the fisherman story, see FO84/1031, Campbell to Clarendon, 1 September 1857, and also Scala, pp. 69–70. Scala adds the rather unlikley detail that Dosunmu was unwilling to accept the throne and that Gollmer sent for Madame Tinubu who persuaded him to do so. Nobody seems to have thought of asking for the Oba of Benin's confirmation on this occasion.
33. FO84/920, Campbell to Clarendon, 10 September 1853; 7 October 1853; FO84/950, Campbell to Clarendon, 10 August 1854. The first gives a figure of 3000–4000 for the Egba warriors; the figure of about 2000 in the last seems more credible. See also Baptist papers, Bowen to Taylor, 7 September 1853.
34. FO84/950, Campbell to Clarendon, 10 August 1854; the payment was approved in Clarendon to Campbell, 23 November 1854. The exact sum was £112 10s. 0d. which obtained 100 bags of cowries, expended in 70 bags to the Egba, 10 bags to the Iso, 17 bags to the chiefs of 'Rame', and 3 bags to the messengers. 'Rame', described as west of Ijebu, presumably refers to Ijebu Remo, at this time hostile to Ijebu Ode.
35. FO84/920, Campbell to Clarendon, 11 September 1853; FO84/954, Bruce to Admiralty, 9 January 1853.
36. *CMR*, xxv, p. 129, extracts from Gollmer's journal, 15 September 1853, 23 September 1853.
37. No name resembling this can be found in the area on the 1:50,000 maps.
38. FO84/920, Campbell to Clarendon, 20 October 1853, enclosing Phillips's report of 10 October 1853. See also FO84/976, Campbell to Clarendon, 17 October 1855, in which the consul writes that the naval force had been intended to cover a landing by the Lagos and the Egba and that the Egba captains subsequently admitted that their interest had been in taking prisoners and not in fighting.
39. Olomowewe does not appear on the map, but the name is said at Epe to be applied still to a village on the coast midway between Orimedu (Palma) and Leke.
40. PP, LXXIII (1854), Phillips to Bruce, 28 October 1853; FO84/920, Campbell to Clarendon, 31 October 1853. According to Losi (1924) pp. 69–70, the Egba on their way through Palma stole a box of gold coins from the house of Mr Coates, a merchant there.
41. FO84/920, Campbell to Clarendon, 30 November 1853.
42. FO84/920, Campbell to Clarendon, 20 December 1853, enclosing a copy of his letter of 13 December 1853 to 'Sagbua and chiefs' at Abeokuta; FO84/950, Clarendon to Campbell, 7 March 1854, approving his action.
43. FO84/920, Campbell to Clarendon, 31 October 1853; FO84/954, Bruce to Admiralty, 21 January 1854.
44. *CMI*, IV (1853) p. 271.
45. In 1858 Norman Bedingfeld, now a captain, accompanied Livingstone and Kirk on their expedition to the Zambezi, but soon resigned after a disagreement with 'the Doctor'. His name has also been spelt 'Bedingfield'. There is a photograph of him, reproduced from the *Illustrated London News*, in Oliver Ransford, *Livingstone's Lake: The Drama of Nyasa* (London, 1968) p. 86.

46. 'Palaver' derives from the Portuguese *palabra*, 'word', and has the double sense of 'trouble' or 'fuss' and 'conference'.
47. FO84/950, Campbell to Clarendon, 29 January 1854; FO84/954, Bruce to Admiralty, 23 January 1854, enclosing Bedingfeld's report of 19 January 1854. None of these show how the British party spent 15 January, but presumably Campbell and Bedingfeld were engaged ashore in the discussions which led to the proposals of the following day.
48. FO84/950, Campbell to Clarendon, 29 January 1854; Irving in the *CMI*, v (1854) pp. 106–9. In FO84/920, Campbell to Clarendon, 29 July 1853, the consul gave his opinion that the African Steamship Company could well engage the enterprising Scala as their agent.
49. A paddle-box boat, when inverted and stored, formed the upper section of the paddle-box, the casing enclosing the upper part of a steamer's paddle wheel.
50. Arekin is even smaller than Agbekin, with the third island, which has no separate name, merely a clump of bushes in its lee. All are covered with low bush interspersed with an occasional palm and umbrella (or 'palaver') tree. They belong to Baiyeku, the Remo village lying opposite them on the north shore, and on a very clear day can be seen from parts of Lagos thirteen miles away.
51. According to tradition in Baiyeku, it was Agbekin on which the conference was held. Irving names the site as 'Orikasie' and says it was in the centre of the lagoon, which accords best with Agbekin. He names the other 'small' island as 'Korisusu'. Neither of Irving's names for the islands are known locally, and perhaps they were a confusion with the Yoruba word for 'island', *erekushu*. Alternative venues suggested to the Epe were Ijede and Langbassa.
52. Losi (1967) p. 42, lists the titles and names of the seven chiefs representing Dosunmu, but omits Ohoro, the Egba captain. Phillips (1966) p. 254, writes that Dosunmu sent seven of his youngest and inferior chiefs, but this interpretation seems to reflect the tone of his missionary sources.
53. The nineteenth-century wars in Yorubaland led to the formation for defence of a number of federated towns such as Abeokuta and Shagamu, where the rulers in the different quarters accommodated themselves reasonably amicably to each other.
54. FO84/950, Campbell to Clarendon, 1 May 1854, 24 November 1854.
55. FO84/950, Campbell to Clarendon, 18 May 1854, enclosing a letter from Gollmer and Gerst of 4 May and his reply of 8 May.
56. FO84/950, Campbell to Clarendon, 1 October 1854, 24 November 1854.
57. For Williams, see numerous references in Kopytoff.
58. FO84/950, Campbell to Clarendon, 24 November 1854. See Scala, pp. 76–89, for his account of the negotiations at Epe. It is colourful, emphasises his own role, places the episode in 1855 instead of 1854, and seems generally unreliable.
59. FO84/950. The Agreement, for which see Appendix B, was contained in Campbell to Clarendon, 1 October 1854, which was lost in the wreck of the mail-ship *Forerunner*, and was copied and commented on in Campbell to Clarendon, 24 November 1854.
60. For the introduction of the silver dollar into West Africa, see Marian Johnson (1970) pp. 335–6.
61. FO84/950, Campbell to Clarendon, 1 December 1854.
62. FO84/976, Clarendon to Campbell, 23 February 1855.

63. FO84/950, Campbell to Clarendon, 24 November 1854.
64. FO84/950, Campbell to Clarendon, 21 December 1854.
65. FO84/950, Campbell to Clarendon, 2 December 1854.
66. See FO84/1002, Campbell to Clarendon, 1 May 1856; FO84/1088, Lodder to Russell, 8 July 1859, Russell to Brand, 22 December 1859; FO84/1115, Brand to Russell, 30 January 1860. Kosoko complained that he would have to distribute any cash payment to his chiefs so said that he preferred presents. In the event plate and dinner and breakfast services were bought for him, but never delivered. The services, in 'white and lilac, slightly gilded', marked 'Athens' and 'Davenport', were discovered at the consulate by Brand in 1860. The cost was £93 14s. 8d., and the Foreign Office in London is perhaps still concerned about the balance of £131 5s. 4d. from a bill for £225 drawn for the purchase by Campbell.
67. Schnapper, p. 173.

Chapter 5

1. FO2/9, Campbell to Clarendon, 30 November 1853, Foreign Office to Campbell, 23 December 1853; FO2/11, Clarendon to Campbell, 31 January 1854; FO2/28, Lodder to Russell, 8 August 1859; FO2/39, Foreign Office to Foote, 24 June 1861. Campbell was also authorised to purchase 'six silver-headed canes' for use when sending messages to the chiefs. For a time Pearce seems to have performed the feat of working for both Campbell and Gollmer.
2. Burton (1863b) p. 213.
3. Correspondence on FO2/11 and FO2/13. The house was obtained from J. Walker of Poplar at a cost of £941, and was shipped at the end of December 1854 in 313 packages and pieces. As well as paying rent, the consul was to keep the house in repair. The consulate, in Yoruba *Ile Ajele*, was used as governor's residence from 1862 to 1885 and later became headquarters of the Nigerian Marine. It was demolished in 1960, the building of the Nigerian Ports Authority being erected on the site. See Miller (1972).
4. FO2/9, Campbell to Foreign Office, 11 October 1853. The boat, which was too large for ordinary use, had been brought out 'some years ago to be used in surveying the Lakes and Lagoons of this part of the Coast'.
5. FO2/13, Campbell to Foreign Office, 1 March 1855, 18 July 1855; Foreign Office to Campbell, 24 May 1855.
6. FO2/20, Campbell to Foreign Office, 3 November 1857; FO2/24; Foreign Office to Campbell, 18 June 1858, 3 November 1858; Campbell to Foreign Office, 16 September 1858.
7. Recent administrative historians do not accept the view that the nineteenth-century Treasury imposed on other departments a policy of economy at all costs. In fact the Foreign Office more than other departments was able to preserve considerable independence in its spending. See M. Wright, *Treasury Control of the Civil Service 1854–74*, London, 1964, passim, also Jones (1971) pp. 22–3, and Cell, pp. 251–3.
8. FO2/11, Foreign Office to Campbell, 29 August 1854; Campbell to Foreign Office,

31 October 1854, 10 November 1854; FO2/13, Foreign Office to Campbell, 26 December 1855.
9. FO2/17, Foreign Office to Campbell, 18 August 1856; Campbell to Foreign Office, 28 June 1856, 30 September 1856; FO2/20, Campbell to Foreign Office, 1 September 1857; Foreign Office to Campbell, 17 November 1857.
10. FO84/950, Campbell to Clarendon, 12 August 1854; FO2/11, Foreign Office to Campbell, 15 December 1854; FO2/13, Campbell to Foreign Office, 1 October 1855; FO2/17, Foreign Office to Campbell, 4 January 1856, 22 August 1856; Campbell to Foreign Office, 23 June 1856. The Foreign Office approved the payment of an outfit allowance to McCoskry, the purchase of a boat, and the hire of four boatmen. Less than a year later Campbell wrote that he had 'hesitated to appoint' him as he had not established himself permanently at Badagry (where Tickel was looking after his interests) and because his implication in the 'conspiracy' of 1855 and his help to Madame Tinubu then had come to light.
11. FO84/950, Campbell to Clarendon, 27 March 1854.
12. FO84/976, Campbell to Clarendon, 2 February 1855; Clarendon to Campbell, 8 May 1855. Clarendon told the Brazilian Minister that Jambo's palm-oil business did not prove that he was not combining this with slaving, as witness the case of Domingo Martinez. See Jennings (1976) for the French Government's condoning of commercial relations between French traders and Brazilian and African slave dealers in the 1840s and 1850s.
13. FO84/1002, Campbell to Clarendon, 16 August 1856. This is presumably Giuseppe Carrena, who later built a fine house for himself on the Lagos waterfront and with whom Scala, his fellow Sardinian, conducted a long feud.
14. See Newbury (1961) pp. 62, 64, fn. 2. Newbury places the opening of the Régis factory in Lagos in 1856, whereas Schnapper, p. 173, says that it was opened in 1854, after an attempt in 1852 or 1853 had failed.
15. FO 84/1031, Campbell to Clarendon, 10 August 1857, 31 August 1857, 2 October 1857.
16. FO84/1061, Campbell to Malmesbury, 30 April 1858, 3 August 1858, also MP, Sierra Leone and Gambia, Weatherby to General Secretaries, 28 April 1858.
17. FO84/1031, Campbell to Clarendon, 6 July 1857, 1 August 1857.
18. FO84/1031, Campbell to Clarendon, 1 December 1857, enclosing questions put to him by Commodore Wise; FO84/1061, Malmesbury to Campbell, 23 February 1858.
19. Ward, pp. 121, 125, 162, 229.
20. Ward, pp. 149–61, 230.
21. FO84/950, Campbell to Clarendon, 1 August 1854.
22. FO84/950, Campbell to Clarendon, 21 December 1854. In January 1856 a suspicious brigantine was run ashore at Lagos, said to have been a slaver sent by Machado at New York to Domingo Martinez; FO84/1002, Campbell to Clarendon, 6 January 1856.
23. FO84/1031, Campbell to Malmesbury, 27 March 1858.
24. FO84/1031, Campbell to Clarendon, 11 May 1857.
25. For example, FO84/1031, Campbell to Clarendon, 11 May 1857 (*Adams Gray* and *W. D. Miller*); Campbell to Clarendon, 5 August 1857 (*Abbot Devereux*).
26. See Ross (1965). Martinez had houses in both Porto Novo and Whydah, and in

addition to exporting slaves owned large oil palm plantations.
27. FO84/920, Campbell to Clarendon, 31 October 1853, no. 24; FO84/954, Bruce to Admiralty, 21 January 1854. The first reference to the revival of the slave trade specifically at Whydah seems to be in FO84/976, Campbell to Clarendon, 2 June 1855, no. 7, reporting the embarkation of slaves there on a French brig.
28. FO84/1002, Campbell to Clarendon, 21 January 1856; FO84/1031, Campbell to Clarendon, 6 August 1857; FO84/1061, Campbell to Malmesbury, 7 April 1858. Shipments from the 'Popo' (Egun) Coast west of Whydah were reported in FO84/1002, Campbell to Clarendon, 18 August 1856, embarkations taking place from beaches between ports so as not to infringe the treaties. Such shipments, Campbell told Clarendon (19 August 1856), encouraged the idea that Britain, exhausted by the Crimean War, was faltering in her opposition to the trade, while the traders were pressing for slaves 'at any cost'.
29. FO84/1031, Campbell to Clarendon, 5 September 1857, no. 35.
30. FO84/1031, Palmerston's minute of 25 June 1857 on Campbell to Clarendon, 4 April 1857, and Clarendon to Campbell, 13 November 1857. Palmerston reverted to the possibility of taking Whydah in his minute of 6 October 1857 on Campbell to Clarendon, 1 August 1857, about possible American designs on Cuba.
31. FO84/1061, Campbell to Clarendon, 6 February 1858.
32. See Ajayi and Smith (1971) pp. 54–5, 123–7, for a discussion of this point, and Hopkins (1968) passim, for an important restatement of the economic causes of the wars, especially in their later stages after 1877. See also Phillips (1966) p. 297.
33. FO84/976, Campbell to Clarendon, 1 October 1855, 2 October 1855, 7 December 1855; FO84/1002, Campbell to Clarendon, 26 February 1856; FO84/1061, Campbell to Malmesbury, 3 March 1858.
34. FO84/976, Campbell to Clarendon, 4 October 1855; FO84/1002, Campbell to Clarendon, 18 February 1856; FO84/1031, Campbell to Clarendon, 14 March 1857, 3 August 1857. Clarendon minuted on that of 14 March 1857 that he 'entirely approve[d]' of Campbell's sending complete information. FO84/1061, Campbell to Clarendon, 28 March 1858; FO84/1071, Campbell to Clarendon, 2 October 1857, enclosing a report by Governor Hill of Sierra Leone.
35. FO84/1061, Campbell to Malmesbury, 27 March 1858 (about slaves who escaped from Martinez at Whydah and sought Campbell's protection at Lagos), 28 March 1858. Lists of persons emancipated at the consulate were not provided until the arrival of Campbell's more professional successor Brand, at the end of the period. Brand's first list, in FO84/1115, Brand to Russell, 18 January 1860, gives figures from 1857(3), 1858(5), and 1859(17). A second list on the same file, in Hand to Russell, 31 December 1860, gives a total of 33 for 1860. FO2/28, Campbell to Malmesbury, 4 February 1859, refers to the provision of passports written in Arabic for emancipated Africans returning to the Muslim interior. There is much valuable information about the official British attitude to the existence of domestic slavery among the Yoruba and in particular in Lagos during the consular period in E. A. Oroge's important thesis (Birmingham Ph.D., 1971) pp. 282–332, which was unfortunately not available to the present writer until this book had gone to press. Oroge describes in detail the 'gradual approach' to the problem adopted by Campbell and followed by his successors at Lagos for most of the period down to 1916.

36. FO84/976, Campbell to Clarendon, 2 February 1855, 12 February 1855.
37. FO84/1002, Campbell to Clarendon, 26 March 1856, 26 May 1856. For other references to Tinubu, see Biobaku (1957) pp. 48, 51, 57, 86, and for a general account of her career see Biobaku in Dike (1960) pp. 33–41.
38. FO84/950, Clarendon to Campbell, 10 September 1854.
39. FO2/20, Campbell to Clarendon, 1 July 1857 and enclosures; Clarendon to Campbell, 12 August 1857. A somewhat similar objection was made at Paris in the seventeenth century by the representatives of Allada to a proposal by the French that their traders should be allowed to cover their factory at Allada with tiles: Akinjogbin, pp. 30–1.
40. FO84/1002, Campbell to Clarendon, 1 October 1856, 4 November 1856. See also MP, Gold Coast, Gardiner to General Secretaries, 6 December 1856.
41. FO84/1002, Campbell to Clarendon, 29 November 1856, with numerous enclosures; FO84/1115, memorandum enclosed in Brand to Russell, 5 April 1860.
42. FO84/1002, Campbell to Clarendon, 24 June 1856, 4 November 1856, 1 October 1856, with minute of 16 November 1856 by Palmerston; FO84/1031, Clarendon to Campbell, 22 January 1857.
43. FO84/1031, Clarendon to Campbell, 3 October 1857; Campbell to Clarendon, 7 April 1857, 4 September 1857, 22 December 1857.
44. FO84/1031, Campbell to Clarendon, 5 January 1857; FO84/1061, Campbell to Clarendon, 2 February 1858; Newbury (1961) p. 58.
45. FO84/1002, Campbell to Clarendon, 30 August 1856, no. 30; Clarendon to Campbell, 14 November 1856.
46. FO2/20, Campbell to Foreign Office, 3 November 1857, no. 23; Foreign Office to Campbell, 22 December 1857; FO2/24, Campbell to Foreign Office, 6 March 1858; FO2/36, Foreign Office to Campbell, 5 December 1860.
47. See FO84/1031, FO2/20, and FO2/24.
48. Crowther, when in Abeokuta in 1853, had traded in cotton on behalf of the mission. See CA2/031(a), Crowther to Venn, 28 November 1853.
49. FO84/950, Campbell to Clarendon, 1 June 1854.
50. FO84/1002, Campbell to Clarendon, 14 May 1856; CA2/031(a), Crowther to Venn, 25 March 1856, 3 May 1856; Newbury (1961) pp. 58–61.
51. FO84/1002, Campbell to Clarendon, 25 September 1856, 29 November 1856, and enclosures to each.
52. The Hansen case is on FO2/11 and FO84/1002. For McCoskry and Sandeman, see numerous references in FO84/1002 and FO84/1031.
53. For this case, see FO2/20, FO2/22 and FO2/24. The Foreign Office substantially upheld Campbell but warned him that as he had no legal jurisdiction he should try to bring the disputants to arbitration, asking the Oba to enforce the arbitrator's decision.
54. FO84/1061, Campbell to Clarendon, 6 February 1858; Scala, pp. 93–154, 230–43; Phillips (1966) pp. 390–2. R. Gray and D. Chambers, *Materials for West African History in Italian Archives*, London, 1965, pp. 147–8, note the existence of a file of letters from Scala in the Archivio di Stato, Sezione Prima, Consular reports, at Turin.
55. FO84/976, Campbell to Clarendon, 2 August 1855, no. 12 (enclosing the draft regulations); Clarendon to Campbell, 18 October 1855 (approval); FO84/1031,

Clarendon to Campbell, 31 January 1857 (article XII).
56. FO84/1002, Campbell to Clarendon, 29 November 1856.
57. FO84/1031, Campbell to Clarendon, 5 June 1857; FO2/24, Campbell to Clarendon, 7 April 1858. Walter Lewis had been brought up in Freetown, where his father was for many years registrar and commissioner in the courts of Mixed Commission, and he had come to Lagos in 1858 as agent for a Liverpool firm. See also Kopytoff, p. 292. He became Chief Clerk at Lagos in 1861, acted at times as Colonial Secretary, and from 1862–72 was registrar of the Vice-Admiralty Court.
58. FO84/1002, Campbell to Clarendon, 29 November 1856, enclosing two letters of support of 10 October 1856 addressed to Commodore Adams by 52 and 71 signatories respectively.
59. FO84/1002, Campbell to Clarendon, 14 May 1856; FO84/1031, Campbell to Clarendon, 7 April 1857; FO2/20, Campbell to Foreign Office, 6 February 1857; FO84/1061, Campbell to Foreign Office, 2 March 1858.
60. CA2/087(a), White to Straith, 18 April 1854. White had enjoyed the favour of Oba Akitoye for whom he 'performed many writing services', and he also seems to have been on good terms with Dosunmu.
61. FO84/920, Campbell to Clarendon, 28 July 1853.
62. According to the *CMI*, III (1852) p. 123, it was the Royal Navy who suggested that the C.M.S. should begin work at Lagos.
63. FO84/950, Campbell to Clarendon, 14 August 1854, enclosing copies of a letter from Irving and of his reply. Irving was in Abeokuta with Townsend between 1854 and 1855, but died in Lagos.
64. Phillips (1966) pp. 305–8, citing CA2/052 and FO84/976, Campbell to Clarendon, 28 May 1855.
65. FO84/950, Clarendon to Campbell, 19 September 1854.
66. FO84/976, Campbell to Clarendon, 4 April 1855 and enclosures; Clarendon to Campbell, 24 May 1855.
67. FO84/976, Skene to Campbell, 10 April 1855, Skene to Irving, 11 April 1855, enclosed in Campbell to Clarendon, 28 May 1855.
68. FO84/976, Campbell to Clarendon, 3 October 1855.
69. FO84/976, Campbell to Clarendon, 7 December 1855, no. 36; FO84/1002, Campbell to Clarendon, 28 August 1856; CA2/031(a), Crowther to Venn, 25 March 1856, 28 July 1856. Crowther admits that Gollmer made an error in his survey of the land.
70. CA2/031(a), Crowther to Venn, 8 May 1855. Crowther's journal (CA2/031(b), 30 April 1855) records that the consul, Commander Skene, and three other naval officers attended Irving's funeral, as did representatives of Oba Dosunmu and the Mewu.
71. CA2/031(a), Crowther to Venn, 28 July 1856.
72. Journal, 21 December 1847, in *CMG* (1849) p. 11.
73. Ajayi (1965) pp. 50–1. Mrs Foote, presumably unaware of Pa Antonio's chapel, expresses surprise at there being no Roman Catholic Church in Lagos in 1861, since the majority of the European residents were Roman Catholics (p. 194).
74. FO84/976, Gardiner to Campbell, 4 October 1855, enclosed in Campbell to Clarendon, 9 October 1855, no. 26; MP, Gold Coast, Gardiner to Hoole, 8 March 1855; Gardiner to Osborn, 10 December 1855 (two letters). It is not surprising that

Gardiner's health broke down in 1856 and that he had to return home early in 1857. Foote, pp. 193–4. See also Ajayi (1965) pp. 78–9, and Kopytoff, pp. 83, 114. When the Rev. E. F. E. Gerst died in 1854, the *CMR*, XXVI (1855) p. 97, noted that he was the first C.M.S. and the third Christian missionary to be buried in Lagos, the other two being a Wesleyan (John Martin) and a Baptist (Mrs Dennard) for whom see Ajayi (1965) p. 98.

75. Ajayi (1965) chap. III and map, p. 125.
76. FO84/950, Campbell to Clarendon, 1 June 1854, no. 14, 11 June 1854, 11 August 1854, 12 August 1854, 14 August 1854. See also the Mewu's account in his letters to Townsend, CA2/06, 19 July 1854 and 18 August 1854.
77. Phillips (1966) p. 285.
78. FO84/950, Campbell to Clarendon, 1 June 1854, 12 August 1854 (and Foreign Office minute of 22 November 1854), 14 August 1854, 6 December 1854; Clarendon to Campbell, 21 September 1854 (numbers 12 and 13); FO84/976, Clarendon to Campbell, 21 February 1855; Campbell to Clarendon, 17 October 1855, enclosing letters to and from the Alake of Abeokuta.
79. CA2/031, Crowther, journal, 17 November 1855; FO84/1061, Campbell to Clarendon, 20 April 1854. See also Folayan (1967) chap. 2.
80. The treaty is enclosed in FO84/920, Wodehouse to Campbell, 28 February 1853.
81. PP, LVI (1854–5), Campbell to Clarendon, 4 May 1854, enclosing Campbell to King of Dahomey, 13 April 1854.
82. A note of scepticism about the report was sounded by T. B. Freeman, the Wesleyan missionary now at Cape Coast: enclosures in FO84/976, Campbell to Clarendon, 30 August 1855.
83. FO84/976, Campbell to Clarendon, 15 February 1855.
84. FO84/1002, Campbell to Clarendon, 26 June 1856 and enclosures; FO84/1031, Campbell to Clarendon, 7 March 1857 and enclosures; FO84/1061, Campbell to Malmesbury, 3 March 1858, 7 April 1858.
85. FO84/976, Campbell to Clarendon, 15 September 1855 and enclosures; Clarendon to Campbell, 5 December 1855, 29 December 1855.
86. FO84/1061, Campbell to Malmesbury, 6 May 1858, 2 August 1858. Protet's report is referred to by Schnapper, p. 160. Campbell does not seem to have been disturbed by, and perhaps never learnt of, the visits to Abomey in 1856 and 1858 by another French naval officer, Lieutenant Vallon.
87. FO2/20, Campbell to Foreign Office, 7 March 1857, 7 April 1857, 30 July 1857; Foreign Office to Campbell, 20 April 1857 and enclosure; FO84/1031, Campbell to Clarendon, 30 May 1857.
88. FO84/976, Campbell to Clarendon, 2 October 1855, 6 December 1855, 7 December 1855, nos 35 and 36, 8 December 1855; FO84/1002, Campbell to Clarendon, 26 February 1856; FO84/1031, Campbell to Clarendon, 1 July 1857; Folayan (1967) 60–2. In FO84/1061, Campbell to Clarendon, 3 March 1858, there is mention of one further Egba expedition and of a projected one which had been abandoned on the advice of the Ketu. 'Esharbay' is said to lie between Mahi country (north of Abomey) and the Niger, so accords well with Shabe. The siege and sacking of Aibo are described in C.M.S. CA2/043, Gollmer to Venn, 2 November 1857, and CA2/043(b), Gollmer's journal for 15 August 1858, cited by Folayan (1967) p. 62. At one point Campbell went so far as to sanction the use by the Egba of

the cannon presented to them by the British Government at Aibo, but then changed his mind: Phillips (1966) p. 340.
89. FO84/976, Campbell to Clarendon, 30 August 1855, enclosing copies of McCoskry to Campbell, 19 August 1855, from Badagry.
90. FO84/976, Campbell to Clarendon, 2 October 1855. The Egba were presumably contrasting their former slaving activities with oil trading. But in a letter to Campbell of 4 July 1856, enclosed in Campbell to Clarendon, 30 August 1856 (FO84/1002), probably drafted by Townsend, the Alake, after congratulating the British on the fall of Sebastopol, claimed that the Egba were originally an agricultural people, but their enemies, especially the Ijebu and Ife, had taught them to make war and thus (by implication) to engage in the slave trade. 'Eshalli' island is identified by both Campbell (FO84/1031, Campbell to Clarendon, 4 April 1857) and H. Macaulay (Ward-Price, p. 100) as being Iddo Island (also called in consular times 'Bruce' and 'Picnic' Island), but Isheri seems a more likely place for the meeting. As the Rev. W. March noted in his journal for 11 June 1845 (CA2/067), it was a regular meeting place for Lagos and Egba traders.
91. FO84/1061, Campbell (in Manchester) to Malmesbury, 30 July 1858, enclosing a copy of the agreement of 22 May 1858. For the burning of Scala's premises, see Scala, pp. 131–9. The Abeokutans still recall Scala's troubles in their town by a song. A couplet of this runs, *Enia ko jagun ko j'owo, Awa la peki Sikala lo*, which seems to mean, 'You can't fight us or conquer us with money, we are the ones who told Scala to pack up and go'. (Professor G. O. Olusanya in a private communication.)
92. FO84/1002, Campbell to Clarendon, 14 July 1856; Clarendon to Campbell, 20 October 1856.
93. A copy of this letter, dated 2 November 1852, is in the C.M.S. file, CA2/08. It would be interesting to know who in Ijebu Ode had sufficient English to write the letter.
94. *CMG* (1855) pp. 109–10; FO84/1088, Lodder to Malmesbury, 7 May 1859; MP, Gold Coast, Champness to General Secretaries, 31 December 1860, Mrs Champness to General Secretaries, 2 September 1861, Champness to Osborn, 7 October 1861 (two letters), Bickersteth to General Secretaries, 7 October 1861.
95. Bosman, pp. 427–8. Beecroft had also taken a hand against the pirates, but in FO2/9, Beecroft to Foreign Office, 19 May 1853, dealing with the destruction of Harrison and Co.'s property, he pointed out that the matter was now the responsibility of the Lagos consulate.
96. FO84/1002, Campbell to Clarendon, 24 March 1856, 26 June 1856, no. 21, enclosing a letter of 16 June 1856 from agents in the river; FO84/1031, Campbell to Clarendon, 2 February 1857, 3 November 1857; FO84/1061, Campbell to Malmesbury, 1 March 1858. See also Ryder, p. 246.
97. FO84/1031, Campbell to Clarendon, 4 April 1857. The second attempt arose from a proposal by Oba Adolo of Benin to recognise Kosoko as ruler of Lagos, for which see Ryder, pp. 242–3.
98. Ryder, pp. 232–3.
99. FO84/976, Campbell to Clarendon, 16 October 1855.

Chapter 6

1. Mabogunje, pp. 21-3.
2. See Curtin (1964) passim, especially chaps 7 and 14. Mortality dropped sharply in the naval squadron during the 1840s, from 58 per 1000 in 1840-2 to 27 per 1000 in 1846-8 (p. 361). This was a 'victory of empiricism', in Curtin's phrase. In FO84/1002, Campbell to Clarendon, 24 June 1856, the consul remarks on the value of the regular use of quinine.
3. FO2/13, Campbell to Foreign Office, 6 June 1856, 20 July 1855; Foreign Office to Campbell, 21 July 1855, 3 September 1855. Campbell thought it singular that as a medical man Irving did not realise that he needed a change of climate.
4. FO2/17, Campbell to Foreign Office, 28 June 1856. Campbell mentions that his only break in three years at Lagos and twenty years on the coast was a visit to Senegal, probably a reference to the cruise for which he had received permission and which he may have taken in November 1855.
5. FO2/24, Campbell to Foreign Office, 1 June 1858, 17 July 1858 (from England); Foreign Office to Campbell, 27 July 1858, 18 November 1858.
6. FO84/1061, Lodder to Malmesbury, 25 December 1858.
7. FO2/20, Campbell to Foreign Office, 2 December 1857; FO84/1061, Campbell to Malmesbury (from 28, Corporation Street, Manchester) 29 July 1858.
8. FO2/24, Campbell to Foreign Office, 7 August 1858, enclosing a newspaper report of the meeting, also Campbell to Foreign Office, 1 November 1858.
9. FO84/1061, Malmesbury to Campbell, 4 September 1858; Campbell to Malmesbury, 18 October 1858.
10. FO2/24, Foreign Office to Campbell, 10 November 1858; Campbell to Foreign Office, 20 December 1858 and Foreign Office minute. Campbell drew his salary of £500 a year while on leave but had paid his own passage, costing £40 10s. 0d.
11. FO84/1061, Malmesbury to Campbell, 21 December 1858; Campbell to Malmesbury, 23 December 1858.
12. FO84/1088, Campbell to Malmesbury, 28 January 1859. Campbell told Lord Malmesbury that Mrs Lightburn was not *anglaise d'origine* as the French alleged but of Portuguese descent, while Mr Lightburn was from South Carolina.
13. FO84/1061, minute by Wylde, 11 May 1858, on the report of 23 March 1858 to the French Minister of Marine. (This is presumably W. H. Wylde, but the signature is unclear.)
14. FO84/1088, Campbell to Malmesbury, 28 January 1859, 4 February 1859 (two dispatches), 7 February 1859.
15. FO2/28, Lodder to Foreign Office, 30 May 1859; FO2/35, Brand to Foreign Office, 12 January 1860, enclosing a memorandum of the conference in February 1859. Lodder writes that the largest tender was for 2000 bags. This seems to be an error.
16. FO2/20, Campbell to Foreign Office, 1 July 1857. Scala does not mention his brick and tile works in his *Memorie*. According to CO147/1, Freeman to Newcastle, 10 February 1862, bricks were being made in Lagos in 1862, though of poor quality. Euler Ajayi ('A Yoruba Historian'), pp. 42-3, writes that 'one Matthias Da Cruz', presumably an Amaro, introduced brickmaking into Lagos in 1859. J. M. Harden, the American Baptist, established his Ebenezer Brickfield in or soon after 1863.

17. FO2/28, Campbell to Foreign Office, 7 February 1859, 1 April 1859; Brand to Foreign Office, 31 December 1859.
18. FO84/1088, Campbell to Malmesbury, 4 March 1859, no. 6; *CMR*, v (NS, 1860) p. 111, Maser's journal, 18 August 1859.
19. FO84/1088, Campbell to Malmesbury, 4 March 1859, no. 6. Tapa was accompanied to his second meeting with Campbell by several Moslem visitors to Epe, one from Morocco and the others from Futa Toro, Futa Jallon, Sokoto, Jenne, and Sego.
20. FO84/1088, Campbell to Malmesbury, 5 March 1859. The Awujale told Williams that 'there are but four crowned heads or legitimate kings in this part of Africa, viz himself, the King of Benin, the Alake of the Egbas at Abeokuta, and the King of Yoruba at Oyo'.
21. FO84/1088, Campbell to Malmesbury, 22 March 1859. The mission carried 'handsome presents' for the Awujale had he consented to reopen the roads to oil supplies. It seems probable that one of the two Europeans was McCoskry.
22. FO84/1088, Campbell to Malmesbury, 6 March 1859, enclosing a letter of 21 February 1859 from the Alake and Campbell's two letters to the Alake of 5 March 1859.
23. FO84/1088, Campbell to Malmesbury, 5 April 1859. Campbell adds that he was delayed in leaving for Porto Novo by events reported in a dispatch of 31 March 1859 and the subsequent 'excitement'. No such dispatch has been traced, and the date seems likely to be mistaken since Campbell *returned* from Porto Novo on 30 March 1859. The delay and excitement could have been occasioned by the reports from and about the Egba described above.
24. FO2/28, Lodder to Foreign Office, 2 May 1859. Lodder's delay in conveying the news to the Foreign Office is probably explained by the infrequency of the mail boat; most correspondence in the consulate seems to have been written for the mail. An attempt to find Campbell's grave in the old Faji or Ajele (consular) cemetery, shortly before all the graves there were removed (December 1971), was unsuccessful. Campbell's sole heir, his daughter in Britain, was the wife of H. St J. Bullen, Medical Officer to the Lambeth Workhouse Infirmary, who, as administrator of the 'small and impoverished estate' (as he called it), had to deal with claims for cotton gins supplied by Venn's friend Thomas Clegg of Manchester for use in the Yoruba country: see FO2/30 and FO2/36. The writer has not traced any descendants of Campbell or Walter Lewis in Lagos.
25. McCoskry estimated in 1865 that 'emigrants' made up one-fifth of the population of Lagos. See his evidence to the Parliamentary Select Committee: PP (1865) p. 68, Q. 1458.
26. *CMR*, xxvii (1856) pp. 55–7; xxviii (1857) pp. 71–3; O. Chadwick, *The Victorian Church*, part I, second ed. (London 1970) p. 464. For Macaulay's school, see *CMR*, v (NS, 1860) p. 109, and Ajayi (1963a) p. 523. Crowther wrote to Venn on 25 March 1856 (CA2/031) that the Europeans in Lagos had been 'shamefully guilty' of Sunday work. See also *CMR*, xxviii (1857), which mentions a report by Crowther that the Hamburg merchant Diederichsen had placed one of Tapa's sons in one of the two C.M.S. schools at Lagos and would perhaps send another to school in Hamburg – an instance of the continuing relationship between the merchant community and the exiles of Epe. 'Emancipadoes' were also sending their children for instruction in English and Yoruba.

27. Burton (1863b) pp. 21–3. Carrena's house must be the 'beautiful mansion built by an Italian' described by Mrs Foote, pp. 190–1. Hutchinson's account (1858) of Lagos, pp. 73–6, with its whitewashed houses and shady trees, is less depressing than Burton's.
28. According to the late Mr K. C. Murray, Fernandez House at the east end of Tinubu Square was probably built at this period. The small Brazilian house called Ile Akitoye at 12 Upper King Street seems to have been built by Oba Akitoye's grandson considerably later.
29. The plan is reproduced in Kopytoff, pp. 90–3, the original being in the Lands Office, Lagos.
30. Burton (1863a) vol. 1, p. 17; Foote, p. 190.
31. Burton (1863b) p. 225. ''Very delightful was this meeting of Moslem brethren.' Perhaps this was the Moroccan who accompanied Tapa to the meeting with Campbell at Ejinrin (n. 19 above).
32. Dr E. R. Turton in a private communication has pointed out that some seventy-six grants of land by Oba Dosunmu were recorded between 1854 and 1860. Only the earliest of these contain the clause 'with the advice and consent' of the chiefs. Professor A. G. Hopkins, in a private communication and elsewhere, has stressed the importance of property rights in the cession and settlement of Lagos. In subsequent years land grants were the subject of much litigation, for example the Marina case in 1916 concerning the firm of John Holt.
33. The Adamorisha play by the Eyo masqueraders, the most prominent of the traditional annual festivals in modern Lagos, is performed only at intervals of several years, in honour of the illustrious dead.
34. Brown (1964) pp. 302–3. The racecourse now constitutes the open space known as Tafawa Balewa Square after one of the greatest of modern Nigerians. Mrs Foote, p. 197, says that she took exercise daily between five and seven (presumably in the evening), 'visiting or sailing on the harbour', and she mentions 'one very pleasant pic-nic' at the harbour mouth.
35. FO2/30, Admiralty to FO, 30 May 1859.
36. For example, see FO84/950, Campbell to Clarendon, 28 August 1854; FO2/28, Brand to Foreign Office, 10 December 1859; FO2/35, Brand to Foreign Office, 9 April 1860.
37. Quoted by G. Townsend (1887) p. 167.
38. Burton (1863b) p. 202. The Western roadstead was known as the 'English' one.
39. FO2/17, Campbell to Clarendon, 8 February 1856.
40. CA2/031(b), Crowther to Venn, 25 September 1856; Hutchinson, p. 73; Burton (1863b) p. 204. Sharks are not commonly seen in the vicinity of Lagos today.
41. Scala, p. 224.
42. Baikie (1856) pp. 21–2.
43. FO2/13, Campbell to Clarendon, 4 September 1855.
44. Burton (1863b) p. 208.
45. Newbury (1961) p. 60.
46. FO84/1088, Lodder to Malmesbury, 7 May 1859.
47. FO84/1088, Lodder to Malmesbury, 5 July 1859; Malmesbury to Lodder, 23 September 1859, no. 4.

48. FO84/1115, Oba Dosunmu to Russell, 4 June 1860, enclosed in Brand to Russell, 6 June 1860.
49. FO84/1115, Awujale to Hand, 19 July 1860, enclosed in Hand to Russell, 13 August 1860.
50. FO84/1115, Hand to Russell, 9 October 1860. These figures do not agree with those in the table in Newbury (1961) p. 58.
51. FO84/1115, Hand to Russell, 13 August 1860, enclosing Townsend to Hand, 9 July 1860, Richards to Hand, 25 July 1860; Hand to Russell, 18 August 1860.
52. FO84/1088, Brand, 9 December 1859, reissue of Campbell's circular of 31 July 1857; FO84/1115, Brand to Russell, 2 May 1860 (about disturbances at 'Ahguay', west of Whydah, settled on the appearance of H.M.S. *Spitfire*), and 5 June 1860 with Foreign Office minute by Wylde, 11 July 1860. See also Newbury (1972) for the rise of local African importers and for the operation of the credit system on the West African coast generally.
53. See Hopkins (1966) pp. 471–9, and M. Johnson (1970) pp. 340–1, also Scala, pp. 203–4. The value of a head (2000) of cowries at Lagos fell from about 4s. in 1851 to about 1s. 9d. in 1859 and 6d. in 1895. The American missionary, Bowen, had discussed difficulties in obtaining cowries in 1853 and reported that some of his colleagues were trying coral beads as a substitute currency: Baptist papers, Bowen to Taylor, 7 September 1853.
54. FO84/1115, Brand to Russell, 18 January 1860; Hand to Russell, 31 December 1860.
55. FO84/1088, Brand to Russell, 31 December 1859. The Foreign Secretary also sent out a draft treaty, enclosed in FO84/1114, Russell to Brand, 17 March 1860, no. 17, abjuring 'the practice hitherto prevailing at Lagos of destroying twin children and one or both of their parents'. In other parts of Yorubaland at this time twins were regarded favourably, but the late Mr K. C. Murray pointed out to the writer that Ibeji (twin) carvings are less prevalent in Lagos than elsewhere, which gives some colour to this allegation. T. J. H. Chappel in 'The Yoruba Cult of Twins in Historical Perspective', *Africa*, XLIV, 3 (1974) considers that the cult represents a reversal of a previous practice of murdering twins at birth and was introduced into Yorubaland between *c*. 1750 and *c*. 1850 as a result of contacts between Yoruba traders and Dahomeans. In any case this treaty seems to have remained unsigned.
56. FO84/1115, Brand to Russell, 25 May 1860; FO84/1114, Russell to Brand, 23 July 1860 (approval).
57. FO84/1088, Lodder to Russell, 2 November 1859. One of the canoes was seventy feet long and ten feet broad, 'capable of carrying several guns'.
58. FO84/1115, Hand to Russell, 3 November 1860 and enclosures.
59. Schnapper, p. 173.
60. FO84/1115, Brand to Russell, 9 March 1860 and numerous enclosures.
61. Ajayi and Smith, pp. 41, 89.
62. FO84/1115, Brand to Russell, 10 April 1860; FO84/1141, Foote to Russell, 9 March 1861, no. 13, enclosing a letter from the Alake; McCoskry to Russell, 5 June 1861; Delany and Campbell, passim, or for extracts from their reports, see Hodgkin (1960) pp. 275–8. On his outward journey, Delany made a similar agreement at Lagos with Oba Dosunmu in October 1859, which was certified and registered by Lodder. MP, Sierra Leone and Gambia, Champness to General Secretaries, 4 April

1861, alleges that the Alake was asleep at the conference with Delany and Campbell 'and did not know what he was doing'. But as the grant was not made in public, it was invalid by Egba custom. Robert Campbell later owned and edited the first locally published newspaper in colonial Lagos, the *Anglo-African*.

63. FO84/1115, Brand to Russell, 8 May 1860, enclosing Alake to Brand, 30 April 1860; Hand to Russell, 3 November 1860.
64. See Smith (1962) pp. 331–2, 346; Ajayi and Smith (1971) pp. 54–5, 63–4, 123–8. Phillips (1966) p. 384, cites a letter from Townsend describing the war as concerning the balance of power in Yorubaland, which is the interpretation of most modern historians.
65. Ajayi and Smith (1971) part I, chap. VII, and part II, passim; Smith (1969a; 1976 ed.) pp. 188–90.
66. FO84/1114, Russell to Brand, 23 May 1860; FO84/1115, minute by Wylde, 11 July 1860, on Brand to Russell, 5 June 1860 and enclosure of 12 May 1860.
67. FO84/1115, Brand to Russell, 9 March 1860, 9 April 1860 and enclosures, including Townsend to Brand, 12 March 1860; Brand to Russell, 16 April 1860, 8 May 1860 enclosing Lodder's report of 7 May 1860 and Alake to Consul, 30 April 1860. For Turner, see Kopytoff, pp. 299–300.
68. FO84/1115, Brand to Russell, 9 April 1860, enclosure from *Iwe Irohin*, 24 March 1860; Brand to Russell, 5 June 1860 enclosing Townsend to Brand, 29 May 1860; Hand to Russell, 8 July 1860.
69. FO84/1115, Hand to Russell, 13 August 1860, 9 October 1860, no. 13.
70. FO84/1115, Richards to Hand, 25 July 1860, enclosed in Hand to Russell, 13 August 1860.
71. FO84/1115, Hand to Russell, 10 September 1860; Hinderer to Hand, 8 September 1860 enclosed in Hand to Russell, 9 October 1860, no. 13. Philips (1966) p. 394, citing CA2/049.
72. FO84/1088, Lodder to Russell, 2 November 1859, enclosing Bowden to Lodder, 10 October 1859.
73. FO84/1115, Brand to Russell, 3 May 1860 and enclosures. The Kroomen were not much use in action. According to Foote, who observed them on the Porto Novo expedition in February 1861, they 'run below at the first shot': FO84/1141, Foote to Wylde, 10 March 1861.
74. FO84/1088, Brand to Russell, 31 December 1859; FO84/1114, Russell to Brand, 17 March 1860, no. 15; FO84/1115, Brand to Russell, 4 May 1860.
75. FO84/1115, Hand to Russell, 10 September 1860, 9 October 1860.
76. FO84/1088, Brand to Russell, 31 December 1859.
77. Glover's journal of the expedition is partially reproduced in Hastings (1926) but it ends before the events alluded to in this section, the last entry being in January 1858.
78. The tangled story can be followed in FO84/1088, Lodder to Russell, 4 August 1859; Russell to Brand, 30 September 1859; FO84/1114, Russell to Brand, 20 April 1860, 21 June 1860, no. 38, 22 June 1860; FO84/1115, Brand to Russell, 8 February 1860 with numerous enclosures; Brand to Governor of Sierra Leone, 10 March 1860; Brand to Russell, 5 May 1860; Hand to Russell, 27 August 1860.
79. FO84/1115, memorandum enclosed in Brand to Russell, 5 May 1860.
80. FO2/20, Clarendon to Campbell, 21 May 1857; Campbell to Clarendon, 29 June 1857, 30 July 1857, no. 15, enclosing Campbell to Dosunmu, 14 July 1857,

Campbell to Hamburg merchants, 20 July 1857. See also Newbury (1961) p. 62.
81. Scala, pp. 188–9, 219–27. Scala was awarded a silver medal by King Victor Emmanuel II 'for introducing Civil Industry into Guinea'.
82. Newbury (1961) p. '62. No references are given.
83. FO84/1088, Lodder to Russell, 3 November 1859, 9 November 1859 enclosing merchants' petition; FO84/1114, Russell to Brand, 20 February 1860; FO84/1115, Brand to Russell, 5 April 1860. The Lemagnière episode is complicated. After being required to leave Lagos in 1855 as a suspected slave trader, at the insistence of Commander Miller, he set up a factory at 'Port Arthur' about nine miles east of Palma. But he was again in Lagos in 1856, expelled a second time, and again returned.
84. Philips (1966) pp. 305, 395–6 citing CA2/04, Irving to Campbell, 15 January 1855, and FO84/1005, memorandum dated 7 October 1859. FO84/1115, Brand to Russell, 9 April 1860, no. 16. In his dispatch of 18 April 1860 Brand told Russell that the King of Dahomey was unpopular at Whydah and it needed little to bring about a revolt there.
85. Argyle, pp. 81–3.
86. FO84/1122, Wylde's minute of 20 April 1860; FO84/1115, minutes of 14 August 1860 on Hand to Russell, 8 July 1860. Gavin (1958) p. 244, seems to attribute the latter minute to Russell, but the signature is clearly 'W'.

Chapter 7

1. FO2/35, Brand to Foreign Office, 6 June 1860; Hand to Foreign Office, 16 June 1860; FO2/36, Admiralty to Foreign Office, 13 August 1860, enclosing Commander Raby's letter of 22 June 1860. Brand was the illegitimate son of John Brand of Auchinblae.
2. FO2/35, Foote to Foreign Office, 14 August 1860 (applying to change posts with Consul Hutchinson at Fernando Po), 1 September 1860 (giving his *curriculum vitae* and minuted by Wodehouse on 18 August 1860 and Russell on 20 August 1860); Phillips (1966) p. 402.
3. Foote, pp. 189–203; FO2/39, Foote to Foreign Office, 1 February 1861, for the repairs to the 'ruinous' consulate. Mrs Foote, who was only four months in Lagos, mistakenly thought that Dahomean territory stretched as far as the harbour of Lagos, and she wrote that the town was constantly under threat of invasion from Dahomey (p. 210).
4. FO84/1141, Foote to Russell, 9 February 1861.
5. FO84/1141, Foote to Russell, 8 January 1861, nos 3 and 4, 8 February 1861.
6. FO84/1115, Brand to Russell, 7 February 1860 and enclosures; FO84/1114, Russell to Brand, 20 April 1860.
7. FO84/1115, Brand to Russell, 14 May 1860.
8. FO84/1141, Foote to Russell, 9 February 1861, nos 6 and 9, 8 March 1861, no. 11, 8 May 1861; Russell to Foote, 23 March 1861 (no. 12). For Tickel, born in Plymouth about 1831, see Folayan (1969). Foote in a private letter of 10 March 1861 to Wylde on FO84/1141 writes that Tickel's father was Government Engineer at Cape Coast.

9. FO84/1141, Foote to Wylde, 10 March 1861.
10. FO84/1141, Foote to Russell, 9 February 1861, no. 10.
11. FO84/1141, Foote to Russell, 4 February 1861.
12. FO84/1141, McCoskry to Russell, 10 July 1861, reporting 499 registrations in the period from 12 March 1861 to 30 April 1861.
13. Ajayi and Smith (1971) pp. 51–2, 126–7. In FO2/35, Hand to Russell, 30 November 1860, the acting consul reported that relief was being provided at the consulate to refugees from Ijaye in order to prevent mothers from selling their children to obtain means of sustaining life.
14. FO84/1141, Foote to Russell, 9 February 1861, no. 11.
15. The figures are somewhat difficult both to extract and to compare. In FO84/1115, Hand to Russell, 9 October 1860, exports of palm oil are given as 3413 tons for January to September 1860 against 2476 tons for the same period in 1859. There seem to be no figures for the first half of 1861, then in FO84/1175, McCoskry to Russell, 7 January 1862 (misnumbered 2), exports of palm oil are given as 3865 tons for the period July 1861 to June 1862. But for the complete year of 1862, according to Newbury (1961) (appendix III, p. 211), the figure was only 1763 tons.
16. FO84/1141, Russell to Foote, 23 January 1861; Foote to Russell, 1 April 1861, enclosing Edmondstone to Foote, 12 March 1861.
17. FO84/1141, Foote to Russell, 9 January 1861; Russell to Foote, 23 February 1861.
18. FO84/1141, Foote to Russell, 9 March 1861. The bursting of muskets on discharge was a frequent cause of casualties in West African wars.
19. FO84/1141, Foote to Russell, 1 April 1861.
20. FO84/1141, Foote to Russell, 8 May 1861. Phillips (1966) p. 413, considers that this agreement 'virtually brought [the Egba] under British protection'. The Alake's assurances were, however, informal and probably not deserving of much weight. Like Burton, and perhaps even Townsend, Foote did not realise that Abeokuta was a confederation representing the three original states of the Egba forest, to which the Owu had joined themselves, and that the Alake was recognised only as the senior among the different crowned rulers of Egbaland. See Smith (1969a) chaps VI, XI.
21. FO84/1141, Foote to Wylde, 6 April 1861; Foote to Russell, 8 May 1861, nos 20 and 21. See also Ajayi and Smith (1971) pp. 103–4.
22. Phillips (1966) pp. 411–14, citing FO84/1148, Edmondstone to Admiralty, 21 March 1861. Printed in Ajayi and Smith (1971) appendix I, pp. 129–40.
23. Printed in Ajayi and Smith (1971) appendix I, pp. 129–40.
24. Ajayi and Smith (1971) pp. 104–5. See also FO84/1141, McCoskry to Russell, 31 May 1861, 4 July 1861, 9 July 1861, no. 7. For criticism of Jones's proceedings by the Methodist missionaries at Lagos, see MP, Gold Coast, Champness to Osborn, 9 September 1861.
25. Phillips (1966) p. 408, asserts that Foote's motive in attacking Porto Novo was to divert King Glele of Dahomey's attention from Abeokuta and to allow the Egba to concentrate on their war with Ibadan. These considerations may well have weighed with him but Phillips's citation of a dispatch, FO84/1115, from Brand to Russell, 30 April 1860, recalling advice from Townsend on these lines (though respecting Whydah rather than Porto Novo) is not conclusive.
26. FO84/1141, Foote to Russell, 8 March 1861.
27. FO84/1141, Russell to Foote, 23 April 1861, nos 15 (containing letters of protest

from Messrs Cotersworth and Powell and others) and 16; McCoskry to Russell, 30 May 1861, blaming the merchants at Badagry for encouraging King Sodji to continue in the slave trade.

28. FO84/1141, Foote to Wylde, 10 March 1861.
29. FO84/1141, Foote to Russell, 1 April 1861.
30. Foote's account of the second expedition is in FO84/1141, Foote to Russell, 9 May 1861, number 22. FO2/39, Foote to Foreign Office, 7 May 1861, shows that the consular interpreter, S. B. Williams, piloted the expedition (whether the first, second or both is not indicated) up the lagoon. Burton (1983b) pp. 194–8, gives a description of both expeditions, from information gathered at Lagos later in the year.
31. FO84/1141, minutes of 13 June 1861 (Russell) and 7 July 1861 (Palmerston) on Foote to Russell, 9 May 1861, also Foote to Wylde, 10 May 1861. The *Iwe Irohin* at Abeokuta, reporting in May the destruction of Porto Novo, wrote that when the officers and sailors walked over the ruins, they 'found many people still remaining in the town'.
32. FO84/1141, McCoskry to Russell, 27 May 1861, no. 2.
33. Burton (1863b) p. 194.
34. FO84/1141, McCoskry to Russell, 28 (18?) May 1861. Mrs Foote does not describe her husband's death in her *Recollections*. She left Lagos, with her daughter and nurse, on 10 June 1861 (pp. 217–18).
35. Gavin (1958) pp. 243–6, who cites the letter of 7 February 1861 from Russell to Newcastle.
36. Cell, pp. 281–2, pointing out that 'There was no specific mention of ending an existing trade in slaves on the island itself.'
37. Newbury (1961) writes, p. 65, that 'Russell's were reasons of state; Brand spoke for the consuls who by the end of the decade were unable to solve the problems raised by the changing economic conditions at the Lagos market, and incapable of ensuring by treaty alone the peaceful conditions of trade among the Gun, Awori, Egbado, and Egba necessary to that market.' But, as Newbury notes, the difference between the consul and his chief was one of emphasis only.
38. FO84/1141, Foote to Russell, 9 January 1861, private. In CO147/1, Freeman to Newcastle, 1 July 1862, the first substantive governor of Lagos reported a story that at some time after his abortive attack on Lagos, Kosoko had made a deal with the French and that the commodore of the French naval squadron regarded himself as 'Protector of Epe'. This seems to be an exaggeration by Lagos gossip of the transactions between Kosoko and Régis or Commander Barbotin.
39. FO84/1141, Foote to Russell, 9 February 1861, private.
40. Cell, chap. 8. See also a review of Cell by G. E. Metcalfe, *JAH*, XI (1970) pp. 615–16.
41. CO96/58, Russell to Newcastle, 7 February 1861, in Newbury (1965) pp. 426–7.
42. FO84/1141, minutes of 3 March 1861 and 4 March 1861 following Foote to Russell, 7 January 1861, but probably misplaced in the file and referring to Foote to Russell, 9 January 1861.
43. FO84/1141, minutes on Foote to Russell, 9 February 1861, number 11; Wylde's minute is dated 16 March 1861, Palmerston's is undated.
44. FO84/1141, Palmerston's minute of 20 March 1861 on Foote to Russell, 9 February 1861, marked 'Private' and unnumbered.

45. FO84/1141, Russell to Foote, 23 March 1861, no. 12; Phillips (1966) p. 405, citing a minute of 30 April 1861 on the same file.
46. FO84/1141, Wylde's minute of 11 July 1861 on McCoskry to Russell, 7 June 1861 (the minute is misplaced on the file and follows McCoskry to Russell, 27 May 1861).
47. CO96/58, Rogers to Wodehouse, 19 June 1861, in Newbury (1965) pp. 428–9. Phillips (1966) p. 421, cites a Colonial Office minute of 18 June 1861, on CO147/1, discussing and opposing the annexation of Lagos, which Newcastle reluctantly overruled in order to meet the views of the Foreign Office about the need to suppress the slave trade and encourage legitimate trade.
48. FO84/1141, Russell to Foote/McCoskry, 22 June and 24 June 1861 and minute of 20 June 1861 on the draft.
49. FO84/1141, McCoskry to Russell, 7 August 1861. CA2/068, Maser to Venn, 9 August 1861.
50. FO84/1141, McCoskry to Russell, 5 August 1861.
51. FO84/1141, Bedingfeld to McCoskry, 8 August 1861, enclosed in McCoskry to Russell, 5 August 1861 (sic).
52. These protests were reproduced in the parliamentary papers respecting the annexation PP, LXI (1862) 2982. They reached Russell through Venn, the secretary of the C.M.S., who received them from the Saro trader, J. P. L. ('Captain') Davies, and consisted of two series of letters, the first dated 8 August 1861 and the second, which included a denunciation of McCoskry, 10 September 1861. The first erroneously assigns the dates 3 August to the palaver (of 5 August) and 4 August to the signature (of 6 August).
53. FO84/1141, McCoskry to Russell, 7 August 1861. Bedingfeld's report of the annexation proceedings is enclosed in Edmondstone to Walker, 22 September 1861, printed in PP, LXI (1862) 3003. For the treaty of cession, see Appendix C. With regard to the land question, Dr E. R. Turton has commented that it was not appreciated at the time of the cession that 'acquisition of territory' did not imply 'acquisition of title to land' (for the distinction see K. Roberts-Wray, *Commonwealth and Colonial Law* (London, 1966) p. 99).
54. Burton (1863*b*) pp. 216–17. Burton was not a witness of the scene but doubtless had an account from McCoskry when he stayed with him shortly afterwards in Lagos. According to Bedingfeld, loc. cit., Dosunmu, after attending the ceremonies at the flagstaff with his chiefs, declined the invitation to dine on the *Prometheus* 'as he could not sit so long'.
55. FO84/1141, minute of 10 September 1861 on McCoskry to Russell, 7 August 1861.
56. Newbury (1961) p. 64, fn. 2; Cell, pp. 273–4.
57. FO84/1114, Russell to McCoskry, 23 September 1861. In FO2/39, McCoskry to Foreign Office, 29 August 1861, the new acting governor wrote that he would continue to correspond with the Foreign Office.
58. FO84/1141, McCoskry to Russell, 4 October 1861, number 21; Russell to McCoskry, 23 November 1861.
59. Captain Jones had adopted this view to the extent that he criticised Hinderer, the C.M.S. agent in Ibadan, for staying at his post. See Ajayi and Smith, p. 105.
60. FO84/1141, Russell to McCoskry, 20 August 1861.

61. Phillips (1966) pp. 453–8, citing FO84/1160, Venn to Layard, 13 November 1861.
62. For Freeman's appointment, see FO2/39, Foreign Office to Freeman, 29 August 1861, 16 November 1861; CO147/2, FO to CO, 18 September 1861, Foreign Office (Layard) to Freeman, 8 October 1861. Freeman had served at Damascus, Tunis, and Ghadames before his appointment to Janina. His selection may have owed something to a recommendation by the Bishop of Sierra Leone in 1859 (FO2/30, Bishop of Sierra Leone to Malmesbury, 19 May 1859) that officials with experience in the Turkish Empire would be suitable for Lagos. While Freeman was taking his extended leave between posts, McCoskry forwarded to the foreign secretary a recommendation from the European merchants in Lagos, which he supported, that Commander Bedingfeld should be appointed governor: FO84/1141, McCoskry to Russell, 7 December 1861, no. 17.
63. FO84/1141, minute of 11 July 1861 by Wylde on McCoskry to Russell, 28 May 1861. Phillips (1966) p. 449, cites FO84/1175, Freeman to Russell, 8 March 1862, to show that McCoskry took over the farming of the Lagos customs in January 1861 for a three-year period, which in the event came to an end on 1 July 1862 with the advent of the British administration. He claims that this was his 'real motivation' in persuading Kosoko to return. In fact, Kosoko seems to have been anxious to return home. Phillips also claims (pp. 416, 449) that McCoskry had been farming the customs since 1859, but see p. 94 above.
64. Burton (1863b) p. 209. With his usual precision, Burton adds that the *Advance* was of 120 tons, drew 6 feet of water, had engines of 80–160 horsepower, and had cost McCoskry £6000. See also CO147/1, Freeman to Newcastle, 10 February 1862.
65. Burton (1863b) p. 213, writes that 'One fellow who calls himself a Captain, upon the strength of having bought a condemned hulk', threatened to drive away the workers clearing the road. This may have been Captain J. P. L. (Labulo) Davies (1828–1906), for whom see Gwam, pp. 36–40. Both Burton, loc. cit., and Losi (1967) p. 91, credit McCoskry with having laid out the Marina, Losi giving December 1861 as the date for this. As the road was in existence during the first half of 1861, when Mrs Foote was in Lagos, it seems either that it was made by McCoskry before he became acting consul or governor or that he improved an existing roadway. C.M.S. correspondence refers to the 'laying out', presumably the improvement or extension, of the riverside road by officers of the *Prometheus* in October–December 1861, when the mission had to cede 20 feet of land: CA2/068, Maser to Venn, 10 October 1861, 10 December 1861. In the 1860s McCoskry traded on the Niger and there is a brief account of his energetic methods in J. Whitford, *Trading Life in Western and Central Africa* (London, 1877, 1967 edn) p. 241. Whitford says that he was 'truthfully reported as one of the most successful men on the West Coast or the interior for dealing with the natives'.
66. Phillips (1966) citing FO84/1175, Freeman to Russell, 8 March 1862.
67. Kosoko died in 1872. His grave and shrine, with his sword and other paraphernalia, may be seen in the Iga Ereko at Lagos. His descendant, the Asajon Oloja, was admitted to the Akarigbere class of chiefs by Oba Oyekan I. Tapa died in 1868; his 'Descendants Union' have erected a monument to him outside his compound in Epetedo, the Iga Oshodi.
68. There seems no trace in official or missionary documents or tradition of resentment by the Ijebu at this second disposal of their territory.

69. Epe seems to have continued as an independent, or semi-independent, enclave in the Ijebu kingdom. In 1883 Awujale Fidipote went into exile there, and in 1892 the town provided a secure base for the British expedition against Ijebu Ode (for which, see Smith, 'Ijebu', in Crowder (1971)). In present-day Epe the Eko (Lagosians), whose head styles himself the Oluepe, live mainly on the waterside, while the Ijebu, ruled by the Oloja, live on the hill. Possu's grandson occupies the Iga Possu, but the Oluepe is descended not from Possu but from Agoro Possu, one of his followers.

Chapter 8

1. CO 147/2, T. L. McLeod to Newcastle, 21 November 1861, suggesting opening up the Lagos hinterland by a timber tram-road from Lagos to Rabba via Abeokuta, Ijaye and Oyo. A minute on the letter dismisses the project as 'preposterous' and 'extravagant'. Scala too speculated, in the last chapter of his *Memorie*, on the possibility of linking Lagos with Abeokuta by a railway. The important dates subsequently are: the Lagos–Ibadan railway, 1896–1900; Lagos harbour works, 1907–14; first Carter Bridge, connecting Lagos with the mainland via Iddo, 1900.
2. G. R. Elton, *Political History – Principles and Practice* (New York, 1970) chap. IV. For another classification of causes, see Robert Smith, 'Event and Portent: the Fall of Old Oyo, a Problem in Historical Explanation', *Africa*, XLI (1971) 3, pp. 189–91.
3. Hargreaves (1963) p. 34.
4. Lloyd, chap. XII. It is impossible to give a date for the ending of the Atlantic slave trade since slavery continued for many years in Cuba and Portuguese West Africa, and occasional coastal slavers may have escaped attention. But by the end of 1865 the trade can be said to have become a thing of the past. In 1867 the African Squadron of the Royal Navy was amalgamated with the Cape Squadron, and it disappeared altogether in 1868.
5. Ajayi and Austen, p. 304.
6. PP, LXI (1862), 3003 Edmondstone to Walker, 22 September 1861, enclosing Bedingfeld's report.
7. CO 147/2, minute on copy of McCoskry to Russell, 7 August 1861, reporting the annexation, cited by Aderibigbe, p. 3.
8. CO 147/6, minute by Barrow, 22 April 1864, on Freeman to Newcastle, 9 March 1864, no. 13, cited by Robinson and Gallagher, p. 36.
9. Newbury (1961) pp. 66–7, 86.
10. Dike (1956a) p. 214. In 1847 the French were prevented by Beecroft (in his capacity of political agent, not yet a consul) and the Royal Navy from concluding a treaty with Old Calabar (Dike, 1956a, p. 94), but until the 1880s there is little further evidence of French interest in the Bight of Biafra.
11. Dike (1956a) pp. 175–81.
12. *CMR*, XXIV (1853) p. 125, extracts from White's journal and from Crowther's letter of 22 November 1852.
13. Robinson and Gallagher, pp. 39–40.

Bibliography and Sources

I. Primary Sources

(a) Government Papers

1. Public Record Office, London
FO 2 series: Consular Correspondence
FO 84 series: Slave Trade, General Correspondence
CO 147 series (1861–2): Colonial Office Correspondence

2. British State Papers
Parliamentary and British and Foreign State Papers (especially prolific under the administrations of Russell and Palmerston) were used to supplement the files in the Public Record Office, some of the first being available in the series reprinted by the Irish University Press. The most important collections are PP 1852 LIV (221), *Papers Relative to the Reduction of Lagos*, and PP 1862 (2982) (3003), *Papers Relating to the Occupation of Lagos*.

3. Nigerian Government Papers
Ward-Price, H. L. (1933). *Commission of Inquiry re the Head of the House of Docemo* (Lagos).
Report (1967) *of the Committe of Enquiry into the Principles and Procedure for the Selection and Appointment of Chiefs in Lagos* (Lagos).

(b) Missionary Papers
Church Missionary Gleaner (CMG)
Church Missionary Intelligencer (CMI)
Church Missionary Proceedings (CMP)
Church Missionary Record (CMR)
Church Missionary Society, London, files in the CA1 and CA2 series
Methodist Missionary Society, London, correspondence filed under (1) Gold Coast and
  (2) Sierra Leone and Gambia

Southern Baptist Convention, Correspondence of the Missionaries of the, 1800–1890 (microfilmed)

(c) Oral Tradition

Oral tradition is not an important source of evidence for the history of the Lagos consulate, very little being remembered specifically about the period. Thus it can be used only to supplement, and then sparingly, the written records. The principal informants, interviewed between 1968 and 1971, were:

> at *Lagos*: H. H. Adeyinka Oyekan II, the Oba of Lagos, Chief Aminu Kosoko, Asajon Oloju, the Olota, the Aromire, Chief T. A. Doherty, the Venerable J. O. Lucas, the Rev. S. A. Pearce, M.B.E., F.R.G.S.; at *Epe*: the Oloja, the Oluepe, Mr A. O. Olukoya the Administrator, Mr Asani Oniga, a grandson of Possu, Mr Olu Bakri, a great-grandson of Possu; at *Badagry*: Chief E. F. Hundeyin, Mr T. Ola Avoseh, Mr. J. Adebayo; at *Isheri Ogun*: Princess Iyalola Olabiyi, the Regent, Prince Amore Adejonlu; at *Isheri Olofin*: Mr Musa Abogunloko, the Bale; at *Baiyeku*: Mr Aliu Maja, the Assistant Bale.

II. Secondary Sources

(a) Printed Sources: Books

Adams, Captain J. (1823) *Remarks on the Country Extending from Cape Palmas to the River Congo* (London).
Ajayi, J. F. A. (1965) *Christian Missions in Nigeria, 1814–1891* (London).
— and Smith, R. S. (1964; 1971 edn) *Yoruba Warfare in the Nineteenth Century* (Cambridge).
Ajisafe, A. K. (1924; 1964 edn) *A History of Abeokuta* (Abeokuta).
Akinjogbin, I. A. (1967) *Dahomey and Its Neighbours, 1708–1818* (Cambridge).
Akintoye, S. A. (1971) *Revolution and Power Politics in Yorubaland, 1840–1893* (London).
Anon. (n.d.: 1852?) *The Destruction of Lagos* (London).
Argyle, W. J. (1966) *The Fon of Dahomey* (Oxford).
Avoseh, T. O. (1960) *A Short History of Epe* (Epe).
Ayandele, E. A. (1966) *The Missionary Impact on Modern Nigeria* (London).
Baikie, W. B. (1856) *Narrative of an Exploring Voyage up the Rivers Kwara and Benue* (London).
Biobaku, S. O. (1957) *The Egba and their Neighbours, 1842–1872* (Oxford).
Bosman, W. (1705) *A New and Accurate Description of the Coast of Guinea* (London).
Bowdich, T. E. (1819) *Mission from Cape Coast Castle to Ashantee* (London).
Bowen, T. J. (1857) *Adventures and Missionary Labours in Several Countries in the Interior of Africa from 1849 to 1856* (Charleston).
Brooks, G. E., Jnr (1970) *Yankee Traders and African Middlemen* (Boston).
Burns, Sir A. (1929: 1947 edn) *A History of Nigeria* (London).
Burton, Sir R. F. (1863a) *Abeokuta and the Camaroons Mountain* (London).
— (1863b) *Wanderings in West Africa* (London).
Cell, J. W. (1970) *British Colonial Administration in the Mid-Nineteenth Century: the Policy-Making Process* (New Haven, Conn.).
Cock, S., ed. (1816) *The Narrative of Robert Adams* (London).

Crowder, M., ed. (1971) *West African Resistance* (London).
Curtin, P. D. (1964) *The Image of Africa — British Ideas and Action, 1780–1850* (Wisconsin).
—, ed. (1967) *Africa Remembered* (Wisconsin).
— (1969) *The Atlantic Slave Trade: A Census* (Wisconsin).
Dalzel, A. (1793) *The History of Dahomey an Inland Kingdom of Africa* (London).
Dapper, O. (1686) *Description de l'Afrique* (Amsterdam).
Delany, M. R. and Campbell, R. (1969) *Search for a Place: Black Separatism and Africa* (East Lansing, Michigan: Univ. of Michigan Press) (comprising Delany (1861) and Campbell (1860)).
Dike, K. O. (1956a) *Trade and Politics in the Niger Delta* (Oxford).
—, ed. (1960) *Eminent Nigerians of the Nineteenth Century* (Cambridge).
Egharevba, J. U. (3rd edn, 1960) *A Short History of Benin* (Ibadan).
Fadipe, N. A., ed. F. O. and O. O. Okediji (1970) *The Sociology of the Yoruba* (Ibadan).
Foote, Mrs (1869) *Recollections of Central America and the West Coast of Africa* (London).
Forde, D. (1951; reprint 1969) *The Yoruba-speaking Peoples of South-Western Nigeria* (London).
Freeman, T. B. (1844; reprint 1968) *Journal of Various Visits to the Kingdoms of Ashanti, Aku, and Dahomi in Western Africa* (London).
Fyfe, C. (1962) *A History of Sierra Leone* (Oxford).
Geary, W. N. M. (1927) *Nigeria under British Rule* (London).
Gollmer, C. H. V. (2nd edn, 1889) *Charles Andrew Gollmer, His Life and Missionary Labours* (London).
Gwam, L. C. (n.d.: 1967?) *Great Nigerians* (Lagos).
Hargreaves, J. D. (1963) *Prelude to the Partition of West Africa* (London).
Hastings, A. C. G. (1926) *The Voyage of the Dayspring* (London).
Herstlet, Sir E. (1909) *The Map of Africa by Treaty* (London).
Hodgkin, T. (1960) *Nigerian Perspectives* (Oxford).
Hutchinson, T. J. (1858) *Impressions of Western Africa* (London).
Johnson, Rev. S. (1921) *The History of the Yorubas* (Lagos).
Jones, R. (1971) *The Nineteenth-Century Foreign Office: An Administrative History* (London).
Kopytoff, J. H. (1965) *A Preface to Modern Nigeria: The "Sierra Leonians" in Yoruba, 1830–1890* (Wisconsin).
Lander, R. L. and J. (1832) *Journal of an Expedition to Explore the Course and Termination of the Niger* (London).
Laotan, A. B. (n.d.: 1943?) *The Torch Bearers or Old Brazilian Colony in Lagos* (Lagos).
Lloyd, C. (1949) *The Navy and the Slave Trade* (London).
Lloyd, P. C. (1971) *The Political Development of Yoruba Kingdoms in the Eighteenth and Nineteenth Centuries* (London).
Losi, J. B. (1914; 1967 edn) *History of Lagos* (Lagos).
— (1924) *History of Abeokuta* (Lagos).
Lucas, J. O. (n.d.: 1947?) *The History of St. Paul's Church, Breadfruit* (Lagos).
— (1952) *The Anglican Church in Lagos, 1852–1952. Centenary Oration* (Lagos).
Newbury, C. W. (1961) *The Western Slave Coast and Its Rulers* (Oxford).
— (1965) *British Policy towards West Africa, Selected Documents 1786–1874* (Oxford).

Payne, J. A. O. (1893) *Table of Principal Events in Yoruba History* (Lagos).
Pereira, Duarte Pacheco, trans. and ed. by G. H. T. Kimble (1937) *Esmeraldo de Situ Orbis* (London).
C.M.S. (1895) *Register of Missionaries 1804–1894* (London).
Robertson, G. A. (1819) *Notes on Africa* (London).
Robinson, R. and Gallagher, J. (1961) *Africa and the Victorians* (London).
Ryder, A. F. C. (1969) *Benin and the Europeans, 1485–1897* (London).
Scala, G. (1862) *Memorie* (Sampierdarena).
Schnapper, B. (1961) *La Politique et la commerce français dans le Golfe de Guinée de 1838 à 1871* (Paris).
Smith, R. S. (1969a; 1976 2nd edn) *Kingdoms of the Yoruba* (London).
— (1976) *Warfare and Diplomacy in Pre-Colonial West Africa* (London).
Sodeinde, E. N. O. (1967) *Souvenir Brochure, Christ Church Centenary Celebrations, 1967* (Lagos).
Stock, E. (1916) *A History of the Church Missionary Society*, 4 vols (London).
Thorp, Ellen (1956) *Ladder of Bones* (London).
Townsend, G. (1887) *Memoir of Henry Townsend* (Exeter).
Verger, P. (1964) *Bahia and the West African Trade, 1549–1851* (Ibadan).
Ward, W. E. F. (1969) *The Royal Navy and the Slavers* (London).
Wood, Rev. J. Buckley (1878) *Historical Notices of Lagos* (Lagos).

(b) Printed Sources: Articles

Ajayi, J. F. A. (1961) 'The British Occupation of Lagos, 1851–1861', *Nigeria Magazine*, no. 69.
— (1963a) 'Political Organizations in West African Towns in the Nineteenth Century – the Lagos Example', seminar paper, *Urbanization in African Social Change*, University of Edinburgh.
— (1963b) 'The Development of Secondary Grammar School Education in Nigeria', *JHSN*, II, 4.
— and Austen, R. A. (1972) 'Hopkins on Economic Imperialism in West Africa', *Economic History Review*, XXV, 2.
Austen, R. A. (1970) 'The Abolition of Overseas Slave Trade: a Distorted Theme in West African History', *JHSN*, V, 2.
Awe, B. (1964) 'The Ajele System: a Study of Ibadan Imperialism in the Nineteenth Century', *JHSN*, III, 1.
Bradbury, R. E. (1959) 'Chronological Problems in Benin History', *JHSN*, I, 4.
Davidson, A. McL. (1954) 'The Early History of Lagos', *Nigerian Field*, XIX, 2.
Dike, K. O. (1956b) 'John Beecroft, 1790–1824', *JHSN*, I, 1.
Folayan, K. (1969) 'The Career of Thomas Tickel in the Western District of Lagos, 1854–1886', *JHSN*, V, 1.
Gavin, R. J. (1961) 'Nigeria and Lord Palmerston', *Ibadan*, 12.
Historian, A Yoruba (Rev. H. T. Euler Ajayi) (1905–6) 'A General History of the Yoruba Country', *Lagos Standard* (page references are to Dr R. C. C. Law's typescript).
Hopkins, A. G. (1966) 'The Currency Revolution in South-West Nigeria in the Late Nineteenth Century', *JHSN*, III, 3.
— (1968) 'Economic Imperialism in West Africa, Lagos, 1880–92', *Economic History*

Review, XXI, 3.
Jennings, L. C. (1976) 'French Policy towards Trading with African and Brazilian Slave Merchants, 1840–1853', *JAH*, XVII, 4.
Johnson, Marion (1970) 'The Cowrie Currencies of West Africa', parts I and II, *JAH*, XI, 1, 3.
Law, R. C. C. (1968) 'The Dynastic Chronology of Lagos', *LNR*, II, 2.
— (1970) 'The Chronology of the Yoruba Wars of the Early Nineteenth Century', *JHSN*, V, 2.
Miller, N. S. (1963) 'Aspects of the Development of Lagos', *Nigerian Field*, XXVIII, 4.
— (1972) 'Ile Ajele, the First British Consulate in Lagos', *Nigerian Field*, XXXVII, 4.
Newbury, C. W. (1972) 'Credit in Early Nineteenth Century West African Trade', *JAH*, XIII, 1.
Ross, D. A. (1965) 'The Career of Domingo Martinez in the Bight of Benin, 1833–64', *JAH*, VI, 1.
Smith, R. S. (1962) 'Ijaiye, the Western Palatinate of the Yoruba', *JHSN*, II, 3.
— (1969b) 'To the Palaver Islands: War and Diplomacy on the Lagos Lagoon in 1852–1854', *JHSN*, V, 1.
— (1970) 'The Canoe in West African History', *JAH*, XI, 4.
— (1973a) 'Peace and Palaver: International Relations in Pre-colonial West Africa', *JAH*, XIV, 4.
— (1973b) 'Giambattista Scala: Adventurer, Trader and First Italian Representative in Nigeria', *JHSN*, VII, 1.
'Supra' (1900–1) 'The Witch of Endor in Yorubaland', *Lagos Standard*.
Verger, P. (1959) 'Notes on Some Documents in Which Lagos is Referred to by the Name "Onim" . . . ', *JHSN*, I, 4.

(c) Unpublished Works
Aderibigbe, A. B. (1959) 'The Expansion of the Lagos Protectorate.' Ph.D. thesis, University of London.
Ayantuga, O. O. (1965) 'Ijebu and its Neighbours, 1801–1941.' Ph.D. thesis, University of London.
Brown, H. B. (1964) 'A History of the People of Lagos, 1852–1866.' Ph.D. thesis, Northwestern University, U.S.A.
Folayan, K. (1967) 'Egbado and Yoruba–Aja Politics, 1832–1894.' M.A. thesis, University of Ibadan.
Gavin, R. J. (1958) 'Palmerston's Policy towards East and West Africa.' Ph.D. thesis, University of Cambridge.
Gbadamosi, G. O. (1968) 'The Growth of Islam among the Yoruba, 1841–1908.' Ph.D. thesis, Ibadan.
Law, Robin (R.C.C.) (1977) 'The Career of Adele at Lagos and Badagry, c.1807–c.1835.'
Mabogunje, A. (1962) 'Lagos: a Study in Urban Geography.' Ph.D. thesis, University of London.
Oroge, E. A. (1971) 'The Institution of Slavery in Yorubaland with particular reference to the Nineteenth Century.' Ph.D. thesis, University of Birmingham.
Phillips, E. H. (1966) 'The Church Missionary Society, the Imperial Factor, and Yoruba Politics, 1842–1873.' Ph.D. thesis, University of S. California, U.S.A.

Index

Abagbon, Lagos war chiefs 6, 7
Abeokuta (Egba capital) 1, 13, 19, 20, 21, 22, 34, 37, 43, 54, 74, 83, 92, 101, 103, 107; British support for 85-6, 95, 103-4, 115-16, 118; commercial agreements, 1858, 1860 88, 101; menaced by Dahomey 22, 85-6, 99, 103, 110; proposed vice-consulate at 112, 113; *see also* Egba
Aberdeen Act 21, 70
Abomey, Dahomean capital 85, 86, 121
Abrinomey, chief of Batere 90
Adamorisha, masquerade 168
Adams, Captain John, cited 8, 10, 11, 99
Adams, Commodore J., R.N. 67, 75, 87
Adams, Robert, cited 10
Adedjuju, first Christian convert in Lagos 38
Adele, Oba of Lagos 14-15, 16, 73
Ado (Addo), Awori town 45, 84
Ado (Addo), river 127
African Steamship Company 35, 98
Agbekin Island, *see* Palaver Islands
Agoueye 114
Aibo, Egbado town 87-8, 164
Ajayi, J. F. A., cited 11, 14, 32, 130, 148
Ajenia, Lagos chief 35, 46, 47, 52, 54, 55, 57, 127
Ajido 28
Ajo Oloye, Lagos council 7
Akarigbere, Lagos chiefs 6, 7
Akinpelu Possu, Lagos chief 35, 46, 47, 52, 54, 55, 57, 60, 127, 175
Akinshemovin, Oba of Lagos 8, 9, 11, 14
Akitoye, Oba of Lagos 11, 16-17, 19, 20, 21, 22, 24, 25, 26-7, 35, 38, 44, 46, 47, 52-5, 84, 90, 129, 148, 156-7
Alafin of Oyo 86
Alake, Egba Oba 87, 92, 101, 115
Albert, Prince Consort 148
Amadie, Hungarian trader 36, 46-7, 71
Amaro, Brazilian and Cuban 'emigrants' 39-40, 82
American slave dealers 2; *see also* Brazilians, United States
Anikilaya, Awujale 42
Anowo (near Badagry) 23
Anti-Slavery Squadron, *see* Preventive Squadron, Royal Navy

Anti-Slavery treaties, Anglo-African 30-1, 35, 48, 119
Antonio, Pa 82
Apa 9
Aplin, Commander, R.N. 72
Ardra (Allada) 10
Arekin Island, *see* Palaver Islands
Aromire, Lagos chief 6, 144-5
Arota, compound head in Lagos 8
Ashanti people 95
Ashipa, Oba of Lagos 4
Ashogbon, Lagos chief 6, 53
Austen, R. A., cited 130
Austin, trader 77
Awori people 2
Awujale 40; *see also* Ijebu Ode
Ayantuga, O. O., cited 42

Badagry 1, 5, 7, 10, 13, 15, 17, 21, 22, 23, 37, 45, 51, 84-5, 112-13, 114, 117, 123; vice-consulate at 68, 112
Badu, husband to Madame Tinubu 74
Bahia 21, 37, 85
Baikie, Dr W. B. 94-5, 107-8
Banner Brothers, traders 36
Baptist Mission, Southern American 83, 97; *see also* Bowen, T. J.
Barbotin, Captain 109, 120
Baring, Sir F. 149
Bashorun of Abeokuta 23
Bedingfeld (Bedingfield), Lieut. N., R.N. 59, 123-4, 130, 157, 175
Beecroft, Consul J. 2, 17, 20, 21, 22, 24, 25, 26-31, 35, 43, 44, 49, 90, 131
Benin, people (Bini): city and kingdom 83, 90, 112; Oba of, 27; relations with Kosoko at Epe 6, 40; relations with Lagos 4, 6, 102, 144; river 5, 75, 89-90, 105
Benin and Biafra, Bights of, consulate of 2, 19
Bickersteth, Rev. E. 89
Blaeu, cartographer 3
blockade, naval 20, 24, 35, 51, 55, 58, 87
Bonny 10
Borghero, Rev. Fr 82
Bosse, Commander 120
Bowden, Commander, R.N. 103, 113
Bowditch, T. E., cited 10
Bowen, T. J., cited 23, 27
Boyle, J. P., consular clerk, trader 67, 107, 112
Brand, Consul G. 99, 102-10, 111, 128, 171

Brazil, Brazilians   9, 10, 21, 34, 39, 68, 106, 123, 130; *see also* Amaro, emigrants, Bahia
brick manufacture, in Lagos   94, 166
Bruce, Captain H. W., R.N.   24, 27-8, 31, 43, 44, 45, 49, 54, 58, 61, 71, 75, 128
Brune, H.M.S., gunboat stationed at Lagos   75-6, 93, 107, 112, 117-19, 121
Burton, Sir Richard   90; cited   8, 26-7, 28, 67, 78, 97, 98, 119, 124, 126

Campbell, Consul Benjamin   44, 47-8; chapters 4 and 5 *passim*, 91-9, 102, 107, 108-9, 112, 113, 117, 129; earlier career of   48, 49-50; death of 96, 167
Campbell, Robert   103, 169
canoes   5, 10, 51, 56; war canoes, warfare   23, 28, 30, 40, 51, 56-7, 118
Carrena, Giuseppe, trader   69, 94, 97, 108, 160, 167
Carrier Pigeon, case of   69
Cell, J. W., cited   120, 121
cession, treaty of, Anglo-Lagosian, 1861 122-4, 140-1
Champness, Rev. T.   89
chieftancy in Lagos   6-7
Christianity, *see* Baptist Mission, Church Missionary Society, Methodist Missionary Society, missionaries, Roman Catholicism
Church Missionary Society (C.M.S.)   13, 19-23, 37, 58; *see also* land, grants of
Clapperton, Captain H., R.N.   14, 15, 108
Clarendon, Earl of   50, 67, 69, 73, 78, 81
Coker, J. B.   38
Columbine, case of   86-7
commercial agreements, Anglo-Lagosian, 1852   36, 46; 1854   77; 1859 93-4
consular matters, Lagos: barge   67, 159; certificates for ex-slaves   73, 102; general   153, 173; jurisdiction, limits of   2, 44, 47-8, 83, 90; magisterial authority   92, 102, 112; premises 50, 67, 81-2, 97, 115, 159
Conto, Signor   46, 57
contract labour   68-70, 86, 129-30; Anglo-French convention on, 1861 68, 100, 131
coral beads, substitute for cowries   169
Cotonou, oil port   96
cotton: cultivation of, in Yorubaland   77; trade in   76, 94
Cotton Supply Association, Manchester 92-3
court, merchants', in Lagos   36, 79
cowries: as currency   36, 77; inflation of 101-2, 169;   *see also* Zanzibar; O'Swald & Co.
Crimean War   68, 165
crowned kings, Yoruba   167
Crowther, Rev. S. A., later Bishop   11, 23, 81-2, 84, 115, 132, 145-6, 148
Cuba   10, 68, 70, 114, 130; Cuban slave dealers   2; *see also* Amaro
customs, *see* export duties, Lagos

Dada Antonio, Lagos chief   40
Dahomey, Fon kingdom of: British attack on, suggested   115; Dahomeans   1, 10, 11, 19-20, 24, 71, 83, 86, 103, 107, 109, 110, 129-30
Dalzel, A., cited   42
Dapper, O., cited   3
Davies, J. and S.   150
Dawson, J.   86
Delany, Dr Martin   103
Denman, Lieut. the Hon. J., R.N.   20, 24
Derby, Earl of   34, 43
Diare, chief of Jakpa   90
Diederichsen, L.   36
Diederichsen, P.   75, 108
Dike, K. O., cited   49, 132
diplomacy, Yoruba   51-2
Dosunmu, Oba of Lagos   58, 59, 61, 64, 73, 74, 76, 77, 79, 85, 90, 96, 98, 100-1, 102, 109, 112, 120-1, 126; accession of   55; attitude to annexation of Lagos   123-4, 174
Duncan, Vice-Consul J.   19
Dutch   76; at Badagry   14

Earl, Thomas   26
Ebute Metta, district of Lagos   4, 58, 63, 74
Edmondstone, Commodore W., R.N. 106, 115, 116, 119
Edo, *see* Benin, Bini
education, missionary, introduction of 96-7, 167
Egba: people   1, 3, 16, 43, 54, 83, 87-8, 95, 99, 125, 129; Egba military support to Akitoye and Dosunmu 23, 46, 55-7, 60; *see also* Abeokuta
Egbado people   1, 3, 99
Egun people   7-8
Ejinrin   7, 94, 95, 100, 101
Eletu Odibo, Lagos chief   6, 7, 16, 60
Elton, G. R., cited   129
'emigrants'   12-13, 39-40, 79-80, 107
Enu Owa, district of Lagos   6, 144
Epe   40, 42, 127, 175; bombardment of, 1863   127; conferences at, 1854 59, 62-3; Kosko's capital in exile   35, 40-3, 50, 56-7, 75, 102, 105; treaty of, 1854   50, 62-5, 81, 138-9
Ereko, district of Lagos   16, 65, 127
Erelu, Lagos female chief   7, 145

Index

'Eshallü' Island (Isheri?) 88, 165
Eshilokun, *see* Oshinlokun
export duties 77, 94; farming of 78, 123, 166, 175

Fanshawe, Commander, R.N. 22
Fanti, canoemen 5, 26, 99
Fernandez House 167
Fernando Po, island of 2, 19, 35, 36
Fidipore, Awujale 42
firearms, gunpowder, trade in, supply of 52, 85, 100, 105, 116, 125
Folayan, K., cited 88
Fon people, *see* Dahomey
Foote, Consul H. G. 99, 111-23, 125, 129
Foote, Mrs, cited 83, 97, 112, 126
Forbes, Commander T. G., R.N. 25, 26, 35, 85
Forster & Smith, traders 45
Frazer, Vice-Consul Louis 44-8, 52, 67, 78, 153, 154
Freeman, H. S., Governor of Lagos 125-6, 174-5
Freeman, Rev. T. B. 13
Freetown 11, 12
French interest in West Africa: Anglo-French relations 14, 24, 109, 120-1, 129-31, 173; French slave-traders 2; *see also* contract labour, Lemagniere
Fulani people 89

Gabaro, Oba of Lagos 9
Gallinas river, operation on 20, 24
Gambia river, British colony on 20
Gardiner, Rev. E. R. 81, 83
Gardner, Commander, R.N. 24, 48, 53
Gavin, R. J., cited 22, 25, 32, 120
Gerst, Rev. E. F. E. 61
Ghezo, king of Dahomey 19, 85-6, 93
Glover, Lieut. J. H., R.N. 107-9
Gollmer, Rev. C. A. 22, 23, 37-9, 44, 45, 50, 53, 55, 61, 64, 80-1, 83, 96
Granville, Earl 25, 34
Gregory, Mr 79
Grote, H., trader 54, 73, 79
gunboat, *see Brune*, H.M.S.
Gun, *see* Egun
Gurney, A. 83

Hamburgers (Hanseatic), traders, interests 47, 97, 108
Hand, Lieut.-Commander H., R.N., Acting Consul 99, 101-8, 110, 112, 129
Hansen, W. R. 64, 75, 78, 94
Harden, J. M. 97
Hargreaves, J. D., cited ix, 130
Harrison & Co., traders 90, 98-9
Hausa people 8, 10, 15, 71, 107, 146; Hausa–Fulani, Holy War of 1

'Hedjenna' 56
Hertz, A. J., trader 104
Heseltine, Commander, R.N. 45
Hewett, Commander W. N. W., V.C., R.N. 103
Hinderer, Rev. D. 88, 96, 105-6
Hopkins, A. G., cited 168
Horsfall & Sons, traders 90
humanitarian party in England 12-14, 21, 31
Hutt, Sir W., M.P. 21
Hutton, Thomas 20, 79, 99; Hutton, Thomas & Co., traders 13

Ibadan, Ibadan empire 72, 84, 86, 88, 94, 95, 105-6, 129
Iddo Island 4, 5, 165
Idejo, Lagos chiefs 4, 6, 38, 144, 151
Idewu Ojulari, Oba of Lagos 15
Ifa oracle, consultation of 6
Ife, people and kingdom 1
Ija Afasegbojo, the 'useless battle' 54
Ijaye 72, 84, 86, 95; Ijaye War 99, 100, 103-6, 110, 125
Ijebu Ode 47, 86, 89, 95, 100, 105, 117, 120; British expedition against, suggested, 100; relations of, with Kosoko, 42, 61;
Ijebu people 1, 2, 3, 4, 5, 43, 54, 94, 119
Ijebu Remo 89, 105, 157
Ijo pirates 89-90
Ijoko Oloye, Lagos council 7
Ijora, district of Lagos 4
Ikorodu ('cradoo') 10, 51, 61, 94, 101
Ikosi 51
Ilaje people, *see* Muhin
Ilorin 86, 88, 95, 105-6
informal empire, rule, system 2, 35, 44, 49, 109; *see also* quasi-protectorate
Irving, Dr E. G. 59, 81-2, 91, 109
Isale Eko, old Lagos 4, 7
Isheri, 11, 143; early Awori settlement 3, 4; *see also* 'Eshalli' Island
Iso ('Issoes'), canoe warriors 56, 155
Italian (Sardinian) interests 108
Iwoye (Iwuye) ceremony 7

Jambo, Senhor 69, 71, 111, 160
Jebba 107
Johns, John 29
Jones, Captain A. T. 116
Jones, Captain L. T., R.N. 23, 28, 30

Keta ('Quittah') 68, 71
Ketu, people and kingdom 103
kingship, Lagos characteristics of 5-6
Kopytoff, J. H., cited 39
Kosoko, Oba and ex-Oba of Lagos 2, 11, 16, 19, 24, 26-30, 40-3, 50, 52-65, 73, 74-5, 82, 86, 94-5, 99, 106-9, 120-1, 126-7, 129-30, 152, 175; *see also* Epe, Ereko

Kroomen, on British naval vessels 106, 117, 170
'Kuramo', origin of name 143

lagoon, Lagos 51, 155
Lagos: battles of, 1851 26-31; harbour 3, 35, 51, 99, 124, 128; origin of name 2; population 7-8, 37, 39, 82, 97; pre-colonial government 5-8; territorial extent 5, 144; treaties, 1852, 1861 30-1, 124, 135-7, 140-1
Laing, T. 83
land grants, land question, Lagos 38, 45, 80, 81-2, 97, 98, 168
Lander, Richard 15, 108; John 15
Landolphe, cited 90
Law, Robin, cited 14, 15
Layard, Sir A. H. 125
Legresley, Mr, trader 94
Leke 40, 127, 152
Lemagnière, Louis 69, 73, 77, 109, 170-1
Lewis, Walter 50, 80, 94, 162, 167
Liberated Africans' Department, Freetown 49
Lightburn, Miss 93
Lightburn, Mrs Isabella 49, 166
Lima, Senhor 40, 54, 57, 63, 152
Lincoln, President 114
Lloyd, C., cited 20
Lloyd, Mr, Foreign Office official 87
Lloyd, P. C., cited 5-6
Lodder, Lieut. E. F., R.N. 92, 103; Acting Consul 92-3, 96-100, 102, 129
Losi, J. B., cited 15, 16
Lugard, Sir Frederick 44
Lyster, Captain, R.N. 29

Macaulay, Rev. T. B. 97
Macaulay & Babington, traders 49
McCoskry, W., trader, Vice-Consul, first Acting Governor 36, 74, 75, 77, 78, 79, 80, 88, 94, 97, 100, 113, 116, 112, 123-6, 160, 175
Machado, Senhor 71
Mahi people 8, 10, 145, 152-3
Mahin (Ilaje), people and kingdom 43
Malmesbury, Earl of 43, 44, 107
Manchester, Campbell's visit to 92-3
Marina, Lagos 97, 126, 175
Marsh, William 11
Martin, Rev. J. 38, 83
Martinez, Domingo 11, 21, 36, 46, 71, 84, 106, 146, 148, 154, 160-1
Martins, Antonio 73
Martins, Ojo 46
Maser, Rev. J. A. 94
Mayo, Commander, U.S. Navy 70
Methodism, Methodist Missionary Society 13, 38, 82-3
Mewu, Porto Novan chief 45, 84
mica, mistaken for gold 77

Miller, Commander T., R.N. 62, 63, 69, 73
missionaries, Christian, introduction of 1, 12, 37
Murray, K. C., cited 167-8
Muslim community in Lagos and Epe 14, 40, 52, 97, 127, 152, 166-7

National Emigration Convention of Coloured Men 103, 169; see also Campbell, R.; Delany
Newbury, C. W., cited 36, 54, 100, 130, 173
Newcastle, Duke of 121-2
Niger Delta 2; Niger Districts, British Protectorate of 2, 130-1; Niger expeditions, British, 1841, 1854, 1857 20, 75, 107
Novelli & Co. Ltd 113
Nupe people 10, 71, 83

Obanikoro, Lagos chief 7
Ogagun, see Abagbon
Ogalade, Lagos chiefs 6, 7
Ogbomosho 84
Ogboni, Yoruba society 7, 17; see also Oshogbo
Ogun, river 3, 5, 16, 23, 43, 51, 88, 103, 116
Ogun Agidingbi, Ogun Ahoyaya (war) 30
Ogun Ajakaiye 4
Ogun Ewe Koko 16, 40
Ogun Olomiro 16
oil, see palm oil
Oliveira, Joao de, trader 9
Olofin, title of rulers of first dynasty at Lagos 5
Ologun Kutere, Oba of Lagos 11, 14
Olokemeji, Egba war camp at 116
Olomowewe 42, 157; raid on, 57, 63
Olumegbon, Lagos chief 6, 60
Oluwole, Oba of Lagos 16, 40
Oni river 51
Onisiwo, Lagos chief 60
Ord, Colonel, boundary commissioner, 1864 127
Orhogbua, Oba of Benin 4
Orimedu, see Palma
Osa, see lagoon
Oshinlokun, Oba of Lagos 14-15, 40
Osho Akanbi, Lagos chief 40
Oshodi Tapa, Kosoko's leading chief 16, 39, 40, 46, 54, 57, 59, 60, 62, 64, 95, 127, 175
Oshun, river 51
Oshogbo, battle of, c. 1838 88
Oshogbo society 7
Osifekunde, evidence of 40
O'Swald & Co., traders 36, 78, 102, 108
Oto (Otto) 4
Otta, Awori town, and kingdom 3, 15, 115
Owiwi war 15

Owu, people and kingdom   1
Oyo, people: and kingdom   1, 3, 10, 86, 95, 100; language   3, 11; *see also* Alafin

Paggi, Vincenzo   94, 108
Palaver Islands, conference on   59-61, 62, 158
palm oil, production, supply, trade   12, 14, 76, 94, 100, 114, 119
Palma (Orimedu), Kosoko's port   40-2, 58, 62, 63, 64, 65, 77, 102, 109, 123, 127
Palmerston, Viscount   19, 20, 21, 22, 23-4, 31-2, 34, 65, 70, 72, 73, 75, 100, 109, 118, 120, 121-2, 125, 130-1
Parliamentary Select Committee, 1865   96, 132
Parsons, Captain   146
Patey, Lieut. R., R.N.   25, 30
Pearce (Pearse), J. B., consular clerk   67, 107
Pearce (Pearse), Samuel, member of C.M.S.   38, 61, 112, 113
Pedro, Senhor   59
Pepple, king of Bonny   35
Pereira, Duarte Pacheco, cited   3
Phillips, Commander C. G., R.N.   46, 54; leads expeditions against Epe, 1853   56-7
Phillips, E. H., cited   32-3, 84, 109, 125
Pittaluga, Emmanuel, trader   94, 108
Plancius, cartographer   3
plots, anti-consular, in Lagos   73, 74
Popo, *see* Egun
Porto Novo: British treaties with, 1852, 1861   35, 119; becomes French protectorate, 1862   131; Consul Foote's expeditions against, 1861   117-19; Egun and kingdom of   10, 15, 68, 71, 84, 85-6, 95-6, 106, 114
Portuguese: slave traders   2, 11, 95, 107; use of language   55, 62
Possu, *see* Akinpelu Possu
Possu, Badagry chief   84
Potts, Fanny   49-50
Pratt, W. H.   49
Preventive Squadron, R.N.   1-2, 12, 20, 35, 49, 53-4, 68, 69, 71-2, 89, 91, 106, 112, 146, 147, 165, 176
Protet, Commodore   86, 121
public funds, British policy   67, 151-6

quasi-Protectorate (British), description of Lagos as   2, 49, 66
quinine, use of   75, 91

racecourse, Lagos   98, 168
railway, suggested   128, 176
Regina Coeli, case of   70, 121
Régis Ainé, traders   65, 69, 71, 93, 94, 102, 109, 120, 127, 131
Richards, Lieut. J., R.N.   101

roads (bush tracks), free movement on, issue of   47, 88, 94-5, 100, 101, 105, 108, 114, 167
Robertson, G. A., cited   19
Robinson, R., and Gallagher, J., cited   1, 132, 150
Rogers, Sir Frederick   122
Roman Catholicism, introduction of   39, 79, 82
Ross, D. A., cited   11
Roy, J. P. da C.   62
Royal Navy: relations with consuls   45, 49, 56-7, 58, 67, 68, 75; relations with missionaries   81, 92; *see also* Preventive Squadron
Russell, Lord John   19, 34, 101, 112, 119, 120-2, 125, 126, 130
Ryder, A. F. C., cited   90

sacrifice, human   85, 87, 90, 93, 104, 109, 119
Sandeman, J. G., trader (representing Steward & Douglas, also Forster & Smith)   36, 45, 50, 59, 73, 75, 77, 79, 80
Saro (Sierra Leonean 'emigrants' of Yoruba descent)   39
Savage, William, trader   74
Scala, Giambattista, trader   36, 59, 64, 74, 77, 78, 79, 94, 108, 151, 160, 165, 170; cited   37, 47
schools, *see* education
Serrano, General   114
Shabe, people and kingdom   87
Sharp, Rev. G.   83, 89
Shasha, river   51
shea butter, grease of, suggested export of   77, 94, 101
Shelburne, Lord   79
Sierra Leone   12, 20
Sierra Leoneans, *see* 'emigrants', Saro
Skelton, Mrs Elizabeth   49
Skene, Commander, R.N.   81
slave trade, on West Coast   66-73, 99, 104, 113-14, 176; at Lagos   9, 10, 13, 66-73
slavery, domestic, predial, plantation   72, 87-8, 92; at Lagos   72-3, 107-8, 109, 114, 161
Smart ('boy')   90
Snelgrave, Captain W., cited   3
Sodji, king of Porto Novo   117-19
Spaniards on West Coast   11, 70, 76
Stanley, Lord   22, 43
steam-powered vessels, introduction of   20, 71-2, 75
Steward & Douglas, traders   36
Stokes, Lieut., R.N.   112; 117
Sunday, observance of, in Lagos   96, 167
Swanzy, Mr   99

Tapa, *see* Oshodi Tapa

Thomas, J. R., trader 105
Tickel, Thomas, trader, Vice-Consul 84, 113
tiles, royal monopoly of use of 8, 74, 94, 161-2
Tinuba, Madame 53, 62, 71, 73, 74, 102, 115, 154, 156
Townsend, Rev. H. 13, 19, 43, 81, 83, 92, 98, 103, 104, 116, 125
trade and commerce in Lagos: consular 76, 98; pre-colonial 3, 5, 9-10, 88, 110
Turner, J. M., trader 89, 105
Turton, E. R., cited 144
twin births 169

U.S.A. 130; anti-slave trade patrol, U.S. Navy 70-1, 106, 114; slave trade of, slavery in 68, 106, 114

Vattel, E. de, cited 34
Venn, Rev. H. 77, 82, 112, 125
Victoria, Queen 92, 124, 148

Walewski, Count 67
war chiefs, Lagos, see Abagbon
Ward, T., Foreign Office official 84
Washington, treaty of, 1861 114
Wawu, Badagry chief 45
Webster—Ashburton treaty 70
Wesleyan Methodism, see Methodist Missionary Society

West Indian troops (British) 104, 115, 116, 121-2
White, Commander, R.N. 45
White, James 38, 53, 66, 132
White Caps, see chieftancy, Lagos
Whydah (Ouida) 9, 19, 44, 47, 69, 71, 72, 85, 94, 99, 106, 110, 117; British occupation of, mooted 72, 110, 118, 120
Williams, George 61
Williams, S. B. 6, 66-7, 88, 95, 107, 172-3
Willoughby, Isaac 94
Wilmot, Commander A. P. E., R.N. 24, 26, 35, 37
witchcraft 113, 147
Wodehouse, Lord 47, 110, 122-3
women, role of, in Lagos 7, 8
Wright, Joseph 11
Wylde, W. H., Foreign Office official 93, 109, 110, 116, 118, 119, 121, 126
Wyse, Commander, R.N. 92, 93

Yevogan, Dahomean official at Whydah 86-7
Yoruba, wars, chronology, interpretation of 72, 87-9, 104, 110, 143, 169-70

Zanzibar, import of cowries from 36, 47, 77, 108

www.ingramcontent.com/pod-product-compliance
Lightning Source LLC
Chambersburg PA
CBHW021708230426
43668CB00008B/760